Contents

Contents

FUTURE *Ready* INVESTING

IDENTIFYING AND MASTERING EMERGING SECTORAL TRENDS FOR WEALTH CREATION IN INDIA

DARSHAN

ISBN
Paperback 979-8-89699-543-2
Hardcase 979-8-89724-784-4

"While the past provides valuable lessons, it is the future that shapes investment outcomes. As investors, we are not merely buying what a company or sector has achieved so far—we are buying into its future potential, its ability to grow, adapt, and thrive in an ever-changing world. The essence of successful investing lies in envisioning this future while ensuring the price we pay today reflects a margin of safety. The art of investing is not just about recognizing what is but imagining what could be, aligning capital with innovation and growth, and participating in the journey of shaping tomorrow's world."

Inside the Book

Comprehensive Understanding of Trends | Demography, Macro and Micro Trend Insights | Practical Guidance Rooted in Real World Examples | A Guide to Value Early Stage & Growth Businesses

The biggest mistake investors make is to believe that what happened in the recent past is likely to persist. They assume that something that was a good investment in the recent past is still a good investment. Typically, high past returns simply imply that an asset has become more expensive and is a poorer, not better, investment.

– Ray Dalio

The future is not ours to see but having a sense of where it might go and being positioned accordingly can significantly increase your chances for investment success.

– Howard Marks

In the business world, the rearview mirror is always clearer than the windshield.

– Warren Buffett

Stay in a Sunrise industry at any cost. Stay out of a Sunset industry at any cost.

– Vijay Kedia

(Extract of Individuals' Investing Philosophy)

A Master Class in Foresight

The crisp chill of an early winter morning brushed against my face as I stepped onto the balcony with a steaming mug of coffee warming my hands. The city below was still asleep, wrapped in a blanket of fog, but the world of social media was already alive, buzzing with thoughts and stories from every corner of the globe. As I scrolled through the stream of consciousness, one post caught my eye. It was about a company that transformed how the world consumes entertainment: Netflix.

The story was Like this

"Once upon a time, in the late 1990s, the entertainment industry was dominated by a giant named Blockbuster. Renting movies meant driving to your local Blockbuster store, picking up a VHS or DVD, and returning it within a few days to avoid hefty late fees. It was a well-established model, seemingly unshakable.

Amidst this landscape, two entrepreneurs, Reed Hastings and Marc Randolph, envisioned a new way to deliver entertainment. Their idea was simple yet radical: why not let people rent DVDs online and have them delivered directly to their homes? In 1997, they founded Netflix and introduced a subscription-based service—no late fees, no trips to the store, just convenience.

In 2000, sensing the potential of their growing company, Hastings and Randolph approached Blockbuster with a proposal to sell Netflix for $50 million. Blockbuster's CEO, John Antioco, and his team dismissed the offer, seeing Netflix as a niche business that could never compete with their vast network of physical stores. The idea of subscription-based rentals, let alone streaming, seemed laughable to them. Blockbuster was comfortable with its dominance and saw no reason to change.

Undeterred by rejection, Hastings and Randolph doubled down on their vision. Netflix refined its subscription model, allowing customers to rent unlimited DVDs for a flat monthly fee. They also began investing in technology, preparing for a future they believed in—a world where movies could be streamed directly to customers' homes.

By 2007, that future began to take shape. Netflix introduced its streaming service, a groundbreaking move that disrupted the entire entertainment industry. The company's technology and user-friendly interface allowed viewers to watch their favourite movies and shows instantly, without ever leaving their homes.

Meanwhile, Blockbuster continued to rely on its brick-and-mortar model, missing multiple opportunities to innovate. Even when they launched a competing subscription service, they struggled to replicate Netflix's success. Blockbuster's reluctance to adapt eventually led to its bankruptcy in 2010, a symbol of how even giants can fall when they fail to embrace change.

Netflix, however, did not stop with streaming. In 2013, it entered the world of original content with *House of Cards*, signalling a shift from being a content distributor to a content creator. The move was revolutionary, cementing Netflix as a leader in the entertainment industry. Today, Netflix is a global powerhouse, with a valuation in the hundreds of billions and a presence in over 190 countries."

This story, though, is not just about missed chances. It is a narrative about vision, foresight, and the ability to disrupt established norms. Reed Hastings and Marc Randolph didn't just aim to make renting movies easier; they foresaw the future of entertainment itself.

For founders, this story underscores the importance of believing in your vision, even when industry giants scoff at your ideas. It was this unwavering belief that enabled Netflix to grow from a DVD rental company into a global leader in streaming and content creation.

For investors, Netflix tale is a masterclass in foresight. It is a reminder that true wealth often lies not in what is, but in what can be. Investing in Netflix during its early days was not just a bet on a DVD rental company—it was a bet on the future of how the world would consume entertainment.

The result? Unparalleled wealth creation.

For India, consider the recent case of Delhivery, a company that, despite it is relatively younger company in the logistics sector, managed to surpass the valuation of older established giants like Blue Dart. Delhivery's success was not built on traditional methods but on an acute understanding of the e-commerce boom. They leveraged technology for last-mile logistics, a trend that was becoming increasingly vital as consumer behaviour shifted online.

This example underscores the importance of identifying macro and micro trends early. Investors who recognized the potential in e-commerce logistics before it became an industry standard were those who reaped significant returns. Delhivery's focus on innovation, from AI-driven route optimization to automated warehousing, positioned it at the forefront of a sector transformation, demonstrating that sometimes, the future belongs to those who can predict and adapt to it.

Similarly, in the retail sector, Trent Ltd. provides a compelling narrative on trend-based investment. While traditional apparel companies focused on maintaining their market share through established channels, Trent foresaw a different trend: the democratization of fashion. With brands like Zudio, they catered to an increasing demand for affordable, yet stylish clothing, tapping into the fast fashion trend that was sweeping across demographics. By aligning their business model with consumer trends towards value-for-money fashion, Trent not only expanded its footprint but also saw its stock value appreciate, even amidst a crowded market.

In today's rapidly evolving world, consumer behaviours, cultural changes, technological advancements, and societal shifts are constantly reshaping industries and economies. What was relevant yesterday may be obsolete tomorrow. For investors, this fast-paced change creates both opportunities and challenges. How do we identify the next big movement in the markets? How do we invest wisely in a future that feels uncertain?

Trend based Investing requires an ability to see the big picture, but also to recognize the smaller, specific changes within broader trends. These "micro-trends" may seem subtle at first, but they can often be the seeds of exponential growth.

Micro-trends are the niche shifts within larger, established trends. While macro-trends like digital transformation, sustainability, and health tech are well-known, micro-trends are the unique pockets within these movements that may initially go unnoticed. However, they represent specific needs, under-served markets, or emerging consumer preferences.

Recognizing these micro-trends allows us to identify businesses that are uniquely positioned to grow, creating opportunities for those who get in early. For example, while "renewable energy" is a well-recognized trend, micro-trends like energy storage solutions offer focused, high-potential investment opportunities within this broader movement.

By focusing on trends that align with future societal and technological shifts, we can find companies that are not only innovative but are also strategically positioned to benefit as these shifts unfold. This approach offers investors a forward-looking method to assess value, capturing opportunities that are often overlooked by traditional, valuation-driven approaches.

My Motivation Behind This Book

During my career of investing, I have observed firsthand how the markets reward those who can foresee change. I have witnessed many investors who have created their wealth from almost nothing by betting on the futuristic and fundamentally sound businesses.

While investing has long been about understanding the fundamentals, we are now in a new era where spotting trends early can be equally powerful. Investing based on sectoral micro trends allows investors to capitalize on growth opportunities before they hit the mainstream.

My initial motivation for authoring this book was to assist myself in researching and identifying futuristic trends. However, as I delved deeper into research papers, consulting reports, and online resources, and gathered knowledge, I realized that this knowledge could help many investors like me and that is where the book came into existence. This book aims to provide the tools and mindset needed to identify, analyse, and practically act on sectoral trends within larger structural shifts, enabling informed and strategic decision-making.

The book is more than just a guide to investment; it is a roadmap for those who want to capture tomorrow's

opportunities, today. Investors who adopt a proactive approach to identifying micro-trends are better positioned to capture value at an early stage, well before these trends become widely recognized. This requires a willingness to look beyond short-term market movements and focus on sectors with the potential to shape the future.

This book is written for everyone interested in staying ahead of the curve in the world of investing. It is particularly suited to stock market investors and early-stage investors who are looking to align their portfolios with future-oriented trends, especially within the Indian market.

Trend Investing is a journey that combines curiosity, patience, and insight. It is about understanding the big picture while also grabbing the specific opportunities that align with India's growth story. Do note that the book has considered only those Macro-Micro trends/themes where the possibility of building a business around is high and investors can capitalize on them.

The data and information presented in this book were gathered **during late 2024 to early 2025**. As the world is ever-changing and dynamic, certain data points may evolve significantly over time, while some trends might remain relevant well into the next decade. Readers are encouraged to interpret the content with this context in mind and consider future developments as they arise.

Chapters D, E, and I of this book contain forward-looking statements related to specific segments and sectors. Readers are advised to conduct their own due diligence before using this information as a reference for investing. These statements are intended for educational purposes only and should not be considered as direct investment recommendations.

Chapter **A**

Vision and Trends: Foundational Concepts

Investing success is shaped by more than just numbers and analysis—it is fuelled by vision. Vision is the ability to look beyond present circumstances, to imagine what could be, and to recognize potential that others might overlook. In a rapidly evolving market like India's, where trends emerge with extraordinary speed, having the foresight to anticipate changes can make the difference between being an early mover and being left behind.

Vision in Investing is not about predictions alone; it is about understanding the driving forces behind change and aligning oneself with opportunities as they unfold.

This requires a blend of creativity, intuition, and analytical thinking—a mindset that is willing to embrace uncertainty while staying grounded in observable shifts. In markets where disruptions are frequent and diverse, the next big opportunity often remains hidden until it is too late for many. Vision allows investors to identify these opportunities early and act with conviction.

One of the most effective applications of vision is the ability to identify macro trends—broad, long-term shifts in demographics, technology, policy, or societal behaviour. These serve as the foundation for understanding the direction in which an economy or industry is headed. However, vision does not stop there. The true art lies in drilling down to uncover micro-trends—smaller, nuanced shifts within the broader narrative that have the potential to grow into significant themes. These micro-trends often hold the key to niche opportunities, offering higher growth potential and less competition than well-known macro trends.

Spotting these trends requires a sharp eye for subtle changes. It could be a gradual shift in consumer behaviour, consumption pattern or regulatory changes that open new avenues for businesses. Visionary investors track these developments not just for their immediate impact but for their ability to transform industries over time.

Ultimately, cultivating vision is about developing a mindset that embraces curiosity and constantly seeks to understand the "why" behind emerging patterns. It is a process of connecting the dots between seemingly unrelated events and asking questions others may not consider. By fostering this skill, investors can position themselves to not only react to changes but to lead in recognizing opportunities others miss. This chapter serves as a guide to understanding vision and trends as foundational tools for long-term investment success.

Cultivate Vision and Visualization Skills

Developing a strong sense of vision and the ability to visualize potential futures is essential for making informed decisions in an ever-changing world. These skills go beyond analysing trends; they involve understanding the deeper forces shaping societies, economies, and industries. Here's how individuals can cultivate these capabilities:

Observe and Decode Human Behaviour

The foundation of vision lies in understanding people—their habits, needs, and evolving preferences. By observing how individuals interact with their surroundings, adapt to challenges, and adopt new practices, one can identify emerging patterns. For example, the shift toward remote work was not merely a technological phenomenon but a response to changing societal needs for flexibility and work-life balance.

Anticipate Sustainability and Lasting Impact

Not every change is permanent. Distinguishing between temporary shifts and enduring transformations requires critical thinking and questioning. Ask: *Will this change become ingrained in daily life, or is it a fleeting response to a temporary condition?* For instance, the focus on renewable energy solutions reflects a long-term global commitment to sustainability, not just a short-term reaction to climate policies.

Understand Broader Forces Driving Change

Visionary thinking requires an understanding of macro-level drivers such as economic shifts, technological advancements, and societal trends. It is not just about observing immediate changes but contextualizing them within larger frameworks like government policy, global market trends, and technological disruption.

Adopt a Long-Term Perspective

True vision involves patience. Understanding that meaningful progress often takes time enables one to stay committed through fluctuations. This is particularly relevant in areas of innovation and emerging markets, where periods of volatility often precede sustained growth.

Learn from Historical Patterns

History often provides clues to the future. By studying previous cycles and disruptions, one can anticipate how current developments may unfold. For example, examining the industrial revolution can offer insights into today's digital transformation and its long-term implications.

Visualize Multiple Futures

Visualization involves imagining a variety of scenarios for how a sector, industry, or society might evolve. This mental exercise sharpens foresight and enables better decision-making. Consider both opportunities and risks: *What challenges might arise? What milestones must be achieved for success?*

Think Beyond the Obvious

Broadening vision means exploring areas outside your immediate scope. For instance, while focusing on technology, also consider its ripple effects on education, healthcare, or urban planning. Seeing the interconnectedness of different domains enhances your ability to anticipate change.

Immerse Yourself in Continuous Learning

Staying informed is key to sharpening vision. Read widely, engage with diverse perspectives, and remain curious about developments across industries and geographies. A well-rounded knowledge base fuels creativity and helps visualize potential futures more comprehensively.

Balance Optimism with Pragmatism

While vision is inherently forward-looking, it must be grounded. This balance ensures that aspirations remain achievable and rooted in practical considerations. Visualize not just the possibilities but also the challenges and trade-offs involved.

By broadening perspective and cultivating the ability to visualize a range of possibilities, one can make better decisions, identify opportunities early, and adapt proactively to the unfolding future. Vision is not just about predicting the next big thing—it is about deeply understanding the forces shaping the world and aligning actions with long-term potential.

The Art of Trend

A trend is a general direction in which something is developing or changing over time. In the context of investing, trends reflect the shifting interests, needs, standards and behaviours of individuals, government, and businesses. Trends are often sparked by innovation, changes in technology, cultural shifts, economic factors, policies, or global events and are typically characterized by their growth trajectory and impact on industries, markets, and societies.

Trends differ from fads in that they are generally more sustainable and can result in significant changes in long term consumer behaviour or business operations over time. While a fad may be short-lived, a trend often signals deeper, more lasting change.

The art of identifying and playing trends is a skill that mostly requires patience, persistence, and practice—it is as much about experience as it is about knowledge. Mastery in this domain is not achieved overnight but is the result of a gradual process of learning, experimenting, and refining. Connecting the dots between seemingly unrelated events, behaviours, or shifts in the market is a nuanced skill that develops with time and effort.

Initially, the process can feel overwhelming. Beginners may struggle to distinguish between passing fads and sustainable trends, or they may fail to recognize the subtle connections between macro shifts and their micro-level implications.

Mistakes in judgment are inevitable in these initial stages—an investor might misinterpret a pattern, overestimate the potential of a trend, or enter too early or too late. However, these missteps are not failures but essential parts of the learning curve.

As individuals invest more time and energy into observing markets, understanding industries, and tracking consumer behaviours, they begin to develop a more intuitive grasp of trends. They learn to identify leading indicators, ask the right questions, and assess the sustainability and scalability of opportunities. With every investment decision, successful or not, they build a repository of insights that sharpens their ability to connect the dots.

Over time, this process cultivates a refined ability to recognize patterns and predict outcomes with greater confidence. The investor becomes adept at distinguishing noise from signal, filtering out distractions to focus on meaningful drivers of change. They learn to balance analytical rigor with creative foresight, blending data with intuition to make informed decisions.

Experience also fosters resilience. An investor who has weathered mistakes and learned from them is less likely to be swayed by short-term setbacks or market volatility. They develop the discipline to stay committed to their convictions, understanding that trend investing is a long-term game requiring patience and perspective.

Ultimately, becoming a master at identifying and playing trends is less about innate talent and more about the willingness to engage in the process of continuous learning. It is about embracing the journey, acknowledging the value of mistakes, and committing to the craft with curiosity and determination. With time, effort, and the accumulation of experience, individuals can transform their initial uncertainties into expertise, positioning themselves to capitalize on emerging opportunities with confidence and skill.

The Evolution of Trends

Trends evolve through a series of stages that represent how they move from novelty to possible mainstream adoption. Understanding these stages helps investors and businesses anticipate when a trend is likely to gain traction or reach sustainability.

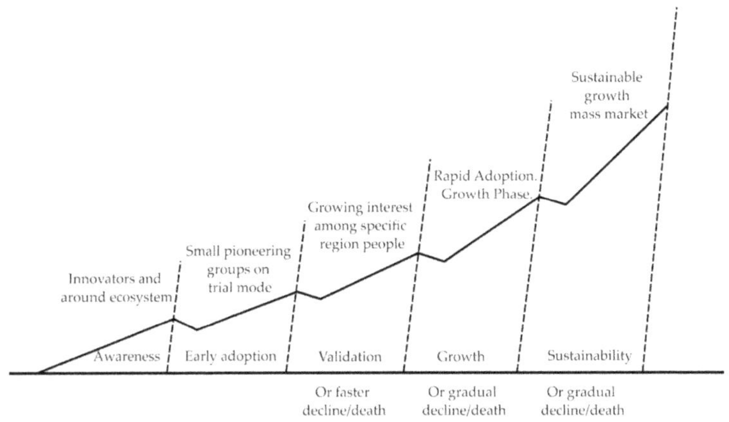

Illustration A.1 Evolution of Trends

Here is a breakdown:

1. **Awareness**: This is the initial exposure to a trend or habit, where only a few people are aware of it. At this stage, the trend is often niche, appealing to innovators or early experimenters who are curious about new ideas or practices. For instance, early interest in plant-based diets or electric vehicles began with a small, environmentally conscious segment.

2. **Early Adoption**: A smaller, pioneering group starts to adopt or try out the trend. These early adopters often influence others, helping spread the idea through word-of-mouth or by demonstrating the trend's benefits. This stage is critical for the trend's visibility, as the experiences of early adopters can either encourage or deter others.

3. **Validation**: Growing interest emerges as more people begin to see value in the trend. As adoption expands, the trend gains validation, often marked by positive reviews, social proof, and an increase in related product offerings. For instance, when fitness apps became popular, they quickly moved from novelty to validation as more people experienced the benefits of on-demand workouts.

4. **Growth**: The trend enters a phase of rapid adoption, becoming widespread and reaching mainstream appeal. Companies and marketers begin to cater to this trend, making it even more accessible. In the case of digital payments, for example, growth was driven by convenience and widespread acceptance across industries.

5. **Sustainability**: In the final stage, the trend becomes deeply integrated into society or daily life, reaching a point where it is likely to remain stable over time. A trend at this stage has moved beyond being a "trend" and is now considered a standard or expectation, such as use of smartphones.

This lifecycle from Awareness to Sustainability demonstrates how habits and trends evolve. Investors and businesses can use this framework to evaluate a trend's potential and assess when a trend might gain sustainable traction.

The point of validation is where the investors should try to get exposure into related businesses keeping business related factors and valuations in mind. Investing at that stage can maximize risk adjusted returns as investors are not paying much for the growth (Valuation Margin of safety) and having reasonable assurance from buyers/users about value for money and product market fit.

Layers of Trends: A Hierarchical Perspective

Investing in trends requires a structured approach to analyse the interconnections between various layers of opportunities. These layers start at the foundational level of a country's demographics and progress to macro, micro, and sub-micro trends. Each layer provides investors with a deeper understanding of how broad forces shape industries and businesses. By recognizing these layers, investors can identify growth opportunities, assess market potential, and align investments with the evolving landscape.

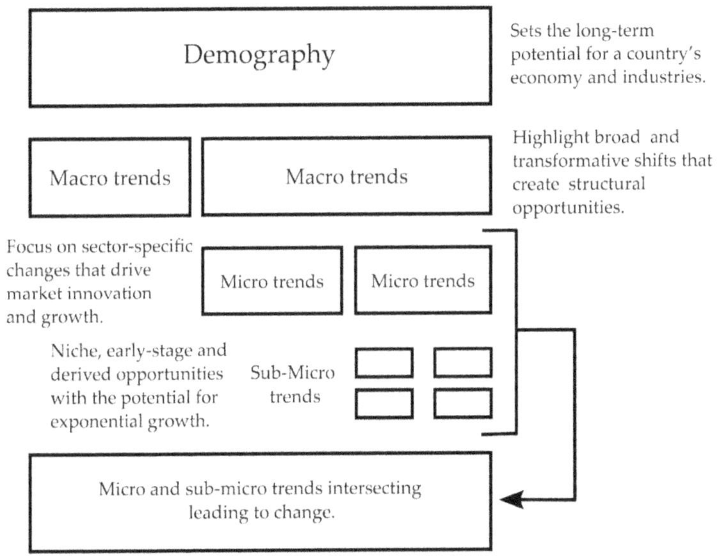

Illustration A.2 Hierarchy of Trends

1. Country's Demography: The Foundational Layer

At the base of all trends lies a country's demography, which defines the long-term trajectory of its economy and growth. Factors such as population size, age distribution, fertility rates, and urbanization patterns drive consumer behaviour and economic policies. For example:

- **India**: With a population exceeding 1.4 billion, a median age of 28 years, and rapid urbanization, India's demographics create a foundation for sustained consumption growth, labour market expansion, and infrastructure demand. This demographic advantage influences sectors like housing, consumer goods, healthcare, and education.

Countries with young populations like India have a natural edge in driving demand, while aging nations like Japan focus more on technology and healthcare to address their demographic challenges.

2. **Macro Trends: The Big Picture Drivers**

Macro trends are large-scale, multi-sector forces that shape economies and industries over decades. These trends arise from demographic shifts, technological revolutions, environmental challenges, or policy reforms. Macro trends provide a broad canvas on which micro and sub-micro trends emerge.

- **Digital Transformation**: The rapid adoption of technology driven by increasing internet penetration and government initiatives like Digital India.

- **Sustainability**: A shift toward renewable energy, electric mobility, and circular economies.

These trends provide the overarching direction for industries and serve as a springboard for more focused opportunities.

3. **Micro Trends: Emerging Themes Within Macro Trends**

Micro trends are sector-specific or industry-level changes that emerge within macro trends. These represent actionable themes where businesses innovate, adapt, and grow to meet evolving consumer demands. Micro trends often highlight sectors poised for growth.

Within the Macro Trend of Digital Transformation:

- Fintech innovations such as UPI-based payment platforms.

- E-commerce growth in Tier-2 and Tier-3 cities.

Within the Macro Trend of Sustainability:

- Solar energy installations and rooftop systems.

- Growth of electric two-wheelers and charging infrastructure.

Micro trends help investors narrow their focus and identify industries that are experiencing significant transformations.

4. **Sub-Micro Trends: Niche Opportunities**

Sub-micro trends are granular, niche opportunities that arise within micro trends. These are often early-stage innovations or specific market segments that hold immense growth potential. Sub-micro trends are where investors can find untapped opportunities by relating with existing sustainable macro trends and finding the link. As Macro trend becomes stronger, the sub micro trends also evolve along with.

Within the Micro Trend of Electronic Manufacturing:

- Rise of refrigerators manufacturing as cold chain logistics

- Manufacturing of electronic components as import reduced in manufacturing.

Within the Micro Trend of Electric Vehicles:

- Battery swapping stations for two-wheelers and three-wheelers.

- Companies specializing in lithium-ion battery recycling.

Sub-micro trends often carry higher risks but can deliver outsized returns when identified and nurtured early.

By understanding the layers of trends—demography, macro, micro, and sub-micro—investors can identify opportunities at varying scales of risk and reward. Each layer provides unique insights:

Whether investing in a focused sub-micro trend, a diversified business spanning multiple layers, or a country itself as a macro trend, this layered perspective equips investors to make informed and strategic decisions aligned with the evolving global landscape.

Overlaps and Conglomerates

As investors delve deeper into the layers of trends, they will often encounter businesses that do not fit neatly into a single trend category. Instead, many companies operate across multiple trends, creating overlaps. These overlaps occur when businesses align with more than one micro or sub-micro trend, leveraging synergies to maximize growth opportunities. Additionally, some conglomerates and large corporations extend their operations across multiple macro and micro trends, creating a unique complexity that investors need to navigate strategically.

Understanding Overlaps in Businesses

Overlapping businesses are those that target more than one trend simultaneously, often by offering diversified products, services, or solutions that cater to various consumer needs. These overlaps can be deliberate, as companies identify opportunities to cross-leverage their capabilities, or they can arise organically as businesses evolve to adapt to changing market dynamics.

Examples of Overlapping Businesses in India:

- Fintech and E-commerce: Platforms like Paytm and PhonePe initially focused on digital payments but have since expanded into areas like e-commerce, digital lending, and financial investments. This positions them at the intersection of the Digital Transformation macro trend and multiple micro trends, such as Fintech Growth and E-commerce Expansion.

- Sustainability and Technology: Companies like Tata Power combine their focus on renewable energy with digital solutions for energy management, such as IoT-based smart meters. This positions them within both the Sustainability macro trend and the Tech-Enabled Infrastructure micro trend.

For investors, overlapping businesses can provide exposure to multiple trends, offering diversified growth potential. However, these overlaps also require a nuanced evaluation of the company's ability to manage its resources and execute effectively across diverse areas.

Conglomerates: Broad-Based Growth Opportunities

Conglomerates are large, diversified businesses that operate across multiple industries, often spanning several macro and micro trends. Their scale, resource base, and ability to enter new markets allow them to capitalize on a broad range of opportunities. However, this diversification can also dilute focus, making it critical for investors to assess how well these companies manage their various business verticals.

Example of Indian Conglomerates:

Tata Group

- Electric Vehicles (EVs): Tata Motors is a key player in the Electric Mobility micro trend.

- Renewable Energy: Tata Power drives initiatives within the Sustainability macro trend.

- IT Services and Digital Transformation: TCS remains a leader in the Technology and Digital Services macro trend.

- E-commerce: Tata Neu integrates services across retail, travel, and digital consumption trends.

Reliance can be cited as another example here. These conglomerates offer exposure to a wide range of growth opportunities, making them attractive to investors looking for diversified bets across multiple trends. However, the challenge lies in evaluating whether the conglomerate's resources are effectively allocated across its verticals and whether each segment operates efficiently.

Patterns of Trends

- **Steady Growth**: Gradual increase in interest or adoption, showing long-term sustainability. Examples: digital payments, renewable energy.

- **Rapid Growth with Stabilization**: Sharp increase in interest initially, followed by stabilization. Examples: social media adoption, e-commerce platforms.

- **Gradual Rise, Mid Decline, Resurgence**: Strong initial interest, a drop in engagement, and later a revival as the trend adapts or finds a new audience.

- **Early Spike and Gradual Decline**: Strong initial interest followed by a gradual decline in interest and usage (Quick Disruption by better solutions).

- **Short-lived Peaks (Fads)**: High but brief interest before quickly fading. Examples: short-term fashion trends.

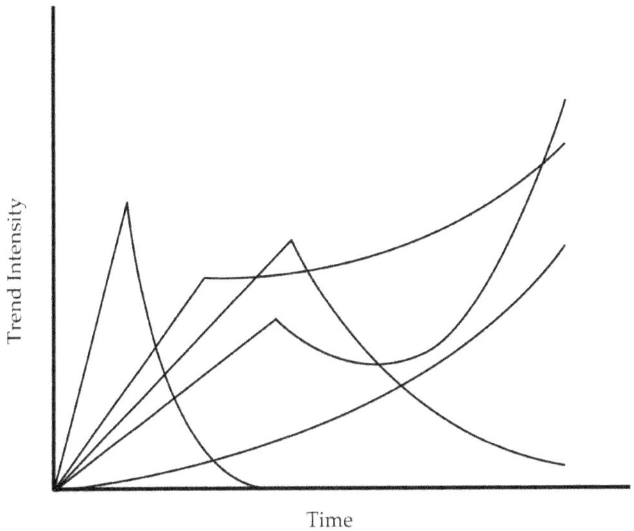

Illustration A.3 Trend Patterns: Intensity vs Time.

Trends Identification

Identifying trends is a mix of observation, analysis, and intuition. It requires being attuned to changes in consumer behaviour, industry developments, and broader cultural shifts. Here are some effective methods for identifying trends:

Monitor Consumer Behaviour and Preferences

Understanding changes in consumer habits is one of the most reliable ways to identify trends early:

- **Observe Everyday Habits**: Look at how people are spending their time and money. Are they adopting new technologies, prioritizing certain values (like sustainability or health), or seeking unique experiences?

- **Identify Pain Points**: Trends often emerge to solve common problems. Observing consumer complaints, challenges, or unmet needs can give early signals of trends. For instance, the growth of meal delivery services was partly driven by a need for convenience and lack of time for home-cooked meals.

Track Digital Platforms and Social Media

Social media and online communities are hubs for trendspotting, as they capture real-time discussions and reflect what's resonating with people:

- **Monitor Hashtags and Trending Topics**: Platforms like Twitter, Instagram, and TikTok highlight popular topics and hashtags, showing what is currently catching public attention. This is more relevant to B2C businesses.

- **Explore Niche Communities**: Online forums and platforms with specialized groups often reflect niche interests and early adoption trends. Communities discussing emerging tech, alternative lifestyles, or health trends can reveal what is likely to gain traction.

- **Follow Influencers and Early Adopters**: Influencers and thought leaders often set trends by introducing new products or ideas to their followers. Observing these individuals can help you spot trends at an early stage.

Analyse Data with Trend Tools and Analytics

Data-driven tools can provide valuable insights into which topics and products are gaining traction:

- **Google Trends**: This tool highlights rising search terms and allows you to track interest in a topic over time. For example, by analysing search interest in "electric vehicles," you could observe a steady increase in interest as the trend gained traction.

- **Keyword Analysis**: Using keyword research tools can show search volume growth for specific terms, helping you gauge which topics are trending in digital spaces.

Follow Industry Publications and Reports

Industry publications, reports, and trade journals often highlight emerging trends within specific sectors:

- **Read Industry Reports**: Major consulting firms (like McKinsey, Deloitte, PwC) and market research companies publish reports that forecast sector trends. These reports are valuable resources for identifying macro and micro trends in various industries.

- **Subscribe to Trade Journals**: Industry-specific publications and newsletters provide insights into shifts within specialized fields, whether it is healthcare, technology, retail, or sustainability. For instance, an Agri-tech journal may discuss the increasing adoption of precision farming tools.

Engage with Conferences, Webinars, and Networking Events

Industry events and expert discussions offer real-time insights into where sectors are headed:

- **Attend Conferences and Webinars**: Conferences often feature discussions on emerging technologies, consumer demands, and upcoming market changes. This is where industry leaders discuss innovations, offering clues about upcoming trends.

- **Join Networking Groups**: Networking groups, both online and offline, provide direct access to industry professionals who are often on the front lines of emerging trends. Conversations with experts can offer invaluable insights into what is evolving within specific markets.

Observe Cultural, Social, and Economic Shifts

Trends are often influenced by broader cultural, social, and economic factors. Paying attention to these forces can help you anticipate trends before they become mainstream:

- **Watch for Cultural Shifts**: Changes in values and attitudes often drive trends. For example, the shift toward sustainability and conscious consumerism reflects growing environmental awareness.

- **Consider Economic Changes**: Economic shifts, like a recession, can impact spending habits and lead to the rise of budget-friendly trends. For instance, during economic downturns, trends around frugality, thrift shopping, or DIY solutions often emerge.

- **Pay Attention to Demographic Shifts**: As generations age or population segments grow, they often influence market demands. For example, India's young demographic has contributed to a digital-first approach in many sectors, including education and finance.

Utilize Your Intuition and Pattern Recognition Skills

Finally, trend identification is not always about hard data. Sometimes, it is about recognizing patterns and making intuitive connections:

- **Observe Repeated Patterns**: Many trends evolve in cycles. By observing patterns from the past, you can anticipate which trends may come back with a modern twist (e.g., the resurgence of vintage fashion).

- **Test and Validate Hypotheses**: When you spot an early trend, test your hypothesis by watching for signs that reinforce or contradict it. For example, if you think wellness travel is a rising trend, you could track the increase in wellness retreats and tourist demand for nature-based activities.

Observe Trends in Developed Nations

Developed nations often serve as early testing grounds for innovations and novel solutions, especially in technology, lifestyle products, and services. Observing how these populations react to innovative solutions can provide a glimpse into trends that might soon emerge in other markets:

- **Adoption Patterns**: If consumers in developed countries show sustained interest in a new product, service, or lifestyle change, it is a strong indicator that this trend addresses real needs or pain points, making it likely to resonate with consumers elsewhere.

- **Adaptations for Local Markets**: Trends from developed nations often require adaptation to fit the cultural, economic, or technological landscape of emerging markets. Observing the adjustments made in other regions can provide clues about how the trend might take shape locally. For example, while ride-sharing apps gained popularity in the U.S., adaptations like cash payment options and smaller vehicle types made the service more accessible and widely adopted in countries like India.

- **Leading Indicators**: Developed countries are often on the leading edge of regulatory, environmental, or technological changes. Watching these markets closely can reveal trends that may gradually influence policies or consumer expectations in other regions. Examples include shifts toward sustainability, privacy-focused technology, or work-from-home adaptations that emerged early in developed countries and later spread globally.

Trend Indicators and Signals to Watch For

Recognizing the early signs that a trend is moving from niche to mainstream can help investors position themselves ahead of the curve. Here are some indicators that signal when a trend is gaining momentum:

Increased Media Coverage

When a trend begins to gain traction, it typically attracts media attention. Early articles may appear in niche publications or industry journals, but as the trend grows, it spreads to mainstream media, news segments, and high-traffic websites.

Pay attention to the type of coverage—if respected publications or analysts start discussing the trend as an important shift rather than a passing novelty, it is likely becoming more established. For instance, the early buzz around "telemedicine" evolved from industry reports to mainstream news, signalling it was here to stay.

Rise in Investment

A surge in venture capital, corporate investment, or even government funding in a particular area can indicate a trend's potential. Investors often seek out high-growth areas with the potential for long-term impact, and tracking these investments can reveal where the market is focusing.

For example, the rise in venture capital investment in renewable energy and electric vehicles over the last decade showed that these were no longer niche interests but were being positioned as the future of energy and transportation.

Product Variations and Market Competition

When a trend gains momentum, companies begin creating variations of products and services to meet diverse consumer needs within that trend. Additionally, more competitors enter the space, indicating that there's significant consumer demand.

For example, when gluten-free diets became popular, food companies introduced a range of gluten-free products, from snacks to beverages. The increased variety and competition reflected a strong consumer demand rather than a fleeting interest.

Adoption by Key Demographics

Certain demographics, especially Millennials and Gen Z, often lead the way in adopting latest trends. If these groups are embracing a trend, it is a good signal that it may become mainstream, as their preferences often influence wider societal and market changes.

Trends in fashion, and technology for instance, often gain early traction with younger consumers who prioritize innovation and values-based choices. Watching adoption patterns within these demographics can help identify which trends have staying power.

Differentiate Between Trends and Fads

Not every new craze is a trend with long-term potential; some are simply fads that capture attention briefly and fade away. Here are key distinctions between trends and fads that can help investors focus on sustainable opportunities:

Depth of Consumer Need

- **Trends** are typically rooted in a deeper, often evolving consumer need, making them more resilient over time. They address genuine concerns, desires, or problems that people are motivated to solve. For example, the trend toward remote work fulfils the needs for flexibility, work-life balance, and productivity, making it more likely to remain relevant.

- **Fads**, on the other hand, are often driven by novelty or a "cool factor" rather than a deep consumer need. They may catch on quickly but lack the substance to persist once initial excitement fades. A good example is the "hoverboard" craze, which did not solve a real need and quickly lost popularity.

Consistency Across Demographics

- **Trends** generally resonate with multiple demographic groups and have cross-generational appeal. When a trend is adopted by a variety of consumer segments—different age groups, socioeconomic backgrounds, or regions—it indicates broad relevance and the potential for sustained growth.

- **Fads** are often limited to specific groups and rarely appeal across demographics. It suddenly comes into craze and gradually or quickly disappear among small groups.

Industry Adoption and Infrastructure Development

- **Trends** are often reinforced when industries and businesses start making long-term investments to support them. Infrastructure, products, and services are developed to cater to the trend, which further solidifies its staying power. Electric vehicles, for example, moved from a niche interest to a sustainable trend as automakers invested heavily in R&D, and governments implemented policies and infrastructure, like charging stations, to support EVs.

- **Fads** rarely see this level of industry commitment. Businesses might capitalize on fads with quick product launches, but they typically do not allocate significant resources to develop long-term infrastructure. For instance, the covid based rise in demand of masks and sanitizers.

Evolution and Adaptability

- **Trends** have the capacity to evolve and adapt to new contexts, technologies, and consumer expectations. They are not fixed; instead, they grow with changing conditions. The fitness trend, for example, has evolved over the years from aerobics in the '80s to today's home workouts, wearable tech, and virtual fitness communities.

- **Fads** tend to be rigid and lack the flexibility to adapt. They capture a moment and quickly become outdated. Once the initial interest fades, fads have limited ability to reinvent themselves or stay relevant.

Longevity and Consumer Retention

- **Trends** demonstrate staying power through consumer retention and repeat engagement. People return to products, services, or experiences that are part of a sustainable trend because it integrates into their lives. For instance, healthy and protein-based foods initially emerged as a trend, but consumer loyalty has persisted, making it a standard choice in food stores.

- **Fads** often show high engagement initially, followed by a steep drop-off as consumers lose interest. Fads might see quick, widespread adoption but struggle to retain users once the novelty wears off, such as when Pokémon Go saw an initial boom but quickly lost daily active users as interest waned.

Track the Lifecycle of a Trend

Understanding the lifecycle of a trend is essential to evaluating its potential for growth, sustainability, or eventual decline. Here is how to assess where a trend is within its lifecycle:

Adoption Rate

Tracking the rate at which consumers adopt a trend can reveal where it stands in its lifecycle. During the initial stages, adoption rates may be slow but will typically pick up as awareness grows.

Metrics to Watch: User sign-ups, first-time purchases, app downloads, and new customer growth are valuable indicators of adoption. A trend with steadily increasing adoption rates—like electric vehicles over the past decade—suggests sustained interest and long-term viability.

Market Expansion and Penetration

As a trend matures, it should expand into new markets or regions and reach broader consumer segments. Early adopters are often the first to embrace a trend, but as it grows, it should attract more mainstream consumers.

Metrics to Watch: Geographic spread, demographic diversity of users, and market share growth. For instance, the expansion of plant-based foods from health-conscious consumers to a more mainstream audience shows the trend's progression toward widespread adoption.

Innovation and Improvement

Sustainable trends are often marked by continuous innovation and product improvement. As a trend matures, companies refine their offerings to better serve consumers and outcompete rivals, pushing the trend further into mainstream markets.

Metrics to Watch: Product development cycles, introduction of new features, or enhancements that improve convenience, quality, or user experience. For example, smartphone technology has continuously evolved, with new models regularly introducing advanced features, keeping the trend relevant and pushing it to new heights.

Consumer Retention and Reengagement

Retention and reengagement rates are important indicators of whether a trend is likely to sustain over time. Trends that provide lasting value often see high retention, as consumers continue to use the product or service repeatedly.

Metrics to Watch: Retention rates, monthly active users, and repeat purchase rates. For example, subscription services like

Netflix have sustained high user retention by consistently offering fresh, relevant content, indicating a trend with lasting power.

Revenue Growth and Profitability

Financial health is a strong indicator of a trend's success and longevity. If companies within a trend are experiencing revenue growth and achieving profitability, it suggests that consumer demand is both high and stable and business models are viable.

Metrics to Watch: Revenue growth, profitability, average order value, and customer lifetime value. A trend with strong financials demonstrates that consumers find enough value in it to justify regular spending, as seen in the growth of e-commerce and online retail.

Cultural and Social Integration

When a trend becomes part of daily life or integrates into cultural norms, it is often a sign that it has reached maturity. Trends that shape consumer habits, values, or social behaviours often indicate they are here to stay.

Metrics to Watch: Mentions in popular media, usage in common language, and alignment with cultural movements. For instance, sustainability has gone from being a niche interest to a social norm, with terms like "eco-friendly" and "carbon footprint" becoming part of everyday conversations.

Shift in Regulatory or Policy Support

Governmental support and policy changes often strengthen a trend's lifecycle, especially in areas like clean energy, data privacy, or health tech. When governments start to create policies supporting a trend, it often indicates that the trend is transitioning from niche to mainstream.

Metrics to Watch: Regulatory approvals, new laws, subsidies, and incentives. For instance, policies supporting renewable energy and electric vehicles have bolstered these trends, making them more viable and attractive to both consumers and investors.

Trend vs Value Migration

Value Migration is the movement of value—economic and shareholder—from one business model or industry to another, driven by changes in customer priorities, technological advances, or inefficiencies in current offerings. Trends are the indications of change, often creating the conditions for value migration by reshaping industries and consumer behaviours. These broader shifts act as catalysts, enabling businesses with superior models to capture value from those unable to adapt. Value migration is not a one-time occurrence but a dynamic process where businesses adapt to or resist trends. Companies that successfully align their models with emerging trends can secure value, while those that fail face value erosion.

Trends serve as the drivers of change, while value migration is the outcome of businesses responding—or failing to respond—to these changes. By understanding the interplay between trends and value migration, businesses can position themselves to capture value, and investors can identify opportunities for growth and avoid pitfalls.

Case Studies of Successful Trend Identification and Investment

Real-world examples offer invaluable insights into how successful companies and investors identify, evaluate, and act on trends. Each case study below highlights a different type of trend, the indicators that signalled its potential, the actions taken, and the outcomes.

Case Study 1:
Shopify and the Growth of E-Commerce

Trend Identified

E-commerce and Online Retail

Background

As internet penetration increased globally, more consumers shifted toward online shopping. Shopify identified the need for an easy-to-use platform that allowed small businesses to set up online stores without complex development.

Indicators

Steady increase in internet access and consumer comfort with online transactions. High demand from small and medium-sized businesses for affordable e-commerce solutions. Growing interest in direct-to-consumer business models, reducing reliance on third-party platforms

Actions Taken

Shopify developed a platform enabling small businesses to create e-commerce websites with user-friendly, customizable features. The company expanded its offerings to include tools for inventory management, payments, and even logistics, providing a comprehensive solution for online businesses. Shopify actively pursued partnerships with social media platforms and introduced integrations that made it easy for merchants to sell directly via social media, capitalizing on another growing trend: social commerce.

Outcomes

Shopify became a leader in the e-commerce platform space, with millions of merchants using its platform to power their online stores. During the COVID-19 pandemic, Shopify experienced significant growth as physical retailers moved online, solidifying its position as a crucial tool for e-commerce.

Key Takeaway

Identifying pain points within a larger trend (e.g., e-commerce) and providing an accessible, scalable solution can drive long-term growth and make a company indispensable to its users. Finding a pivotal point (e.g., Covid) will allow investors to make massive wealth.

Indian Cases

Case Study 2:
Jio and the Digital Connectivity Revolution

Trend Identified

Digital Connectivity and Affordable Internet Access

Background

India had long faced high data costs, which limited internet access for many people, especially in rural areas. Recognizing the potential demand for affordable digital connectivity, Reliance Jio launched a disruptive model focused on low-cost, high-speed data.

Indicators

India's large population of young, tech-savvy consumers and rising smartphone adoption. An increase in digital services, mobile applications, and demand for online entertainment, indicating a potential market for affordable data. A push from the Indian government for digital inclusion through initiatives like Digital India, highlighting the need for broader internet access.

Actions Taken

Jio entered the market in 2016 with aggressive pricing, offering free data and calls for an initial period, quickly building a massive user base. The company invested heavily in 4G infrastructure, allowing them to deliver high-speed internet at a fraction of the cost compared to competitors. Jio capitalized on its ecosystem approach by offering bundled services (like Jio-TV, Jio-Saavn for music, and Jio-Cinema for video streaming), creating a digital-first ecosystem that attracted millions of users.

Outcomes

Jio added over one hundred million users within six months of its launch, fundamentally transforming India's telecom industry and forcing competitors to lower their prices. The influx of affordable internet access accelerated India's digital economy, leading to increased adoption of online services, mobile payments, and e-commerce. Today, Jio is one of India's largest telecom operators, and its success has propelled Reliance into new sectors, including digital payments, e-commerce, and AI.

Key Takeaway

By identifying the need for affordable digital access and implementing a customer-focused pricing model, Jio captured and fuelled the digital connectivity trend, reshaping the entire telecom industry in India.

Case Study 3:
Zomato and the Food Delivery Ecosystem

Trend Identified

Online Food Delivery and Digital Convenience

Background

As smartphones and internet access became more affordable, consumer demand for convenience grew. Zomato identified the potential for online food delivery in urban areas, leveraging India's large population and rising middle class.

Indicators

Increasing smartphone penetration and data affordability due to telecom developments (notably Jio's market disruption). A cultural shift toward convenience in urban centres, where consumers increasingly sought quick, accessible food options. Rising disposable incomes among young professionals and an expanding base of double-income households in cities, contributing to demand for food delivery services.

Actions Taken

Zomato expanded from a restaurant discovery platform into food delivery, building a user-friendly app and partnering with local restaurants. The company invested heavily in logistics, developing a fleet of delivery personnel to reach consumers quickly and efficiently. Zomato also incorporated digital payment options, making transactions easy and promoting frequent use. Additionally, they introduced loyalty programs and exclusive memberships to retain customers.

Outcomes

Zomato became one of India's top food delivery platforms, with millions of active users and a significant presence in urban and semi-urban areas. The company went public in 2021, marking a landmark moment for Indian tech IPOs, and its stock debut highlighted investor confidence in digital convenience trends. Zomato's success accelerated the online food delivery trend, paving the way for other entrants and the expansion of India's gig economy.

Key Takeaway

By combining consumer insights on convenience with investments in digital payments and logistics, Zomato capitalized on the shift toward online food delivery, helping shape India's food tech industry.

Lessons from These Case Studies

Each of these examples illustrates different approaches to trend identification and execution. Look for early indicators of growth potential, including consumer interest, regulatory support, or shifts in technology. Trends succeed when products or services are accessible and user-friendly, broadening the appeal to mainstream audiences.

Building necessary infrastructure or vertical integration can enhance a trend's adoption and ensure long-term sustainability. Strategic partnerships can accelerate a trend's growth by improving distribution and making products more accessible.

How Demography Shapes the Future

Demographics, a crucial pillar of macroeconomics, significantly shape a nation's economic trajectory. Fertility rates, population size, age distribution, migration, and dependency ratios have far-reaching implications for productivity, consumption, investment patterns which ultimately defines the growth trajectory. This chapter delves into the macroeconomic implications of demographics worldwide, with a particular focus on India.

The dynamics of population growth vary significantly across continents, shaping their economic and social trajectories. Africa stands out with a young and rapidly expanding population, projected to double by 2050. High fertility rates and an untapped economic potential position the continent as a promising yet challenging frontier, requiring substantial investments in education, infrastructure, and governance.

Asia, the world's most populous continent, presents a mixed demographic picture. East Asian nations such as Japan, South Korea, and China face declining fertility rates and aging populations, leading to shrinking workforces and rising dependency ratios. In contrast, South Asia, particularly India, continues to experience steady population growth, driven by a younger demographic and a fertility rate nearing stabilization.

In Europe and North America, aging populations and persistently low fertility rates present long-term economic challenges. Europe's average fertility rate of approximately 1.5 and Japan's notably lower rate of 1.3 reflect demographic stagnation, increasing the burden on shrinking workforces to sustain aging populations.

Meanwhile, in developing economies like India, where the fertility rate is approaching the replacement level of 2.1, a demographic sweet spot emerges. This stabilization offers a window of opportunity for accelerated economic growth, provided the country capitalizes on its youthful workforce through employment and education reforms.

The average age across continents further highlights these contrasts. Aging economies such as Japan and Italy, with average ages above 47 years, grapple with workforce shortages and rising healthcare costs. On the other hand, young economies in Africa and South Asia, with average ages below 30, exhibit economic vibrancy but face pressing challenges in creating jobs, improving education systems, and building sustainable infrastructure. These demographic realities underscore the diverse pathways countries must navigate, balancing opportunities with significant socioeconomic hurdles.

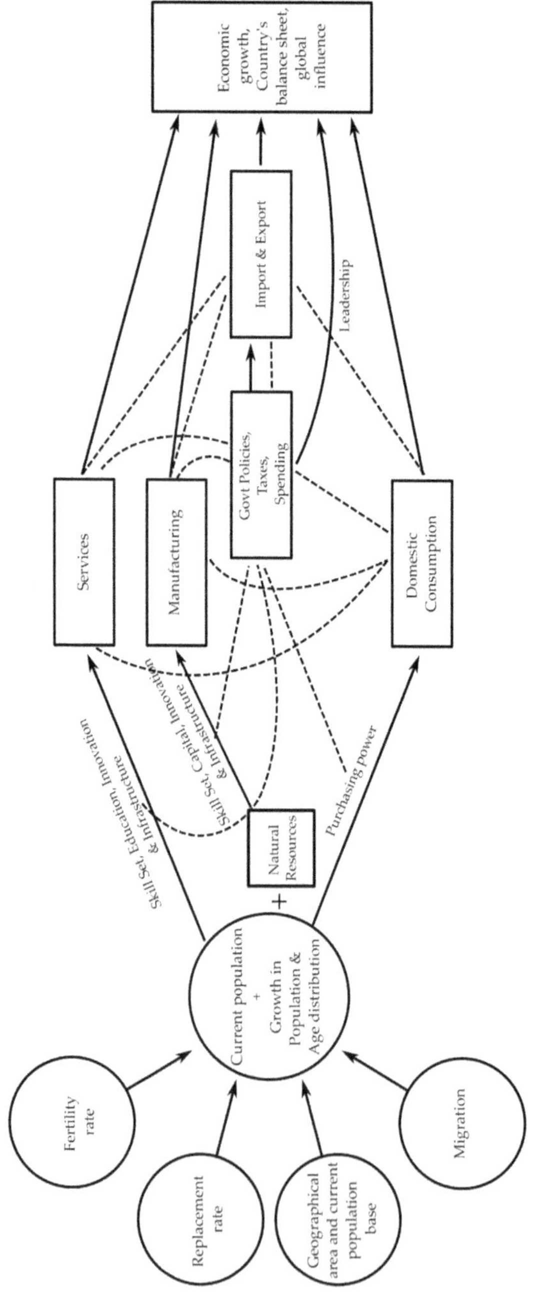

Illustration B.1 Major factors affecting Demographics and their relationships to economic parameters.

The interplay of demographic factors such as fertility rates, population size, age distribution, migration, and dependency ratios form the foundation of global economic dynamics. These elements not only influence labour markets, consumption patterns, and fiscal policies but also shape a nation's capacity to innovate, adapt, and sustain growth. Countries with youthful populations, like India and much of Africa, hold the promise of robust economic expansion, provided they address challenges in education, healthcare, and job creation. Conversely, aging economies must leverage technology, innovation, and migration to maintain stability and growth. Understanding these demographic relationships is crucial for investors, businesses, and policymakers to anticipate shifts, harness opportunities, and mitigate challenges in an ever-evolving global landscape.

Youthful Economies and Growth Potential

Youthful economies, characterized by a high proportion of young people in their populations, present immense opportunities for economic growth, innovation, and global influence. These economies often possess a demographic structure conducive to labour-intensive industries, robust consumption, and technological adaptation, which collectively form a solid foundation for long-term growth.

Demographic Dividend

A youthful population translates into a larger workforce, which can drive economic productivity and increase national income. Countries like India, where over 50% of the population is below the age of thirty, are poised to benefit from this demographic dividend for decades.

Younger populations are active consumers, fuelling demand for goods and services across various sectors, including technology, entertainment, housing, and transportation.

Younger demographics tend to exhibit entrepreneurial enthusiasm, driving innovation, startups, and economic diversification. For instance, economies with high youth populations often become hubs for emerging industries like fintech and e-commerce.

Opportunities in Key Sectors

Education and Skilling: Youthful economies require significant investments in education and vocational training to ensure the workforce is equipped with the skills needed in the modern economy. For example, programs like India's Skill India initiative aim to upskill millions of workers annually.

Technology Adoption: Young populations are typically early adopters of technology, accelerating the digital transformation of economies. The proliferation of smartphones, internet connectivity, and digital platforms in countries like Indonesia and Kenya highlights this trend.

Infrastructure Development: To cater to the needs of a growing and urbanizing population, youthful economies invest heavily in infrastructure, including transportation, energy, and housing, which creates further growth opportunities.

Economic Resilience and Flexibility

Adaptability to Change: Youthful economies can adapt more quickly to changing global trends due to their openness to innovation and risk-taking. For instance, Vietnam has rapidly integrated into global supply chains due to its agile and young workforce.

Labour Cost Competitiveness: Young and growing workforces often allow for lower labour costs, making these economies attractive destinations for outsourcing and manufacturing.

Challenges of Youthful Economies

Job Creation: While a young workforce is an asset, insufficient job opportunities can lead to high unemployment and social unrest. Ensuring that economic growth keeps pace with population growth is crucial.

Education and Healthcare: Providing quality education and healthcare to a large and young population requires substantial public investment and effective governance.

Urbanization and Infrastructure Stress: Rapid urbanization due to youth migration to cities can strain infrastructure, housing, and public services, leading to congestion and inequality.

Political and Social Stability: Large youth populations demand inclusive policies and governance. Marginalizing this demographic can lead to discontent and instability.

Examples of Youthful Economies

India: With a median age of 28, India exemplifies the potential of a youthful economy. The country is witnessing rapid growth in consumption, technology, and innovation, with significant global investment in sectors like IT and manufacturing.

Africa: As the youngest continent, with a median age of 19, Africa represents a vast untapped market. Nations like Nigeria and Ethiopia are emerging as key players in technology, agriculture, and logistics.

Indonesia: With a young and tech-savvy population, Indonesia has become a leader in Southeast Asia's digital economy, excelling in sectors like e-commerce and fintech.

Long-Term Growth Implications

Sustainable Development: Leveraging youthful populations for sustainable development can position countries as future economic powerhouses. This requires strategic investments in human capital and forward-looking policies.

Global Influence: Youthful economies have the potential to shape global markets and geopolitical trends, supplying skilled labour and innovative solutions to aging economies.

Regional Leadership: Economies with youthful demographics often emerge as regional leaders, attracting foreign direct investment (FDI) and forming key trade networks.

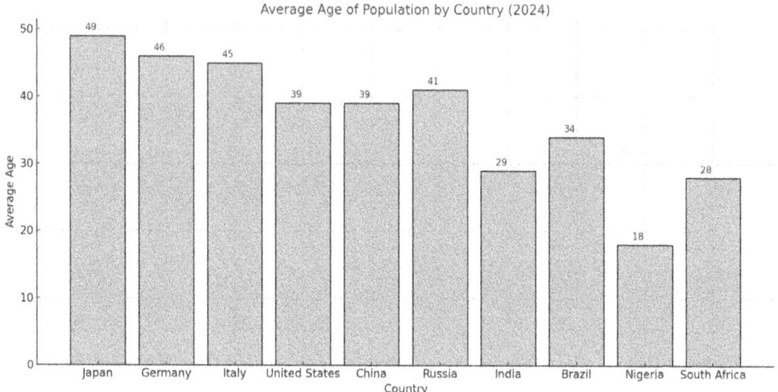

Illustration B.2 Average Population Age of major countries (2024)

Aging Economies and Their Challenges

Aging populations are becoming a critical challenge for many advanced economies, particularly in regions such as Japan, Western Europe, and parts of North America. This demographic shift arises from declining fertility rates and increasing life expectancies, which together lead to a higher proportion of elderly individuals relative to the working-age population. This phenomenon has profound economic, social, and political implications.

Economic Impacts

Shrinking Workforce: A declining working-age population reduces the labour force, leading to slower economic growth and, in extreme cases, labour shortages in essential industries. Japan, for example, has seen its economic expansion suppressed by its shrinking labour pool.

Rising Dependency Ratios: With fewer workers supporting more retirees, the burden on social welfare systems, such as pensions and healthcare, increases significantly. These dynamics put pressure on government budgets and potentially necessitates higher taxes or reduced benefits.

Consumption Patterns: Older populations tend to spend more on healthcare, pharmaceuticals, and leisure but less on durable goods and technology. This shift alters economic activity and affects industries reliant on younger consumers, such as fast fashion and tech gadgets.

Strains on Social Systems

Healthcare Costs: Aging populations require more medical care, leading to escalating healthcare expenditures. For instance, countries like Germany and Italy allocate substantial portions of their GDP to healthcare, creating long-term fiscal stress.

Pensions and Social Security: Many pension systems were designed for societies with higher birth rates and shorter lifespans. The imbalance caused by aging populations threatens the solvency of these systems, necessitating reforms like raising retirement ages or increasing contributions.

Impact on Productivity

Declining Innovation: With fewer young workers entering the labour force, the influx of fresh ideas and energy may dwindle. Younger demographics are often the drivers of technological adoption and innovation.

Need for Automation: To counter labour shortages, aging economies are turning to automation and robotics. Japan, for instance, is a global leader in robotics, driven by the need to sustain productivity with fewer workers.

Geopolitical and Societal Implications

Shift in Global Power: Aging economies may lose their competitive edge to younger nations with vibrant workforces, such as India and parts of Africa, altering global economic and political power balances.

Immigration Policies: To counteract workforce shrinkage, many aging economies adopt immigration policies to attract younger workers. However, such policies can lead to social tensions and require careful management of cultural integration.

Intergenerational Inequality: An aging society often requires younger generations to bear a heavier financial burden through higher taxes and reduced benefits, potentially causing resentment and social unrest.

Opportunities in Aging Economies

Silver Economy: Businesses catering to the elderly, such as healthcare technology, assistive devices, and senior living communities, are thriving. Companies innovating in this space can capture significant market share.

Upskilling the Workforce: Aging economies can mitigate labour shortages by encouraging lifelong learning and upskilling among older workers, enabling them to stay active in the workforce longer.

Lessons and Adaptation

Countries with aging populations, like Sweden, have successfully mitigated challenges by implementing robust social welfare systems, promoting gender equality in the workforce, and investing in automation and productivity-enhancing technologies. These measures highlight the importance of innovation, inclusivity, and forward-looking policymaking. Below is the chart illustrating Japan's population trend since 2014.

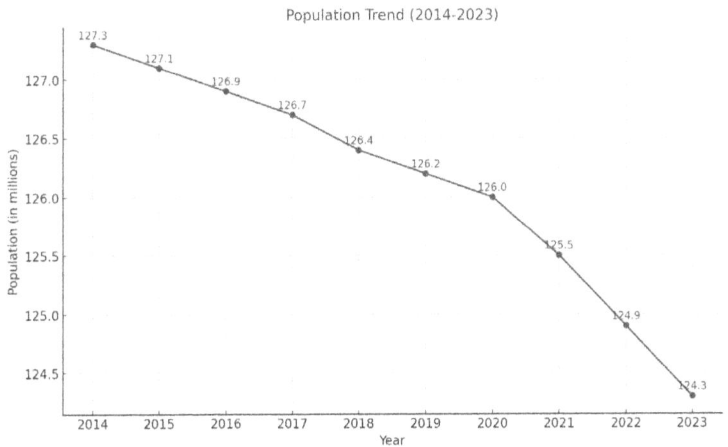

Illustration B.3 Japan's Population Trend

The Role of Fertility Rates

Fertility rates play a pivotal role in shaping the demographic and economic trajectory of nations. Defined as the average number of children born to a woman during her lifetime, fertility rates influence the size, structure, and dynamics of populations, impacting labour markets, economic growth, and social systems.

Replacement Rate and Population Growth

The replacement fertility rate, typically around 2.1 children per woman, is considered necessary to maintain a stable population. Rates above this indicate population growth, while lower rates signal potential decline.

Countries with high fertility rates, such as many in sub-Saharan Africa, experience rapid population growth, leading to opportunities and challenges in economic development, infrastructure, and governance.

In contrast, nations with fertility rates below replacement, such as Japan and South Korea, face shrinking populations and aging demographics, resulting in labour shortages and increased dependency ratios.

Regional Trends

Developed Economies: Most developed nations, including those in Europe, North America, and East Asia, have fertility rates well below the replacement level. This has prompted policies to attract immigrants or boost family-friendly programs to offset population declines.

Emerging Economies: Countries like India, Indonesia, and Brazil are transitioning from high to moderate fertility rates, balancing youthful populations with gradual aging.

Africa: Fertility rates in sub-Saharan Africa remain among the highest globally, providing a significant demographic advantage if investments in education and healthcare are prioritized.

Fertility Rates and Long-Term Economic Trends

Demographic Dividend: Countries with moderate fertility rates can benefit from a demographic dividend—a period when the working-age population grows faster than dependents, boosting economic productivity.

Urbanization: Declining fertility rates often correlate with increased urbanization, where smaller family sizes are more feasible, and women have greater access to education and employment.

Women's Workforce Participation: Lower fertility rates frequently coincide with higher female labour force participation, contributing to economic growth and gender equity.

Global Contrasts and Case Studies

China: With a fertility rate of 1.3, China's population is shrinking faster than anticipated, raising concerns about long-term economic growth and labour shortages despite its current global economic position.

India: India's fertility rate has declined to 2.0, just below the replacement level, positioning it for a sustained demographic dividend, with a growing young workforce set to fuel economic expansion.

Japan: Fertility rates in Japan have remained below 1.5 for decades, leading to one of the world's oldest populations and prompting policies to encourage childbearing and immigration.

Africa: Fertility rates across Africa average 4.3, with countries like Nigeria exceeding 5. This presents vast opportunities if economic policies and infrastructure development keep pace with population growth.

Global Migration and Workforce Redistribution

Migration has always been a critical driver of economic and social change, redistributing labour, skills, and economic opportunities across the globe. In the context of changing demographics, migration is becoming even more significant as nations grapple with aging populations, labour shortages, and disparities in economic opportunities.

Economic Drivers of Migration

Labour Market Needs: Countries with aging populations and declining fertility rates, such as Germany, Japan, and Canada, increasingly rely on immigrants to fill workforce gaps in key sectors like healthcare, construction, and technology.

Economic Disparities: Differences in income levels and job opportunities between regions push individuals to migrate from low-income to high-income countries, seeking better living standards and opportunities.

Skill Redistribution: Skilled migration is reshaping industries globally, as countries compete to attract high-tech talent through visa programs, such as the H-1B in the United States or Canada's Express Entry system.

Impact on Sending Countries

Brain Drain: Countries like India, the Philippines, and Nigeria often lose highly skilled workers to emigration, creating talent shortages in critical sectors like healthcare and engineering.

Remittances: Migrants send billions of dollars back to their home countries, bolstering local economies. For example, remittances accounted for nearly 10% of GDP in the Philippines in recent years.

Cultural Ties: Migration fosters international connections and knowledge sharing, contributing to globalization and cultural exchange.

Impact on Receiving Countries

Economic Growth: Immigrants contribute to GDP growth by filling labour shortages, increasing productivity, and boosting consumption.

Diversity and Innovation: Diverse workforces are proven to drive innovation, creativity, and problem-solving, particularly in advanced economies like the US and Canada.

Strain on Resources: Influxes of migrants can strain public services, housing, and social systems, especially if integration policies are inadequate.

Migration Trends and Patterns

North-South Divide: Workers from developing countries in Asia, Africa, and Latin America continue to migrate to developed economies in North America, Europe, and the Middle East.

Intra-Regional Migration: Regions like the European Union and ASEAN encourage intra-regional labour mobility to balance workforce needs and economic integration.

South-to-South Migration: Migration between developing countries, such as within Africa or Latin America, is growing and often overlooked.

Challenges and Policy Implications

Integration Challenges: Successful migration depends on policies that ensure social and cultural integration, preventing hostility or racism.

Regulatory Barriers: Immigration laws and restrictions can hinder the movement of workers, affecting global economic dynamics.

Brain Waste: Highly skilled migrants often face underemployment or credential recognition issues in destination countries, wasting talent and economic potential.

Humanitarian Concerns: Refugees and forced migrants due to war, climate change, or persecution face severe challenges in accessing opportunities and rights.

Long-Term Economic Impact

Migration helps address global demographic imbalances by redistributing labour to where it is most needed. It creates economic opportunities for individuals, enriches societies through diversity, and fosters international cooperation. However, balancing the benefits of migration with its challenges requires robust policies, international cooperation, and a commitment to equity and integration.

Global migration and workforce redistribution are powerful tools for mitigating demographic challenges and enabling economic growth. By addressing barriers and fostering inclusivity, countries can harness the immense potential of migration to build resilient and dynamic economies.

Political Stability and Leadership: Pillars of a Nation's Future

Political stability and effective leadership are among the most critical factors shaping a country's long-term growth and development. They serve as the foundation upon which social cohesion, economic prosperity, and innovation are built. For a country to fully leverage its demographic potential, political and leadership structures must align with the nation's aspirations and challenges. Below, we explore how these elements influence a nation's trajectory.

Fostering Economic Growth and Stability

Political stability reduces uncertainty, creating an environment conducive to investment and economic activity. Stable governments can implement and sustain long-term policies that attract domestic and foreign investments, foster industrial growth, and support entrepreneurial ecosystems. For instance, nations like Singapore have demonstrated how consistent leadership and sound governance can transform a small economy into a global financial hub.

Leadership plays a pivotal role in prioritizing economic reforms and ensuring efficient policy implementation. Importantly, stable leadership can also ensure fiscal discipline, maintaining manageable debt levels and a healthy national balance sheet. This fiscal prudence creates room for public investments in innovation and infrastructure while keeping long-term economic risks in check.

Prioritizing Innovation and Fostering Business Ecosystems

A key responsibility of leadership is to encourage innovation by supporting research, development, and technology adoption. Leaders who prioritize innovation create opportunities for a nation to stay competitive in global markets, adapt to technological shifts, and capture emerging trends. For example, investments in artificial intelligence, renewable energy, and advanced manufacturing can give countries a competitive edge in high-growth sectors.

Political stability provides the foundation for building a robust business ecosystem. Stable governments can implement policies that ease doing business, encourage entrepreneurship, and support small and medium enterprises (SMEs). A healthy business ecosystem ensures job creation, diversifies economic output, and boosts domestic and international trade. Additionally, stable, and transparent regulations create confidence among investors and foster long-term partnerships.

Ensuring a Sustainable Fiscal Position

Maintaining fiscal discipline is crucial for economic resilience. Stable political leadership ensures prudent management of the country's finances, including maintaining a healthy balance sheet and avoiding excessive debt burdens. By focusing on creating multiple revenue streams—such as developing robust tax systems, boosting exports, and monetizing natural resources—countries can enhance their financial resilience.

Examples include countries like Germany and South Korea, which have leveraged their manufacturing and technology sectors to become global export powerhouses. Similarly, a focus on diversifying revenue streams allows nations to absorb external shocks more effectively and sustain economic growth.

Demographic Advantage: Leadership in Action

Leadership is crucial in harnessing the potential of a youthful demographic. Countries with a young population, like India and several African nations, require forward-thinking leaders to invest in education, healthcare, and job creation. Targeted skill development programs can prepare the workforce for future industries, while investments in health infrastructure ensure a robust and productive labour pool. Political stability ensures that such programs are not disrupted by frequent policy changes or shifts in governance.

Managing Crises and Navigating Uncertainty

Strong leadership is often tested during crises, be it economic downturns, pandemics, or geopolitical tensions. Political stability ensures continuity and resilience in decision-making during such times. Effective leaders rally nations, mitigate risks, and guide them toward recovery. For instance, timely policy interventions during global financial crises have proven crucial for countries like India to maintain their economic stability and continue a growth trajectory.

Conversely, political instability or weak governance can exacerbate crises, leading to economic stagnation, capital flight, and public discontent. Examples from countries with prolonged political unrest highlight how instability can derail even the most promising economic and demographic potentials.

Attracting Global Partnerships

In a globalized world, political stability and leadership significantly impact a country's ability to form and sustain international alliances. Stable governments inspire confidence among global investors and trade partners, while visionary leadership can elevate a nation's stature on the world stage. For example, countries with consistent foreign policies and strong diplomatic engagements are better positioned to attract foreign direct investments (FDI) and participate in global supply chains.

Building Institutions and Rule of Law

Political stability enables the strengthening of institutions that uphold the rule of law, ensure justice, and protect property rights. Strong institutions foster trust among citizens and businesses, which is essential for long-term economic and social stability. Leadership that emphasizes governance reforms, anti-corruption measures, and institutional transparency ensures sustainable development and equitable growth.

Future Projections and Scenarios

The 21st century is marked by rapid shifts in global demographics, economic power, and geopolitical influence. These changes, driven by population growth, technological advancements, and economic transformations, are shaping the world's future. Here is an expanded look at population projections, GDP growth forecasts, and potential shifts in global superpower dynamics.

Population Projections

The world's population is expected to reach 9.7 billion by 2050, according to the UN. However, growth is uneven, with some regions booming and others shrinking. Africa will account for more than half of global population growth, with its population expected to double to over 2.5 billion by 2050. This presents significant opportunities but also challenges in terms of infrastructure, education, and governance.

Asia, despite slowing growth, will remain the most populous continent, with India surpassing China as the world's most populous country by 2024. Europe and Japan will see population declines, with shrinking workforces and aging populations posing economic challenges.

By 2050, nearly 16% of the global population will be over 65, with the proportion reaching 28% in Japan and 30% in Europe. Aging societies will face rising healthcare costs, pension burdens, and labour shortages, necessitating automation and immigration.

Over 68% of the global population will live in urban areas by 2050, up from 55% today. Emerging economies like India and Nigeria will see the fastest urban growth, spurring opportunities in infrastructure, real estate, and urban technologies.

GDP Growth Projections

By 2050, emerging economies are projected to dominate the list of the world's largest economies. According to PwC, countries like India, Indonesia, and Nigeria could see the fastest GDP growth rates, reshaping global economic rankings. India is expected to grow to a $35 trillion economy by 2050, becoming the world's second-largest economy after China.

China's growth, while slowing, will continue to cement its position as the largest economy, with a GDP projected to surpass $58 trillion by 2050. Advanced economies like the United States, Japan, and Europe will grow at slower rates due to aging populations and saturated markets.

The US is expected to remain a key player but may face challenges in maintaining its global economic dominance. Technology and services will drive growth in developed economies, while manufacturing, infrastructure, and renewable energy will play critical roles in emerging markets.

The Superpower Shift

Asia is poised to become the global economic hub, with China and India leading the way. Their growing influence will extend beyond economics into geopolitics, innovation, and culture. ASEAN countries will also play an increasingly key role as a collective economic bloc, rivalling the EU.

Africa's young workforce and untapped resources position it as a future economic powerhouse. If governance, infrastructure, and education systems improve, countries like Nigeria, Ethiopia, and South Africa could become major players. The US is expected to remain a global leader, particularly in technology, innovation, and military power, but may face intensified competition from emerging powers.

Europe's influence could diminish unless it addresses demographic decline and fragmented political dynamics. China's Belt and Road Initiative and technological advancements are expanding its geopolitical reach. However, domestic challenges like an aging population and regulatory crackdowns on innovation could hinder its ambitions. India's combination of a young workforce, democratic governance, and growing economic heft positions it as a balancing power between the US and China.

Future Scenarios

Multilateral Collaboration

Nations work together to address global challenges like climate change, migration, and technological ethics. A more equitable global order emerges, with shared leadership among the US, China, India, and Europe.

Regionalism and Fragmentation

Economic and political fragmentation leads to regional blocs dominating trade and geopolitics. Innovation continues but is unevenly distributed.

Technological Dominance

Technologically advanced nations dominate the global order, with AI, renewable energy, and biotech driving growth. Emerging economies that fail to innovate risk falling behind.

Population Challenges

Aging and declining populations in major economies like China, Europe, and Japan strain global growth. Africa and India's youthful demographics lead to a shift in labour-intensive industries.

The global economic and demographic landscape is set for profound transformation. Population dynamics, GDP growth, and shifts in superpower influence will create new opportunities and challenges. For investors, understanding these trends and preparing for their implications is key to navigating the future successfully.

Factors to Analyse Potential and Stability of a Country

When assessing a country's potential and stability for investment, growth, or long-term opportunities, several key factors need to be examined. These factors span economic, demographic, political, social, and technological dimensions, providing a comprehensive understanding of the nation's prospects.

Category	Factors	Description
Demographics	Population Size	The total population and its implications for workforce and consumption.
	Fertility and Replacement Rates	Indicates population growth
	Age Distribution	The proportion of young, working age, and elderly populations.
	Dependency Ratios	The ratio of dependents (young and elderly) to the working-age population.
	Migration Trends	Net migration inflows or outflows and their impact on workforce and diversity.
Economic Indicators	GDP Growth Rate	Measures economic expansion over time. Past and expected in future.
	Per Capita Income	Indicates standard of living and consumer spending power.
	Unemployment Rate	Highlights job availability and economic health.
	Inflation Rate	Assesses price stability and purchasing power.
	Debt-to-GDP Ratio	Measures the sustainability of public debt levels.
	Export-Import Balance	Shows the trade surplus or deficit and the nation's global trade strength.
Fiscal Position and Public Finances	Tax Revenue Base	Evaluates the country's ability to generate revenue through taxation.
	Fiscal Deficit	Indicates how much the government spends over its revenues, highlighting fiscal discipline.

Category	Factors	Description
	Public Spending Efficiency	Assesses how effectively public funds are utilized for development and welfare.
Governance and Stability	Political Stability	Indicates the nation's ability to maintain consistent policies and avoid disruptions.
	Leadership Vision	Reflects the ability of leaders to guide the nation toward sustainable growth and innovation.
	Regulatory Framework	Assesses the efficiency and transparency of laws and governance.
	Corruption Index	Measures the level of corruption, which impacts business and foreign investments.
Geopolitical Environment	Strategic Location	The nation's geographical importance in global trade, defence, and diplomacy.
	Global Alliances	Membership in trade or political alliances (e.g., WTO, G20, BRICS) and their benefits.
	Trade Policies	Free trade agreements, tariffs, and regulations affecting exports and imports.
	Diplomatic Relations	The country's ability to maintain peaceful and cooperative relationships with other nations.
Infrastructure	Physical Infrastructure	Includes transport, energy, and urban development facilities.
	Digital Infrastructure	Broadband, mobile connectivity, and technology adoption rates.
	Health Infrastructure	Access to healthcare facilities and systems.
	Education Infrastructure	Quality of schools, universities, and vocational training.

Category	Factors	Description
Innovation and Business	R&D Spending	Indicates the nation's investment in innovation and future technologies.
	Ease of Doing Business	Measures the regulatory and operational environment for businesses.
	Entrepreneurship and Startup Ecosystem	Assesses the vibrancy and support for innovation-led businesses.
	Intellectual Property Protection	Indicates how well patents and innovations are safeguarded.
Technological Advancements	AI and Automation Adoption	Highlights progress in adopting transformative technologies in various sectors.
	Digital Transformation	Assesses how sectors like banking, healthcare, and manufacturing are leveraging technology.
	Cybersecurity Infrastructure	Measures readiness to combat digital threats and maintain data integrity.
	Technology Exports	Value of tech products and services exported globally.
Natural Resources and Energy	Availability of Resources	Includes mineral, agricultural, and water resources critical for economic activity.
	Energy Independence	Assesses reliance on domestic vs. imported energy sources.
	Sustainability Initiatives	Efforts toward renewable energy adoption and environmental conservation.
Export Capabilities and Global Integration	Export Diversification	Examines the range of products and services exported by the nation.

Category	Factors	Description
	Global Market Share	Evaluates the country's competitiveness in international trade.
	Foreign Direct Investment (FDI)	Tracks inward FDI as a measure of investor confidence.
	Supply Chain Resilience	Assesses the nation's ability to maintain stable exports during global disruptions.
Cultural and Social	Cultural Diversity	Reflects the richness of the nation's cultural fabric and its influence on creativity and global appeal.
	Gender Equality	Indicates inclusivity and equity in workforce and leadership roles.
	Literacy and Education Rates	Highlights skill availability and workforce quality.
	Urbanization	Tracks migration to cities and the potential for economic agglomeration effects.

A Land of Opportunities Waiting to Be Seized

India's economic journey has been one of remarkable transformation. From its post-independence years through periods of rapid globalization, the country has evolved in ways that few could have anticipated. Understanding the evolution of India's economic ecosystem is essential for identifying the trends shaping the future, as each historical phase has left a lasting imprint on the current landscape of opportunities. Glimpse of past helps us connect the dots efficiently referring similar possibilities and challenges.

The Foundation: Post-Independence Industrialization

In the years following independence in 1947, India embarked on a journey of industrialization, largely driven by public sector enterprises. This period was characterized by heavy state intervention and a focus on self-reliance. Industries such as steel, textiles, and manufacturing were prioritized, and large public enterprises were established to achieve economic stability and infrastructure development. While this strategy built a robust industrial base, it also led to limitations in efficiency and flexibility, creating the need for economic reforms.

The 1991 Economic Liberalization: A New Dawn

In 1991, India faced a severe balance of payments crisis, prompting a radical shift in economic policy. The government introduced sweeping economic reforms that liberalized the economy, inviting foreign direct investment (FDI), reducing tariffs, and easing regulations. This transformative period, often called the liberalization era, sparked a wave of entrepreneurship and exposed Indian businesses to global competition and innovation.

With the right influx of the foreign capital, new industries emerged—technology, telecommunications, and finance began to thrive, opening the door for a new class of investors. Liberalization ignited a shift in consumer behaviour, as Indians began to experience greater choice and a taste for global goods. This era set the stage for India's growing middle class and laid the foundation for consumerism, which continues to drive growth.

The Technology Boom: Rise of the IT and Digital Economy

India's IT revolution, which began in the 1990s, turned cities like Bengaluru into global tech hubs. Indian IT companies capitalized on a skilled English-speaking workforce, providing software services and support to companies worldwide. This phase not only contributed significantly to GDP but also nurtured an entrepreneurial spirit, inspiring generations of engineers and innovators to create solutions for both local and global markets.

By the early 2000s, technology had become integral to India's economy, creating wealth and jobs, and spurring the growth of adjacent sectors such as e-commerce and digital payments. The IT boom paved the way for the digital economy that continues to thrive, with Indian consumers quickly adapting to digital products, creating demand for fintech, edtech, health tech, and other sectors driven by innovation.

The Start-Up Revolution and New-Age Consumerism

In the past decade, India has witnessed an explosion of startups across various sectors, from e-commerce and food delivery to financial technology and sustainable products. Fuelling revolution is a young population that is tech-savvy, mobile-first, and increasingly aspirational. The consumer landscape has evolved, with urbanization, rising disposable incomes, and digital penetration reshaping purchasing patterns.

Today's Indian consumers are not only digitally engaged but also increasingly conscious about sustainability and quality, paving the way for niche trends. Health and wellness, organic products, electric mobility, and homegrown brands are gaining traction, highlighting a distinct shift toward responsible and value-driven consumption.

The Present Ecosystem: A Confluence of Tradition and Innovation

India's current economic landscape is a blend of tradition and modernity, where centuries-old practices coexist with innovative technology. Small and medium-sized enterprises (SMEs), many of which are family-owned, are now experimenting with digital tools to reach a wider market. Agriculture, once rooted in conventional methods, is now embracing Agri-tech solutions that optimize resources and increase yields.

At the same time, India's regulatory framework is adapting to accommodate innovation, with initiatives like 'Make in India,' 'Digital India,' and 'Atmanirbhar Bharat' (Self-Reliant India) encouraging domestic production, technological advancement, and sustainable practices. This ecosystem creates unique opportunities for investors who can look beyond well-established sectors to uncover emerging areas poised for growth.

India's Demographics and Opportunities

Population Base: India recently overtook China as the world's most populous country with a base of over 1.4 billion people. A vast working-age population (15-64 years) makes up 67% of the total, a proportion that will peak by 2040.

Average Age: India's median age is approximately 28 years, compared to thirty-eight in the U.S., forty-two in China, and forty-eight in Japan. A younger population translates into a lower dependency ratio, enhancing savings, investments, and consumption.

Workforce Expansion: An annual addition of 12-15 million individuals to the workforce is a potential driver of economic growth, provided there is adequate skilling and employment. Sectors like manufacturing, IT, and renewable energy can absorb this expanding workforce.

Fertility Rate and Urbanization: India's fertility rate has dropped from 3.6 in 1991 to ~2.0 in 2023, nearing replacement level. Urbanization trends indicate a shift toward city-centric economic activities, with urban areas projected to host 40% of India's population by 2030.

GDP Growth: India's economy, currently valued at $3.7 trillion, is the world's fifth largest. It is expected to grow to $10 trillion by 2035. Key growth areas include IT, pharmaceuticals, manufacturing, and renewable energy. Initiatives like "Make in India," "Startup India," and infrastructure investments underpin sustained GDP growth.

Governance Stability: India's political environment has fostered structural reforms like GST and digitization, creating a stable investment climate. Strong diplomatic ties with countries like the U.S. and Japan, and leadership in forums like G20, enhance India's geopolitical standing.

Innovation: India is home to over one hundred startup unicorns and leads in fintech, edtech, and deep-tech innovations. Government and private sectors are increasing investments in research, particularly in AI, robotics, and space technology.

Export Capabilities: India remains a global leader in IT services, contributing $194 billion to exports annually. Electronics, automotive, and textiles are rapidly expanding, with export-friendly policies and subsidies driving growth.

Internal Consumption: Rising disposable incomes in urban and semi-urban areas are fostering demand for goods, services, and infrastructure. A burgeoning middle class of over three hundred million offers opportunities for consumer-focused industries.

Savings and Investments: A younger population with fewer dependents tends to save more, boosting capital formation. Rising domestic investments can support infrastructure, housing, and technological innovation.

Challenges

Job Creation: The challenge of creating 10-12 million jobs annually to prevent unemployment and underemployment. Skilling initiatives, such as PMKVY (Pradhan Mantri Kaushal Vikas Yojana), must be scaled effectively.

Income inequality: As nation grows and create wealth for individuals and businesses, it creates massive inequality among people where top 1% corners significant wealth compared to bottom 50%. K shaped wealth distribution may harm nation in terms of demand and purchasing power.

Regional Disparities: Demographic dividends are uneven across states; Southern states are aging faster, while Northern states continue to grow younger. Many states are far behind in terms of basic infrastructure and job creation while few of them are leading a nation.

Healthcare and Aging: Although currently young, India's aging population will surpass three hundred million by 2050, necessitating robust healthcare and pension systems.

Social Infrastructure: Education, healthcare, and housing infrastructure need significant investments to support the growing population.

Lack of global brand: India is yet to witness a multinational company having a differentiating technology and niche offering as compared to countries like USA and China enjoying certain global brands.

India's Investment Climate: A Dual Edge

India's investment climate is unique—on one hand, it offers vast untapped potential, but on the other, it poses certain challenges. The rapid pace of change, coupled with evolving consumer behaviour and market shifts, can create volatility. Yet, it is precisely this volatility that creates opportunities for investors who are prepared to act decisively.

While large-scale, well-established businesses often provide stability, it is the smaller, emerging companies that tend to exhibit the most potential for growth. These companies are agile, adaptable, and frequently at the forefront of innovation. However, they are also high-risk investments, which is why understanding the balance between risk and reward is critical. The ability to manage risk while capturing the upside potential of high-growth businesses is a defining characteristic of successful investors in India's emerging markets.

While we discuss the opportunities and economic evolution of the country, it is essential to look at the risks, challenges, and downside of the nation to ensure we have broader picture of nation's potential.

One discussion which has remained among investing ecosystem is India's economic growth, though impressive, has consistently struggled to break the 8% barrier, falling short of China's double-digit growth during its peak years. This disparity can be attributed to a combination of structural, policy, and investment factors that have shaped the trajectories of the two nations differently.

Unlike China's manufacturing-led growth, which benefited from robust government support and extensive special economic zones, India's growth has been service-driven. While the services sector has propelled GDP growth and attracted global recognition, it lacks the scalability and job-creation potential of manufacturing. Furthermore, China's early investment in infrastructure transformed its industrial efficiency and logistics, whereas India's infrastructure, though improving, still faces significant gaps, hindering industrial productivity.

India's regulatory framework, marked by bureaucratic hurdles and slower reforms, has often stifled business operations and delayed critical investments. In contrast, China's centralized governance enabled swift implementation of pro-growth policies and large-scale economic reforms. While India's democratic fabric ensures checks and balances, it also leads to protracted political debates over reforms, delaying economic momentum.

Another critical differentiator is workforce readiness. Despite its demographic dividend, India's education and skill development systems have not sufficiently aligned with market demands, limiting productivity. Conversely, China strategically focused on equipping its labour force with industry-relevant skills, ensuring its workforce was ready to meet manufacturing demands.

China's aggressive capital investments, often exceeding 40% of its GDP, fuelled infrastructure, technology, and industrial growth. India's investment rate, while commendable, lingers around 34%, insufficient to drive transformative growth at the same scale.

Furthermore, fragmented domestic markets and stiff international competition have constrained India's industries, whereas China's protected domestic market allowed its companies to mature and achieve global competitiveness.

While India holds immense potential with its burgeoning youth population, thriving startups, and growing global integration, bridging these gaps will require bold reforms, targeted investments, and an unwavering focus on improving infrastructure and human capital. Learning from China's trajectory while leveraging India's unique strengths could unlock sustained high-growth potential in the coming decades.

On the other hand, stable growth has its own merits which India is enjoying compared to China which is now witnessing lower GDP growth. While rapid economic growth can often dominate headlines, the long-term health of an economy is determined by the sustainability and stability of that growth. India, with its steady economic expansion, has demonstrated the merits of stability compared to China, which is now facing a slowdown after decades of high GDP growth.

Stable growth fosters investor confidence by providing a predictable environment, crucial for long-term investments and reducing the risks of sudden capital flight. It also enables consistent policymaking, minimizing the shocks associated with abrupt economic or regulatory shifts.

From an economic perspective, stable growth helps manage inflation by preventing overheating, ensuring balanced economic progress. It also allows for better resource management, avoiding the pitfalls of boom-and-bust cycles that can deplete natural resources or strain infrastructure. Socially, sustainable growth promotes inclusivity, reducing income disparities and fostering a more equitable distribution of wealth. Environmentally, it aligns with practices that protect natural ecosystems, in contrast to rapid industrialization, which often prioritizes growth over sustainability.

Furthermore, stable growth underpins long-term resilience by encouraging sector diversification, reducing over-reliance on any single industry. This, in turn, makes the economy more adaptable to global shifts. Financially, it mitigates the risks of over-leveraging, which can lead to debt crises in economies that pursue unchecked rapid expansion.

As China grapples with the challenges of slowing growth and an aging population, India's steady trajectory offers a blueprint for balanced development. By focusing on sustainable practices, fostering inclusivity, and ensuring financial and environmental stability, India is not only laying a foundation for enduring prosperity but also positioning itself as a resilient player in the global economy.

India Itself a Macro Trend to Play

India itself represents a compelling macro trend, driven by its unique combination of demographic advantages, economic growth potential, and evolving global positioning. With a population of over 1.4 billion, India boasts a vast consumer base, a young median age of 28 years, and a workforce that continues to grow while other major economies face aging populations.

This demographic dividend offers unparalleled opportunities for businesses across sectors, from consumer goods and services to technology and infrastructure. India's rising middle class is driving consumption patterns, creating robust demand for housing, healthcare, education, and entertainment. Coupled with the government's focus on "Make in India," digital transformation, and infrastructure development, the nation is setting the stage for sustained long-term growth.

On the global stage, India's strategic initiatives, such as becoming a key player in renewable energy, emerging as a hub for global supply chains, and leveraging its tech-savvy workforce, position it as a critical participant in shaping future global trends.

Political stability, a democratic framework, and progressive economic policies like the rollout of GST, production-linked incentives (PLI), and privatization of public sector undertakings (PSUs) further solidify India's growth story. The country's burgeoning startup ecosystem, backed by an ever-growing base of tech-enabled consumers, demonstrates its ability to innovate and compete in global markets.

Moreover, India's export capability is expanding, with different sectors like pharmaceuticals, software, and specialty chemicals gaining prominence. The integration of digital public infrastructure such as UPI and Aadhaar fosters financial inclusion and efficiency, enabling small businesses and startups to thrive.

With projected GDP growth rates surpassing many developed and emerging markets, India presents a unique blend of stability, growth, and opportunity. As global investors seek alternatives to aging economies and over-reliance on China, India's macroeconomic trends, entrepreneurial ecosystem, and policy-driven reforms make it a must-watch market and an enduring investment theme for the next decade and beyond.

A Call to Action for Investors

"The best time to invest in India was in 1991 when Manmohan Singh presented his liberalisation budget and the second-best time to invest in India is today."

– Ramesh Damani, BSE Member

Investing in India is not just about buying into industries; it is about recognizing the pulse of the market, the evolving consumer preferences, and the unique challenges that drive innovation. From rural startups introducing affordable tech solutions to urban innovators creating sustainable models, Indian businesses are a study in contrasts and resilience.

For investors, the appeal of business investing lies in the potential for exponential growth. Unlike traditional asset classes such as bonds or real estate, investing in businesses—especially those in emerging sectors—allows for the possibility of significant returns. India's entrepreneurial spirit, especially in recent years, has driven the creation of countless innovative companies, many of which have experienced rapid growth against the backdrop of favourable demographic and technological trends.

One thing Investors should keep in mind that the valuations of rightly aligned businesses in India will not be reasonable as their potential is seen. One need to be valuation sensitive while picking the stories as chances of overheating the valuations in some segments due to futuristic hyper growth would be quite high. Paying for growth is reasonable and sensible but do not overpay for stories.

India's fast-growing economy offers the right kind of environment for such investments, where the pace of growth in key sectors far outstrips global averages. However, achieving wealth through these investments takes time. It requires a long-term perspective and the foresight to see how micro-trends will evolve into major industries.

Action	Description
Identify Micro Opportunities	Start with the big picture—identify India's structural trends. Within these macro trends, seek out micro-trends that align with them.
Start Small, Think Big	Begin with small allocations to test your hypotheses and build confidence in specific themes. As you gain conviction, scale your investments.

Action	Description
Balance Optimism with Discipline	Be optimistic about India's growth story but remain disciplined in evaluating businesses and valuations.
Track Emerging Risks and Headwinds	Regularly monitor market developments, government policies, and global factors that could impact your investments.
Focus on Quality of Businesses	Conduct due diligence on financials, business models, and management before investing.
Commit to Learning	Stay curious about industries, consumer behaviour, and technological shifts shaping India's future.
Be Patient	Understand that India's growth story is long-term. Commit to holding quality investments for 5-10 years or more to maximize returns.

The greatest wealth creation stories are those that are aligned with the broader growth narrative of a country. For Indian investors, this narrative is one of resilience, rapid urbanization, and technological innovation. It is the story of a young, digitally native population demanding more from the economy and driving change at a scale that few nations can match.

D

Deep Dive into Major Trends of India

Before we dive into the macro, micro, sub-micro trends, it's important to recognize that some of these trends might already feel familiar—you may have witnessed or even experienced their impact. However, trends are rarely static; they evolve and often present new opportunities as innovation reshapes their trajectory. What seems established today may still have untapped potential to play out further, either in similar ways or through entirely new dimensions driven by constant advancements.

It is also worth noting that within these ongoing trends, more innovative and efficient businesses may emerge, challenging the dominance of existing pioneers. This dynamic nature can diminish the significance of even the most established players, as disruptors with superior technology or execution redefine the trend. Understanding this evolution is crucial, as it highlights the importance of staying vigilant, adaptable, and forward-looking when navigating trends.

This chapter is designed to guide you through the intricate web of trends shaping industries, markets, and economies. While it may seem like an extensive list, think of it as a map—a way to navigate opportunities across layers, from broad, overarching macro trends to the more focused micro and sub-micro trends. Each trend is an avenue to explore, not just a statistic to memorize. To make it understand both sides of trends, we've included overviews, their growth drivers and risks/concerns to help you connect these trends to your investment decisions.

Approach this chapter with curiosity, see each trend as a story of change, and let it inspire you to identify opportunities that align with your vision and mental models. Remember, it is not about reading them all at once but understanding how these trends and drivers interconnect and evolve to shape the future.

Try exploring one macro trend at a time, or if you prefer, you can skip to Chapter F and later revisit the trends as you work on identifying specific investment opportunities. This approach allows you to engage with the content at your own pace, ensuring it aligns with your immediate interests and needs.

Note: *We have considered only those sectoral/structural trends which are likely to have annual growth more than 10% for at least next five years.*

Macro Trend 1

Digital Transformation in Consumer Services

Digital transformation is rapidly reshaping consumer services by enhancing customer experience, ease of doing, operational efficiency, and revenue potential. Here are the core micro and sub-micro trends driving this transformation. (For the next upcoming macro trends, consider this flow: Macro Trend – Micro and Sub-Micro Trends).

Fintech and Digital Payments

With the rise of digital payments, traditional financial services are being complemented or replaced by mobile wallets, UPI (Unified Payments Interface), buy-now-pay-later (BNPL) options, and cryptocurrency transactions. Many countries are exploring or have begun piloting their own digital currencies. CBDCs could potentially offer a new form of money that is digital, backed by the state, and could revolutionize how transactions are conducted, especially cross-border payments.

Decentralized Finance (DeFi) platforms are expanding, offering financial services like lending, borrowing, and trading without traditional intermediaries. This trend leverages blockchain for transparency and security, aiming to provide broader access to financial services. Financial services are being integrated directly into non-financial platforms (like e-commerce, automotive, and retail). This allows for seamless payments, loans, insurance, and more, enhancing customer experience by reducing the need to switch between different service providers.

The concept of a super app, where one application offers a multitude of services including digital payments, insurance, mutual funds has gained traction. Companies are looking to emulate the success of apps like WeChat or Grab by providing an ecosystem where finance is just one part of a larger service offering. As virtual worlds gain popularity, there is an emerging trend of integrating payment systems within these spaces. This involves virtual currencies, NFTs, and traditional digital payments for virtual goods and services.

The trend towards contactless payments has not slowed down, with NFC technology becoming standard in many regions for its speed and convenience. BNPL services are evolving, not just as a payment option but integrating into broader financial ecosystems, offering more flexible payment solutions for consumers.

The rapid growth of fintech and digital payment solutions is driven by multiple factors. Consumer convenience and the speed of instant payments have boosted adoption, with platforms like Google Pay, Paytm, and UPI gaining widespread traction in India. The globalization of e-commerce has further increased the demand for seamless international payment systems. Regulatory support from governments aiming to reduce cash dependency has also played a key role.

Technological advancements such as blockchain and AI enhance security and efficiency, while solutions like microfinance and digital wallets improve financial inclusion. Additionally, increased internet and smartphone penetration, coupled with the rising popularity of Buy Now Pay Later (BNPL) models, has expanded access and appeal, especially among younger consumers.

Regulatory changes could reshape market dynamics, increasing operational costs or stifling innovation and sometimes losing market shares to conventional ways/other players. Data security and compliance with evolving protection laws remain critical, as breaches could lead to financial losses and reputational damage.

The unpredictable adoption of new financial products and intense competition raises questions about the sustainability of customer bases, while reliance on emerging technologies introduces risks of failure. Investors in fintech often grapple with concerns about long-term viability, especially for companies with high burn rates or heavy reliance on venture capital without a clear path to profitability. Fintech firms offering credit or investment services are particularly sensitive to economic cycles, where downturns or defaults could significantly impact performance.

Quick Commerce and Hyperlocal Delivery

Quick Commerce refers to a model of e-commerce where goods, particularly groceries, essentials, and sometimes even non-essential items, are delivered to customers within a noticeably short time frame, often within minutes. Companies like Blinkit, Swiggy Instamart, Zepto, and others in India exemplify this trend with promises of 10–30-minute deliveries.

Hyperlocal Delivery, while related, often emphasizes delivery from local shops or services within a specific geographic area, ensuring that the product comes from a nearby source. This can include everything from food to services like laundry, beauty, or repair services.

The growth of quick commerce is being fuelled by several key factors. Urbanization and increasingly busy lifestyles have created a demand for convenience and rapid delivery services. The COVID-19 pandemic further accelerated this trend, with consumers shifting towards contactless shopping and deliveries. Advances in logistics technology, including sophisticated routing algorithms, real-time inventory tracking, and experiments with drone delivery, have significantly improved the efficiency of these systems.

Changing consumer behaviour, with a preference for instant gratification, now extends beyond essentials to categories like clothing, electronics, and other non-perishables. Platforms integrating local vendors and "kiranas" into the digital economy have enhanced the hyperlocal e-commerce ecosystem, while data-driven personalization leverages consumer insights to tailor offerings and optimize delivery times.

Quick commerce platforms face significant challenges, including high operational costs that often result in losses, raising investor concerns about when or if profitability will be achieved. Regulatory risks, such as labour rights, urban delivery restrictions, or environmental mandates, could disrupt current business models.

Market saturation, with numerous players entering the space, has intensified competition and price wars, while customer retention remains challenging as speed often outweighs brand loyalty or product quality. Heavy reliance on tech-driven logistics and inventory systems introduces risks of system failures, complicating scaling efforts across regions with diverse infrastructure and consumer behaviours.

Ensuring stock availability for ultra-fast deliveries adds logistical and financial strain and growing environmental concerns could spark backlash against services perceived as unsustainable.

OTT Platforms

Over-the-Top (OTT) platforms refer to media services offered directly to viewers via the internet, bypassing traditional distribution channels like cable or satellite television providers. These platforms provide a wide range of content, including movies, TV shows, documentaries, and original programs, accessible on various devices like smartphones, tablets, smart TVs, and computers.

Major players include Netflix, Amazon Prime Video, Disney+, local giants like Hotstar, Jio-cinema and ZEE5. This sector has seen exponential growth, especially highlighted during periods like the global health crisis, where demand for home entertainment surged.

The explosion of original content, including movies, series, exclusive sports events, and live streaming, has captivated audiences and fuelled subscriber growth. Affordable, high-speed internet has made streaming accessible to a broader demographic, enabling global reach, and tapping into diverse markets with ease. Personalization algorithms enhance user engagement by suggesting tailored content, while the rise of binge-watching culture keeps viewers hooked.

The cord-cutting movement, spurred by the flexibility and cost-efficiency of OTT services compared to traditional cable TV, has further accelerated adoption. Mobile viewing has become a dominant trend, especially in regions with high smartphone penetration but limited TV ownership. Moreover, platforms' investments in exclusive original programming differentiate them from competitors and foster subscriber loyalty.

High churn rates add to the uncertainty, as subscribers can easily unsubscribe if content fails to meet expectations consistently. Regulatory risks, such as content regulation, data privacy laws, and internet neutrality issues, further complicate business models, especially in markets with strict oversight.

Dependence on third-party ISPs for content delivery introduces vulnerabilities like service quality issues or potential throttling. Additionally, the evolving landscape of content consumption demands frequent strategic pivots.

The ongoing need for technological investments, global intellectual property management, and complex licensing agreements adds another layer of operational and financial complexity to the OTT business model.

Profitability remains a challenge, with excessive costs for content acquisition and production often leading to delayed or uncertain returns. The crowded market, filled with numerous competitors, forces platforms to constantly innovate to retain subscribers, while content saturation risks viewer fatigue, making it harder for any single offering to stand out.

E-Commerce and Direct-to-Consumer (DTC)

E-commerce refers to the buying and selling of products or services using the internet, facilitated through online platforms or marketplaces. It encompasses a broad range of activities from retail sales to B2B transactions.

Direct-to-Consumer (DTC) is a business model where manufacturers or brands sell their products directly to the end consumer, bypassing traditional retail channels like wholesalers and brick-and-mortar stores. This can be done through e-commerce websites, subscription models, social media or even physical pop-up stores but primarily relies on direct online interaction.

The e-commerce and DTC landscape is thriving, driven by increasing digital literacy and trust in online transactions. Platforms like Amazon and Shopify empower merchants to easily enter the market, while consumers enjoy the convenience of shopping anytime, anywhere, with options like same-day delivery.

DTC brands leverage direct control over storytelling and customer engagement, fostering loyalty and creating unique experiences. The use of consumer data enhances personalized marketing and product offerings, while subscription models boost retention and revenue predictability. Integration with social media simplifies purchasing for younger demographics, and a focus on niche markets and customization helps brands meet specific consumer needs.

The Direct-to-Consumer (DTC) space faces mounting challenges, starting with market saturation as the crowded landscape makes it difficult for new entrants to differentiate themselves. The initial excitement around DTC brands has waned, prompting investor caution about scalability and the uniqueness of emerging ventures.

High customer acquisition costs, driven by intense competition in digital advertising, raise concerns about the sustainability of growth. Scalability poses another hurdle; while DTC models can begin small, expanding logistics, customer service, and quality control at larger volumes often proves challenging.

Many DTC brands prioritize rapid growth over profitability in their initial stages, which can deter investors seeking immediate returns or sustainable business models. Channel conflict further complicates the picture, as DTC efforts may strain relationships with traditional retail partners. Additionally, handling consumer data directly increases exposure to cyber threats, requiring expensive cybersecurity measures. Economic sensitivity also plays a role, as DTC sales can decline during downturns when consumers cut back on discretionary spending.

Lastly, managing logistics and fulfilment, especially returns, can be a costly and operationally demanding task, significantly affecting margins and efficiency. These factors collectively make the DTC model a complex and nuanced investment proposition.

ONDC (Open Network for Digital Commerce)

The Open Network for Digital Commerce (ONDC) is an initiative by the Indian government aimed at creating an open, unbundled, and interoperable network for digital commerce. Launched to foster inclusivity in the e-commerce sector, ONDC seeks to democratize digital commerce by enabling sellers, even small and medium enterprises (SMEs), to reach a broader audience without being restricted to proprietary platforms. It operates on the principle of an open network, like how UPI functions for digital payments, where buyers and sellers can transact across different platforms without intermediaries.

The ONDC initiative is reshaping India's digital commerce landscape by empowering SMEs and local vendors, integrating them into the vast unorganized retail sector. Backed by government policy support, it ensures inclusivity while reducing transaction costs, making online commerce more accessible for smaller merchants. With major platforms like Paytm and PhonePe integrating ONDC, its reach and adoption continue to grow. By fostering competition among sellers, ONDC meets consumer demand for greater choice and better pricing, driving the evolution of India's e-commerce ecosystem.

One key issue is execution and scalability—while ONDC has shown rapid growth, achieving the operational efficiency and scale of established giants like Amazon and Flipkart demands overcoming significant logistical and technological hurdles. Additionally, ensuring data privacy and security in a decentralized environment is crucial, as any lapses could erode trust in the platform.

Standardization and interoperability pose another challenge, as participants with diverse technological capabilities and business models must adhere to uniform standards for seamless operations. Large e-commerce platforms may also resist or disengage from ONDC, citing competitive concerns or conflicts with their established business models. This resistance could limit the network's ability to attract and retain key market players.

Quality assurance across a wide network of small sellers is critical to maintaining consumer trust, but variability in product and service quality could hinder this effort. Furthermore, ONDC's dependency on the participation of large buyer-side apps could create vulnerabilities if these key players seek to renegotiate terms or withdraw support. Public perception and sustained consumer adoption remain vital—beyond the initial excitement and price incentives, ONDC must deliver a reliable, user-friendly ecosystem to win long-term consumer loyalty.

Cab Aggregators and Ride-Hailing

Cab aggregators and ride-hailing services involve platforms that connect passengers with drivers for transportation needs. These services are accessed via mobile apps or websites, allowing users to request a ride from their current location to a desired destination.

Companies like Uber, Ola prominent in this space, offering various service types including rides in personal cars, electric vehicles, luxury cars, carpooling, and even two-wheeler transportation in some markets.

Urbanization and traffic congestion are driving the popularity of ride-hailing services as a convenient alternative to personal car ownership. Enabled by widespread smartphone penetration, these platforms offer time-efficient, hassle-free transportation while creating flexible work opportunities for drivers.

With the integration of electric vehicles, ride-hailing appeals to eco-conscious consumers, and technological advancements like AI-driven route optimization and safety features enhance service quality. Changing consumer preferences, especially among younger demographics, further solidify ride-hailing as a preferred choice over traditional taxis for its reliability and transparency.

Regulatory risks are mounting globally, with stricter licensing requirements, safety standards, labour laws, and environmental policies potentially driving up operational costs and limiting expansion.

Market duopoly in many regions makes it increasingly difficult for new entrants to gain traction and for incumbents to sustain growth. Profitability remains a significant hurdle, as companies contend with high driver acquisition costs, user subsidies, and intense price wars. Maintaining a steady supply of drivers is further complicated by evolving labour laws and worker dissatisfaction.

Consumer safety and trust are critical concerns, as incidents can damage a company's reputation and erode user confidence. Additionally, the rise of autonomous vehicles may pose a potential technological disruption in future, threatening companies that fail to adapt their business models. Intense competition exacerbates these issues, leading to aggressive pricing strategies that may be unsustainable in the long term.

Privacy and data security risks also loom large, as companies handle vast amounts of personal data, making them targets for breaches that could result in financial and legal consequences.

Digital Public Infrastructure

Digital Public Infrastructure (DPI) refers to digital systems and frameworks provided by governments or public-private partnerships to facilitate the delivery of public services, enhance economic activities, and promote digital inclusion. DPI includes components like digital identity systems (e.g., India's Aadhaar), payment interfaces (e.g., UPI in India), and data exchange platforms that enable secure and efficient transactions and information sharing. It is designed to be interoperable, inclusive, and accessible, serving as the digital backbone for a modern society.

Government initiatives worldwide are driving the adoption of Digital Public Infrastructure (DPI) as a cornerstone for economic growth and financial inclusion. By enabling digital identities and payment systems, DPI empowers unbanked populations to participate in the digital economy. It enhances efficiency in service delivery, as seen in India's direct benefit transfers, and serves as a catalyst for innovation through open APIs. DPI also proven invaluable during crises, enabling rapid response measures like emergency fund distribution, while aligning with Sustainable Development Goals, particularly those focused on poverty reduction, education, and healthcare.

Privacy and security are critical concerns, as the collection and management of vast amounts of personal data make DPI systems vulnerable to misuse and cyberattacks. The digital divide poses another risk, as inadequate implementation could exacerbate inequalities, leaving less developed or remote regions further behind. Technological failures or glitches in DPI systems can disrupt essential services, leading to public dissatisfaction and loss of trust.

The dependency on government policies and funding introduces risks, as political shifts could impact the stability and direction of DPI initiatives. Interoperability between different systems within the DPI framework is another technical hurdle, essential for seamless functionality. Scalability and ongoing maintenance require substantial investment and expertise to ensure that DPI can serve large populations while remaining secure and efficient.

Regulatory and legal frameworks are also critical, as they must balance user rights, data protection, and fair competition. Cultural and social adoption challenges, including resistance to change and lack of digital literacy, can further slow progress. Ethical concerns, such as potential misuse of DPI for surveillance or political control, highlight the importance of implementing transparent and inclusive policies to mitigate risks and build public trust.

Data Economy and Personalization

The Data Economy and Personalization trend encompasses the collection, management, and use of data for creating personalized experiences, products, and services. In this economy, data is seen as an asset, where its value is derived from its insights, which can be used to tailor offerings to individual preferences, behaviours, or needs. This trend spans industries from marketing and advertising to healthcare, finance, entertainment, and beyond, leveraging technologies like AI, machine learning, and big data analytics to deliver more relevant, engaging, and efficient customer interactions.

The surge in data availability, driven by the widespread adoption of digital services and IoT devices, has elevated personalization to a critical business strategy. Advancements in AI and machine learning enable companies to analyse vast datasets and predict individual preferences, meeting the growing consumer demand for tailored experiences.

This not only enhances customer satisfaction and loyalty but also improves marketing efficiency, translating to higher ROI. While privacy legislation like GDPR and CCPA presents challenges, it also fosters trust through transparent data practices, underscoring the economic value of data-driven personalization in today's market.

Data privacy and security concerns are paramount, as high-profile breaches and regulatory scrutiny can deter consumers and result in fines or lawsuits. Complying with global data protection laws is complex and costly, particularly for companies operating internationally. Over-personalization or perceived invasions of privacy can lead to consumer backlash, fatigue, or mistrust, undermining the effectiveness of such efforts.

The quality of data plays a crucial role, as poor or biased data can result in flawed personalization, damaging customer experiences and brand reputation. Monetizing data remains challenging, with many consumers reluctant to share their information freely. Additionally, heavy reliance on technology makes companies vulnerable to system failures or being outpaced by competitors with more advanced solutions.

Ethical concerns, including issues of consent, data ownership, and potential manipulation, are increasingly prominent, requiring companies to tread carefully. Market saturation further complicates the landscape, as differentiation becomes harder, and consumers may grow weary of excessive personalization efforts. Integrating data from disparate sources to create a unified system is technically demanding and resource intensive.

Finally, measuring the return on investment (ROI) for personalization initiatives can be difficult, making it harder to justify these strategies to stakeholders despite their perceived benefits.

Live Commerce

Live Commerce, also known as live shopping or live stream commerce, combines e-commerce with live streaming video where sellers showcase products in real-time, interact with viewers, and often enable direct purchases through the stream. This trend has gained substantial traction, particularly after being popularized in China through platforms like Taobao Live. It is now expanding globally, with companies like Amazon, Instagram, and TikTok integrating live commerce features into their platforms.

Live commerce has revolutionized the shopping experience by merging entertainment and e-commerce. The real-time interaction allows viewers to ask questions, see products in action, and make informed decisions, driving higher engagement and trust. Leveraging influencers and celebrities adds social proof, boosting sales through their follower base. The convergence of shopping and entertainment creates an engaging experience, increasing consumer interest and time spent on platforms.

This format often achieves higher conversion rates due to the immediacy and persuasiveness of live presentations. In culturally aligned regions, like parts of Asia, live commerce has become a shared social activity, enhancing its appeal. By integrating brand storytelling with internet and mobile penetration, live commerce not only enriches the customer experience but also sets new standards for interactive and dynamic shopping.

Market saturation is a significant concern, as more brands and platforms adopt live commerce, making it increasingly difficult to stand out and potentially leading to viewer fatigue. Technological barriers also limit participation, as not all viewers or sellers have access to the necessary technology or reliable internet speeds for high-quality live streaming. Additionally, compliance with e-commerce regulations, consumer protection laws, and data privacy standards is complex, particularly for businesses operating across borders.

Scalability poses another hurdle, with live commerce requiring robust technical infrastructure to manage simultaneous viewers and transactions seamlessly. Maintaining quality in live presentations is essential, as poor experiences can harm brand reputation. Over-reliance on influencers for driving sales is risky, as their effectiveness or public image can change unpredictably. Global live commerce further complicates operations due to time-zone differences, which may not align with peak shopping times across regions.

Impulse buying, while beneficial for sales, raises concerns about encouraging excessive or unnecessary spending. Economic fluctuations also affect live commerce, as discretionary spending tends to decrease during downturns, reducing consumer participation. Note that Live commerce is yet to emerge in India.

Everything as a Service

"Everything as a Service" (XaaS or EaaS) is a business model where virtually any product, process, or service traditionally sold as a one-time purchase is instead offered on a subscription or usage-based model. This trend has expanded from Software as a Service (SaaS) to encompass Infrastructure as a Service (IaaS), Platform as a Service (PaaS), and now includes everything from hardware to even traditional goods like cars or appliances, where consumers pay for usage rather than ownership. This has become possible due to tech.

The "Everything as a Service" (XaaS) model offers flexibility and scalability, but it also presents several challenges. Companies often become heavily reliant on external service providers, posing significant risks if these services are disrupted. The continuous connectivity required for XaaS increases vulnerability to cyber threats, making data security and privacy critical concerns. Consumers and businesses alike may experience subscription fatigue, where an overload of subscriptions leads to cancellations or hesitation to adopt new services.

Over the long term, the cumulative cost of subscriptions can exceed the cost of outright purchases, especially for services used extensively. Service reliability and quality are paramount, as downtime or inconsistent performance can disrupt operations and impact user satisfaction. Vendor lock-in is another concern, where high switching costs can limit competition and flexibility for businesses tied to a provider's ecosystem.

Adoption challenges also arise in traditional industries or sectors resistant to change, where transitioning to a service-based model can be slow and complex. Regulatory compliance, particularly for services handling sensitive data or critical infrastructure, adds further complexity and expense. Finally, market saturation intensifies competition, making it harder for providers to differentiate their offerings and maintain sustainable growth in the crowded XaaS landscape.

Conclusion

With the rise of technology and related business models, IT and related companies helping build digital platforms and infrastructure will benefit the most. Although the IT service and IT development market is fragmented, one should look for established players having an edge in terms of technology and network clients.

The Trends	Expected Growth Rate (2025-2030)	Sources
Fintech and Digital Payments	~30-35% annually	PwC, Indian Brand Equity Foundation (IBEF)
Quick Commerce and Hyperlocal Delivery	~30-50% annually	RedSeer, FICCI
OTT (Over the Top) Platforms	~20-25% annually	KPMG, FICCI Frames
E-commerce and DTC	~25-30% annually	IBEF, McKinsey & Company
ONDC (Open Network for Digital Commerce)	Variable, potentially high; specifics unclear	Government of India, ONDC's initiative documents
Cab Aggregator and Ride-Hailing	~15-20% annually	BCG, LocalCircles
Digital Public Infrastructure	~20-30% annually	NITI Aayog, MeitY reports
Data Economy and Personalization	~30-35% annually	NASSCOM, Deloitte India
Live Commerce	~40-45% annually	Analysis based on trends in China and emerging interest in India
Everything as a Service (XaaS)	~25-30% annually	Gartner, Zinnov

These expected growth rates are based on current and futuristic sentiments and trends of users, investment interests, policies, external factors and industry analysis. Growth rates may be higher or lower than stated here depending on the fluctuations in the underlying factors affecting the overall growth.

Macro Trend 2

Renewable Energy and Sustainability

Solar, Wind, Nuclear Power, and BESS

Solar Power utilizes photovoltaic (PV) panels to convert sunlight directly into electricity. It is rapidly growing due to technological advancements and declining costs. Wind Power Involves the conversion of wind energy into electrical power using wind turbines. Wind energy has become one of the fastest-growing renewable sources. Nuclear Power generates electricity by controlled nuclear reactions, typically fission. It is a significant source of low-carbon energy but faces challenges regarding safety, waste disposal, and public perception. With the rise of solar, wind and nuclear, related accessories, infra and services would also gain significantly, and investors may find good businesses around such sub micro trends.

Battery Energy Storage Systems (BESS) store electrical energy during times of low demand for use during peak times or when renewable generation is low. BESS is crucial for managing the intermittent nature of solar and wind power.

The global energy landscape is driven by ambitious renewable energy goals, technological advancements, and the urgency to combat climate change. Falling costs of solar panels, wind turbines, and battery energy storage systems (BESS) have made renewable energy highly competitive, while innovations in nuclear technology, like small modular reactors (SMRs), offer scalable and safer alternatives.

Governments worldwide are supporting this transition with incentives, mandates, and policies, while rising environmental awareness among consumers fuels demand for cleaner energy. Additionally, the need for energy security and grid stabilization through advanced storage solutions underscores the growing momentum behind solar, wind, nuclear, and BESS technologies.

Solar and wind energy, despite their appeal, suffer from intermittency due to reliance on weather conditions, requiring advanced storage solutions or backup systems to ensure reliability. Additionally, these energy sources have environmental and land-use concerns. Solar farms often require large tracts of land, which can conflict with agricultural or natural ecosystems, while wind turbines face criticism for visual pollution, noise, and their impact on wildlife, particularly birds.

Nuclear power, another key player, struggles with safety concerns stemming from past accidents like Chernobyl and Fukushima, leading to public apprehension. Challenges with long-term radioactive waste disposal, high capital costs, and lengthy construction times further complicate its viability. Battery Energy Storage Systems (BESS), critical for managing renewable energy variability, face issues such as fire risks, degradation over time, and dependence on scarce resources like lithium and cobalt.

All these technologies are heavily influenced by policy, which can shift with political changes, creating uncertainty. Integration of variable renewable energy into existing grids demands substantial investment in infrastructure and advanced grid technology. Market saturation and high supply intensifies pricing competition. Regulatory hurdles, including stringent safety standards for nuclear and zoning laws for solar and wind, further slow progress.

Electric Vehicles (EVs) and Charging Infrastructure

Electric Vehicles (EVs) refer to cars, trucks, buses, and other vehicles that are powered partially or entirely by electricity stored in rechargeable batteries. The charging infrastructure for EVs includes home chargers, public charging stations (Level 2 AC and Level 3 DC fast chargers), and destination charging at workplaces, shopping centres, etc.

The electric vehicle (EV) revolution is accelerating, driven by stricter environmental regulations, technological advancements, and growing consumer awareness. EVs offer cost efficiency through lower operational and maintenance costs, supported by innovations in battery technology and faster charging solutions. Government incentives and an expanding range of EV models make them accessible across consumer segments, while corporate fleets increasingly adopt EVs for sustainability goals. Urbanization further enhances EV suitability, reducing emissions in densely populated areas. Additionally, EV adoption contributes to energy security by decreasing dependence on oil imports, making them a cornerstone of a greener, more sustainable future.

One of the most pressing issues is the gap in charging infrastructure, which may struggle to keep pace with rising EV adoption, leading to range anxiety and inconvenience for consumers. While the total cost of ownership for EVs is often lower, the high upfront purchase price compared to traditional vehicles remains a barrier for many buyers. Additionally, the supply of essential battery materials like lithium and cobalt poses scalability concerns, potentially disrupting production and increasing costs.

Charging time is another hurdle, as even fast-charging options cannot yet match the speed of traditional refuelling, making EVs less convenient for some users. Grid capacity is a looming issue, with widespread EV charging likely requiring significant upgrades to electrical infrastructure, especially during peak times. Resale value also raises questions, with battery degradation being a key factor affecting long-term value retention.

Consumer adaptation to the lifestyle changes EVs demand, such as planning for charging, varies, and equitable access to charging stations remains a concern, particularly in underserved areas. Rapid advancements in battery technology risk rendering older models obsolete, while unique risks like battery fires could lead to higher insurance premiums or stricter safety regulations. In regions where electricity generation still relies heavily on fossil fuels, the environmental benefits of EVs may be diminished.

Market saturation, increasing competition, and potential price wars further complicate the landscape. Finally, shifts in government policy or incentives could significantly impact market growth, making the EV sector highly dynamic but fraught with challenges requiring strategic innovation and adaptation.

Waste Management and Recycling

Waste Management and Recycling involves the collection, transportation, processing, and disposal of waste materials in an environmentally responsible manner. It includes traditional waste collection, composting, recycling of materials like paper, plastics, metals, electronic components, and glass, as well as advanced methods like waste-to-energy conversion, water treatment, chemical recycling, and the circular economy principles where waste is minimized, and materials are reused or repurposed. In short, it works on reduce, reuse, recycle.

Growing environmental awareness and stricter regulations are propelling advancements in waste management and recycling. The shift towards a circular economy emphasizes reusing and recovering resources, supported by innovations like waste sorting and chemical recycling. Resource scarcity and economic incentives make recycling both environmentally and financially viable.

Urbanization and the global plastic waste crisis further highlight the need for efficient waste management solutions, while waste-to-energy technologies offer dual benefits of reducing landfill use and generating alternative energy. Corporate social responsibility and EPR (Extended producer responsibilities) also plays a significant role, as companies adopt sustainable practices to meet both regulatory demands and consumer expectations.

Market fluctuations for recycled or leftover materials make operations unpredictable, as the value of these materials can drop significantly, affecting profitability. Contamination in mixed waste streams reduces the quality and recyclability of materials, often rendering them economically unviable. Additionally, many regions lack the necessary infrastructure to support effective recycling, resulting in low rates despite high waste generation.

Public behaviour is another hurdle, as successful recycling heavily depends on education and consistent participation, which can vary widely. Technological limitations also persist, especially f or complex plastics or composite materials that are difficult or costly to recycle. High investment costs for advanced recycling facilities or innovative technology can deter adoption, while navigating regulatory requirements adds complexity and expense to operations.

In some areas, landfill dependency remains an issue, as it is often cheaper to dispose of waste in landfills than to recycle it. Illegal dumping and enforcement challenges further hinder progress in waste management. The debate between resource recovery (recycling materials) and energy recovery (incinerating waste for energy) can lead to inconsistent policies. Poorly managed waste poses significant environmental and health risks, particularly in developing regions.

Finally, adopting new recycling technologies faces resistance due to excessive costs, regulatory barriers, and uncertainties around long-term viability. These factors collectively make scaling effective recycling systems a significant but necessary challenge for global sustainability efforts.

Green and Biodegradable Products

Green and biodegradable products span a diverse range of items designed to minimize environmental impact throughout their life cycle. These include goods made from renewable resources, those that naturally decompose without harming ecosystems, and those suitable for composting. This trend encompasses sectors such as packaging, textiles, personal care, agriculture, construction, energy (biodiesel), and industrial chemicals (biochemicals and fertilizers), all aimed at reducing waste, pollution, and reliance on non-renewable resources.

The rising demand for sustainability is driving innovation in eco-friendly alternatives, supported by advancements in biodegradable plastics, natural fibres, and bio-based fuels. Consumer awareness, stricter environmental regulations, and corporate commitments to sustainability are accelerating the adoption of green solutions across industries. Concepts like the circular economy and initiatives in sustainable agriculture and food packaging emphasize waste reduction and resource efficiency.

Eco-friendly products not only contribute to climate change mitigation efforts but also offer businesses a competitive edge through brand differentiation. For instance, biodiesel and biochemicals present low-carbon alternatives to conventional fossil fuels and petrochemicals, while biodegradable fertilizers reduce soil and water pollution, promoting sustainable agriculture. These innovations address waste management challenges and encourage a transition to a greener economy.

However, challenges remain. Many green products struggle to match the performance and durability of traditional materials, leading to consumer hesitation. High production costs often require subsidies or premium pricing to compete, creating market entry barriers. Misleading claims, or "greenwashing," undermine trust in genuinely sustainable products, eroding consumer confidence.

The absence of universal certification standards adds to consumer confusion, making it difficult to differentiate between truly sustainable products and superficial claims. Scaling up production is another challenge, as raw material availability and manufacturing capacity remain limited. End-of-life disposal issues are significant—many biodegradable products, such as certain plastics and fertilizers, require specific conditions for effective degradation, which may not be universally available or well-understood.

Supply chain complexities, including ethical sourcing and logistical challenges, also pose hurdles. Market saturation further complicates differentiation as more companies enter the green space. Additionally, while biodiesel and biodegradable plastics are marketed as eco-friendly, improper disposal or incomplete degradation in natural environments (e.g., oceans) can result in unintended environmental harm.

The adoption of green and biodegradable products, though fraught with challenges, remains critical for a sustainable future. Innovations in bio-based materials, supportive policies, and consumer education will play pivotal roles in overcoming barriers and ensuring meaningful progress toward global sustainability goals.

Decarbonization and Carbon Credits

Decarbonization refers to the process of reducing carbon emissions and transitioning towards a net-zero or low-carbon economy.

This involves replacing fossil fuels with renewable energy, improving energy efficiency, and implementing carbon capture and storage technologies. Carbon Credits are a market-based mechanism used to incentivize these reductions. One carbon credit represents the reduction of one tonne of carbon dioxide (or its equivalent) from the atmosphere. They can be traded through carbon markets, allowing entities to offset emissions they cannot eliminate directly.

The global push for decarbonization, driven by climate agreements like the Paris Agreement, corporate net-zero pledges, and regulatory pressure, has elevated the demand for carbon credits. With growing ESG investing, technological advancements in renewable energy and carbon capture, and heightened consumer awareness of environmental responsibility, carbon credits have become a critical tool for achieving sustainability goals. Additionally, carbon pricing and the emergence of new markets for green technologies highlight the economic opportunities tied to emissions reduction efforts. This union of factors underscores the increasing relevance of carbon credits in global climate strategies.

Concerns about the quality and integrity of carbon credits arise from doubts over the actual environmental impact of offset projects, with issues such as additionality, permanence, and leakage undermining their value. Market volatility is another critical issue, as carbon credit prices are overly sensitive to policy changes, supply and demand dynamics, and geopolitical factors.

Regulatory risks further complicate the landscape, with shifts in climate policies potentially affecting the value and viability of carbon credits or altering compliance markets. Greenwashing is a prevalent concern, where companies claim carbon neutrality while relying heavily on credits instead of reducing their emissions. Verifying the actual carbon savings of projects remains a challenge, leading to over-crediting or ineffective offset initiatives.

Scalability is also limited, as carbon credits cannot replace the need for direct emission reductions. Technological limitations in carbon capture and storage technologies hinder their scalability and impact. Economic dependency on carbon markets, particularly in developing countries, creates vulnerabilities if the market collapses or policies change.

The lack of standardized international regulations complicates cross-border credit trading, while risks of carbon leakage and double counting undermine global decarbonization efforts. Additionally, speculative trading in carbon markets could divert focus from meaningful emission reductions, highlighting the need for robust governance, transparency, and innovation to realize the potential of carbon credits as a tool for climate action.

Grid Optimization and Infrastructure

Grid optimization and infrastructure development are central to the energy transition. As electricity consumption rises and renewable energy adoption increases, grid networks must evolve to handle the complexities of integrating intermittent energy sources like solar and wind. Optimized grids focus on enhancing efficiency, reliability, and resilience while supporting decentralized energy generation and storage. Key elements include smart grids, advanced metering infrastructure (AMI), transmission lines, substations, and energy management systems.

A modernized grid is vital for achieving energy security, decarbonization goals, and accommodating emerging demands from electric vehicles (EVs), data centres, and distributed energy resources (DERs). Grid infrastructure upgrades and optimization are not only about technology but also about creating a robust framework for sustainable and scalable energy distribution.

The demand for grid optimization is driven by the global shift toward renewable energy, increasing electricity consumption, and the rise of decentralized energy generation. Renewables like solar and wind require advanced grid technologies such as inverters, smart meters, and grid-scale batteries to manage variable supply patterns and ensure stability. Smart grids, with IoT and digital tools, enable real-time monitoring and demand-side management, reducing downtime and improving efficiency.

Additionally, the electrification of transport and industrial processes, coupled with EV adoption, has necessitated infrastructure upgrades to manage higher energy loads. Government policies promoting clean energy transitions, alongside incentives for grid modernization, further accelerate growth. Decentralized energy sources like rooftop solar and microgrids also require advanced systems for bi-directional energy flow and seamless integration, enhancing energy security and reliability.

Despite these drivers, grid optimization faces significant risks. Upfront capital requirements are high, particularly for emerging economies, and the ROI may take years, discouraging private investments. Technological integration, though necessary, is complex and increases cybersecurity vulnerabilities. Aging infrastructure in many countries raises reliability concerns and adds to modernization costs.

Environmental impacts, such as ecosystem disruption from new transmission lines, pose challenges, while regulatory hurdles and policy inconsistencies can delay projects. Additionally, passing upgrade costs to consumers may lead to resistance, underscoring the importance of public awareness and education.

Green Hydrogen and Related Accessories

Green Hydrogen refers to hydrogen produced through the electrolysis of water using renewable energy sources like wind or solar power. The process is clean, with hydrogen being stored and used as a zero-emission energy carrier. Related accessories include electrolysers for production, hydrogen storage solutions, fuel cells for energy conversion, and the infrastructure for distribution.

Green hydrogen is emerging as a cornerstone of global decarbonization efforts, particularly in hard-to-electrify sectors like heavy industry, shipping, and aviation. Its ability to store excess renewable energy enhances grid stability, making it integral to renewable energy integration. Backed by strong policy support, advancements in electrolyser efficiency, and innovations in storage and transport, green hydrogen is becoming more cost-effective. Industrial applications, growing demand in fuel cell technologies, and the push for a global hydrogen economy further highlight its potential. Rising carbon pricing and the need for energy security also position green hydrogen as a vital solution for a sustainable future.

Currently, green hydrogen is more expensive than grey hydrogen produced from fossil fuels, though costs are expected to decline with advancements in technology and scale. Efficiency losses during production, storage, and conversion into electricity or other uses reduce its overall energy utility, while its low volumetric energy density and flammability present challenges for safe storage and transport.

A significant barrier is the lack of infrastructure for hydrogen distribution, which limits its accessibility. Scaling up electrolyser production to meet demand poses both technical and economic challenges, and the availability of renewable energy—critical for green hydrogen production—is uneven across regions. The nascent nature of the green hydrogen market creates investment uncertainty, further compounded by heavy reliance on governmental support and favourable policies for growth.

Environmental concerns also arise, as the lifecycle emissions and water usage in hydrogen production require careful management. Public perception remains a hurdle, with a need to educate industries and consumers on the safety and benefits of hydrogen technology. Additionally, the absence of global standards for green hydrogen production, quality, and safety complicates scaling and market integration.

Conclusion

As power and energy become essential pillars of progress, it is equally important for a country to adopt a sustainable approach while minimizing environmental impact. Segments and players involved across the entire value chain of sustainable development are poised for significant growth as the world increasingly prioritizes green solutions and renewable energy innovations.

Trends	Expected Growth Rate (2025-2030)	Source
Solar, Wind, Nuclear Power, and BESS (Battery Energy Storage Systems)	Solar: ~25-30% annually, Wind: ~15-20%, Nuclear: Stable, BESS: High growth potential	MNRE, IEA, TERI
EVs and Charging Infrastructure	EVs: ~30-35% annually, Charging Infrastructure: ~40% annually	NITI Aayog, Deloitte India, FICCI
Waste Management and Recycling	~15-20% annually	CPCB, World Bank, FICCI
Green and Biodegradable Products	~20-25% annually	Market research, sustainability reports
Decarbonization and Carbon Credits	Variable, potentially high; specifics depend on policy implementation	MoEFCC, Carbon Market Watch, TERI
Grid Optimization and Infrastructure	~15% annually	Power Grid Corporation of India Limited, IEA
Green Hydrogen and Related Accessories	Potentially 30-40% annually, starting from a low base	NITI Aayog, Hydrogen Council, TERI

These expected growth rates are based on current and futuristic sentiments and trends of users, investment interests, policies, external factors and industry analysis. Growth rates may be higher or lower than stated here depending on the fluctuations in the underlying factors affecting the overall growth.

Macro Trend 3

Contract Research, Development, Manufacturing, and Outsourcing

Pharmaceutical Contract Research and Manufacturing (CRAMS)

The Pharmaceutical Contract Research and Manufacturing Services (CRAMS) sector stands as a critical component in the global pharmaceutical industry, providing an outsourced solution for drug development, clinical research, and manufacturing. This sector has evolved significantly, with companies outsourcing more of their operations to focus on core competencies like drug discovery. CDMO is a specialized category within the larger CRAMS framework, focusing on development and manufacturing.

The trend shows a shift towards more integrated services where CRAMS not only manufacture but also engage in drug development from initial stages to commercialization. While CRAMS may also include services like early-stage research (discovery and preclinical), CDMOs concentrate on development and manufacturing. CDMOs often specialize in biologics, biosimilars, and high-value drug products, whereas CRAMS might include broader, lower-value or generic pharmaceutical services. This sector's growth is propelled by the pharmaceutical industry's need for flexible, scalable, and cost-effective solutions, especially as the complexity of new drugs increases with the rise of biologics and personalized medicine.

Cost reduction remains a primary motivator, as outsourcing to countries like India and China offers substantial financial advantages due to lower labour and operational costs, particularly for generic drug production and Active Pharmaceutical Ingredient (API) synthesis. Simultaneously, the increased investment in R&D by pharmaceutical companies has led to a surge in demand for contract services, especially for managing expanded pipelines, clinical trials, and niche manufacturing needs.

The rising demand for biopharmaceuticals, including biologics, biosimilars, and cell therapies, further propels CRAMS, CDMO growth. These products require highly specialized manufacturing capabilities, which many CRAMS providers are well-equipped to deliver. Additionally, the complex and dynamic regulatory landscape encourages pharmaceutical companies to rely on CRAMS partners with the expertise to navigate stringent compliance requirements efficiently, particularly in evolving markets like India.

Technological advancements also play a pivotal role, with CRAMS providers adopting innovations such as continuous manufacturing to improve efficiency, quality, and speed to market. This, coupled with strategic outsourcing, allows drug companies to accelerate product development, mitigate risks, and foster innovation through collaborative partnerships.

Quality and compliance are critical, as any lapse in adhering to global standards can lead to significant setbacks, including product recalls, regulatory sanctions, and loss of client trust. Intellectual property (IP) challenges also pose risks, with concerns over IP leakage or disputes, particularly in regions with less stringent IP laws or enforcement mechanisms. Over-reliance on key clients is another vulnerability, as a shift in strategy or financial difficulties of major clients can destabilize CRAMS providers. Regulatory changes further complicate the landscape, potentially increasing compliance costs.

Rapid technological advancements demand continuous investment in new equipment and processes to stay competitive, but these investments are risky if technologies quickly become obsolete. Supply chain vulnerabilities, including disruptions from natural disasters, geopolitical tensions, or pandemics, can halt production and inflate costs. Additionally, environmental and sustainability pressures are growing, with expectations for green manufacturing practices necessitating costly operational upgrades.

Electronics Manufacturing Services (EMS)

The Electronics Manufacturing Services (EMS) industry is experiencing robust growth, characterized by companies outsourcing their electronic manufacturing needs to specialized firms. EMS providers offer services ranging from design, prototyping, component sourcing, assembly, testing, to final product manufacturing.

This trend is driven by the electronics industry's rapid evolution, where companies rely on EMS to accelerate product development cycles, manage supply chain complexities, and navigate the increasingly intricate landscape of electronic components and devices. The global reach of EMS firms, particularly in Asia, has made it possible for original equipment manufacturers (OEMs) to focus on innovation, marketing, and sales while leveraging the manufacturing expertise of EMS providers. The industry is also seeing a shift towards more integrated services, where EMS companies are not just assemblers but partners in product design and lifecycle management.

The Electronics Manufacturing Services (EMS) industry is thriving due to the increasing complexity of electronic devices, which require specialized skills and advanced manufacturing technologies like automation and robotics. OEMs are outsourcing to EMS providers, particularly in cost-effective regions like India, China, and Vietnam, to achieve scalability and economic efficiency. These providers excel in managing global supply chains, mitigating risks, and ensuring inventory control, which is vital in today's environment of frequent disruptions.

China+1 is the biggest factor for Indian EMS industry as more businesses shifting towards Indian players reducing dependency on China. With shorter product lifecycles driven by rapid technological advancements, EMS firms enable faster time-to-market. Additionally, their ability to implement eco-friendly practices aligns with growing environmental regulations, while allowing OEMs to focus on core competencies such as R&D and market expansion.

Supply chain vulnerabilities are a constant concern, as global events, geopolitical tensions, or natural disasters can disrupt production schedules and inflate costs. Intellectual property (IP) risks arise when outsourcing exposes Original Equipment Manufacturers (OEMs) to potential IP theft, particularly in regions with less stringent legal protections. Ensuring consistent quality control across multiple manufacturing facilities worldwide is another challenge, with lapses potentially leading to product defects, recalls, and reputational damage.

Price competition in the EMS market is intense, often leading to narrow profit margins and pressure on quality and service levels. Providers must also invest heavily in technological upgrades to remain competitive, a capital-intensive and risky endeavour given the rapid pace of innovation. Dependency on major clients poses another risk, as shifts in client strategies or market conditions can significantly impact an EMS company's revenue.

Navigating international regulatory frameworks adds complexity, with non-compliance risks leading to fines or restricted market access. Cybersecurity threats are growing with the rise of connected manufacturing systems. Economic fluctuations also affect the EMS sector, as demand for electronic products often correlates with broader economic cycles. Additionally, geopolitical tensions, including trade wars, tariffs, and policy shifts, can alter cost benefits in outsourcing regions, forcing companies to adapt rapidly.

Precision Machinery and Engineering

The trend in Precision Machinery and Engineering reflects a global push towards higher manufacturing quality, efficiency, and innovation. This sector involves the design, development, and manufacturing of precision equipment used in various industries like aerospace, automotive, medical devices, semiconductor production, and more. The demand for precision machinery is driven by the need for products that offer higher performance, greater reliability, and reduced tolerances.

The advent of Industry 4.0, with its focus on smart manufacturing, automation, and data exchange, has significantly influenced this sector. Precision engineering not only pertains to the machines themselves but also includes the tools, processes, and technologies that enable the production of highly accurate parts and components. This trend is also characterized by the integration of advanced materials and innovative technologies like 3D printing, nanotechnology, and smart sensors into machinery design and manufacturing.

The precision engineering sector is witnessing significant growth due to multiple converging trends. Industry 4.0's integration of IoT, AI, and robotics demands machinery with unparalleled accuracy, while the trend towards miniaturization in electronics and medical devices necessitates even finer precision. Consumers and industries increasingly demand high-quality products, fuelling the need for precision in manufacturing. Customization, the use of advanced materials, and technological advancements in CNC, additive manufacturing, and metrology further elevate the standards for precision machinery. Global competition, the push towards renewable energy solutions where precision enhances efficiency, and the critical need for accurate medical devices all contribute to the expanding landscape of precision engineering.

The precision engineering industry faces significant challenges despite its critical role in high-tech manufacturing and innovation. One of the primary barriers is the high capital investment required to acquire and maintain advanced precision machinery. This initial cost, coupled with the need for continuous technology upgrades to avoid obsolescence, makes entry and sustainability financially demanding. Additionally, the industry suffers from a global shortage of skilled technicians and engineers, which can limit growth and operational efficiency.

The rapid digitalization of precision machinery introduces cybersecurity risks, as connected systems become vulnerable to cyber-attacks. Supply chain complexity is another concern, as reliance on global networks for components and materials makes the industry susceptible to geopolitical or economic disruptions.

Environmental regulations are tightening, often necessitating costly redesigns of processes and equipment to comply with sustainability goals. The industry is also economically cyclical, with demand closely tied to sectors like automotive and electronics. Intellectual property theft remains a risk, particularly in less regulated markets, threatening the competitive edge of innovators.

Meeting stringent quality and precision standards is an ongoing challenge, as defects in high-precision applications can lead to significant financial and reputational costs. Furthermore, growing competition from established firms and new entrants intensifies price pressure, potentially squeezing margins.

Electronic Components and Semiconductor Chips

The Electronic Components and Semiconductor Chips sector is undergoing dynamic transformations, driven by the ever-increasing demand for electronics across various industries. This trend includes the manufacturing of semiconductors, integrated circuits, sensors, resistors, capacitors, and other electronic components essential for modern technology.

The semiconductor industry is at the forefront of innovation, with chips becoming smaller, faster, and more energy efficient. This sector is critical for enabling advancements in AI, IoT, 5G technology, electric vehicles, renewable energy systems, and consumer electronics. The global chip shortage in recent years has highlighted the sector's importance to the economy, pushing countries to rethink their semiconductor supply chains for resilience and security.

The semiconductor industry is experiencing robust growth driven by several key factors. The proliferation of smart devices, including smartphones and IoT gadgets, has heightened the demand for advanced semiconductor technologies. Advancements in AI and machine learning necessitate chips with superior processing capabilities, while the global expansion of 5G networks pushes for innovations in chip technology to support faster data transfer. The automotive sector's transition to electric and autonomous vehicles further escalates the need for high-performance electronic components.

Moreover, the expansion of data centres for cloud computing, continuous evolution in consumer electronics, and applications in renewable energy and industrial IoT all contribute to this growth. The healthcare sector's reliance on advanced medical devices adds another layer of demand. Additionally, geopolitical strategies are prompting nations to bolster their own semiconductor production capabilities, aiming for self-sufficiency in this critical technology domain.

The semiconductor industry, a cornerstone of modern technology, faces numerous challenges that complicate its growth and operations. Supply chain disruptions, as highlighted by the recent global chip shortage, can cause significant delays and increased costs, impacting a wide range of industries reliant on semiconductors. Technological barriers also pose a challenge, as chips continue to shrink, requiring advanced materials and innovative manufacturing methods to overcome the physical limitations at the nanoscale.

The industry's capital intensity is another hurdle, with the construction of state-of-the-art semiconductor fabrication facilities (fabs) requiring massive investments, often deterring new entrants, and limiting competition. Intellectual property theft is a persistent risk, especially in regions with less stringent IP laws, threatening the value of proprietary technologies. Geopolitical tensions, such as trade wars and sanctions, further disrupt global supply chains and partnerships, particularly for key players like TSMC and Samsung.

The semiconductor market's cyclical nature adds volatility, where periods of high demand can quickly flip to oversupply, affecting profitability. Environmental and ethical concerns are growing, as semiconductor production consumes significant energy and water and involves hazardous substances, raising sustainability issues. Talent scarcity remains a critical bottleneck, with a global shortage of skilled semiconductor engineers and technicians slowing innovation and expansion.

Cybersecurity risks are increasing as semiconductors play a vital role in critical infrastructure, making secure design practices essential. Regulatory compliance, especially around security and trade policies, adds further complexity and costs to manufacturing and distribution. These challenges underscore the need for strategic innovation, collaboration, and policy support to ensure the semiconductor industry's resilience and sustainability.

Consumer Electronics and Electrical Goods

The consumer electronics and electrical goods market continues to evolve rapidly, shaped by technological innovation, changing consumer behaviours, and global economic factors. This sector includes a wide array of products like smartphones, tablets, televisions, home appliances, wearables, and IoT devices. The trend is towards smarter, more connected devices that integrate seamlessly into our daily lives, enhancing convenience, entertainment, and efficiency. The rise of smart homes, wearable technology, and the integration of AI in consumer products are pivotal, reflecting a shift from purely functional to intelligent, data-driven devices that offer personalized experiences. Moreover, the focus on sustainability and energy efficiency is increasingly influencing product design and consumer choice, with companies striving to meet both regulatory demands and consumer expectations for greener technologies.

The electronics market is propelled by a mix of technological advancements and evolving consumer behaviours. Innovations in display technologies, battery efficiency, processing power, and AI integration keep consumers engaged with new product releases. The widespread adoption of 5G enhances device connectivity, opening avenues for IoT and smart home solutions.

Rising disposable incomes in emerging markets fuel demand, while a preference for interconnected devices caters to the modern consumer's lifestyle. Health and wellness trends have spurred interest in wearables, and there is a growing market for sustainable products. Entertainment technologies like gaming, streaming, and

VR/AR drive device upgrades, while the global shift to remote work and education has significantly increased the need for personal electronics. Coupled with shorter product replacement cycles due to rapid tech evolution, these factors ensure a vibrant growth trajectory for the electronics sector.

Market saturation in mature markets, where smartphones and other devices have high penetration, has led to slower growth as consumers delay upgrades. Supply chain vulnerabilities, exacerbated by geopolitical tensions, natural disasters, or pandemics, can result in delays and component shortages, particularly for critical items like semiconductors.

Intense competition in the industry drives price wars, which erode profit margins and push companies to innovate or cut costs aggressively. The rapid pace of technological change contributes to product obsolescence, generating increased electronic waste and challenging companies to manage shorter product cycles responsibly. Cybersecurity risks also grow with the proliferation of connected devices.

Consumer privacy is another pressing issue, as the integration of AI and IoT devices raises concerns about data security, potentially affecting trust and adoption rates. Regulatory and environmental compliance add further complexity, with increasing standards for energy efficiency, recycling, and material use driving up production costs. Additionally, the shift towards subscription models, such as streaming and cloud gaming, may reduce long-term demand for physical hardware.

Economic downturns present another vulnerability, as consumer electronics are discretionary purchases. Geopolitical risks, including trade tensions and dependence on imports, can disrupt operations and supply chains. Finally, the rapid pace of innovation heightens the risk of intellectual property disputes, which can be costly and time-consuming for companies to resolve.

BPO, KPO and GCC

Business Process Outsourcing (BPO), Knowledge Process Outsourcing (KPO), and Global Capability Centres (GCCs) represent evolving trends in how businesses manage their operations globally. BPO involves outsourcing operational functions like customer service, technical support, or back-office work to third-party providers, often for cost efficiency. KPO, a subset of BPO, deals with processes requiring advanced analytical and technical skills, such as research, analytics, or legal services. Global Capability Centres, initially referred to as captives, are offshore or nearshore units set up by companies to conduct high-value activities like software development, innovation, and R&D, which are strategic to the company's core business. It is not a new, but the trend has been towards more strategic outsourcing and offshoring, with a shift from pure cost-saving to value creation, innovation, and accessing specialized talent pools.

The growth of Business Process Outsourcing (BPO), Knowledge Process Outsourcing (KPO), and Global Capability Centres (GCC) is driven by distinct advantages each offers. BPO thrives on cost reduction, allowing companies to focus on core competencies by outsourcing routine tasks, offering scalability, and leveraging advanced tech infrastructures for 24/7 operations. KPO, on the other hand, caters to the demand for high-skill services, providing innovation, research, regulatory compliance, and complex problem-solving capabilities. Meanwhile, GCCs facilitate control over strategic functions, offering access to a global talent pool, driving innovation, managing risks associated with sensitive data, and ensuring seamless integration with parent company operations. Together, these models provide organizations with the flexibility, expertise, and strategic advantages needed in today's competitive landscape.

For BPOs, ensuring consistent service quality from third-party vendors can be difficult, especially when cultural and language barriers lead to miscommunication and customer dissatisfaction. Data security concerns are prominent, as outsourcing often involves sensitive information, raising risks of breaches. Over-reliance on external providers also poses a risk if service levels decline or providers face business challenges.

In KPO, the outsourcing of high-level tasks brings intellectual property risks, as safeguarding proprietary knowledge and data becomes critical. High attrition rates among specialized knowledge workers exacerbate the challenge, causing frequent talent loss. Additionally, seamless integration of KPO services with a company's broader operations can be complex and resource intensive.

For GCCs, the high investment required for setup and operations is a significant barrier, compounded by the need to navigate local labour laws and compliance requirements. Talent retention is another hurdle, as skilled workers are often in high demand, leading to high turnover rates. Political and economic instability in foreign countries adds another layer of risk, and maintaining operational control to ensure alignment with the parent company's global strategy and culture can be challenging.

Across all outsourcing models, market fluctuations due to economic downturns can impact strategy viability. Technological disruptions, particularly automation and AI, may reduce the demand for traditional BPO/KPO services. Geopolitical tensions and evolving privacy regulations like GDPR and CCPA further complicate operations, requiring stringent data handling practices. Ethical and sustainability concerns, including corporate social responsibility (CSR), also influence decisions about where and how to outsource, underscoring the need for resilient and adaptive strategies.

Make in India and China+1

The "Make in India" initiative and the "China Plus One" strategy are two interconnected trends in global manufacturing and trade. "Make in India" is a campaign launched by the Indian government aimed at encouraging multinational companies to manufacture in India, enhancing investment, fostering innovation, and creating jobs. It emphasizes sectors like electronics, pharmaceuticals, automobiles, and textiles.

The "China Plus One" strategy, on the other hand, is adopted by companies looking to diversify their manufacturing bases beyond China due to distinct reasons including trade tensions, supply chain risks, and labour costs. India is often viewed as a prime beneficiary of this strategy, given its large market, skilled workforce, and supportive government policies.

The "Make in India" initiative and the "China Plus One" strategy are driving significant growth in India's manufacturing sector. "Make in India" is bolstered by government incentives like the Production Linked Incentive (PLI) schemes aimed at attracting manufacturing investments across various sectors. The development of industrial corridors, alongside improvements in logistics and transport infrastructure, further supports this growth. India's vast and expanding consumer market presents an enormous opportunity for manufacturers looking to sell domestically and internationally.

On the other hand, the "China Plus One" strategy is primarily motivated by geopolitical risks and the desire to increase supply chain resilience following global disruptions like the COVID-19 pandemic. Increasing labour costs in China have also made India a more competitive destination for manufacturing, encouraging companies to diversify their production bases.

However, these growth drivers come with their set of risks and concerns. For "Make in India," regulatory and bureaucratic hurdles can still pose significant challenges to investors, potentially offsetting the benefits of incentives. Infrastructure, while being developed, remains uneven across India, which can hamper large-scale manufacturing projects in certain regions. There is also the critical issue of skill development to ensure the workforce is prepared for sophisticated manufacturing processes.

In terms of the "China Plus One" strategy, there is the risk of market saturation as multiple countries compete for the same pool of manufacturing investments, which might not distribute benefits evenly. Companies also face the challenge of adapting to new cultural and business environments in India, which requires understanding local customs and practices. Finally, maintaining the quality and consistency of manufacturing outside of China's established ecosystem can be demanding, requiring significant effort to match or exceed existing standards.

Conclusion

As the manufacturing industry thrives in a nation with robust resources in place, innovation, technological advancements, and cost efficiencies are likely to attract increasing interest from global players. Companies positioned within the value chain of scalable manufacturing stand to gain significant traction. For investors, identifying manufacturing players with a strong domestic revenue focus or those operating in areas aligned with emerging macro trends can unlock substantial growth opportunities.

Trends	Expected Growth Rate (2025-2030)	Source
CRAMS (Contract Research and Manufacturing Services)	~10-15% annually	IBEF, Frost & Sullivan
Electronics Manufacturing Services (EMS)	~15-20% annually	IBEF, EY India
Precision Machinery and Engineering	~10-15% annually	Engineering Export Promotion Council of India, Deloitte
Electronic Components and Semiconductor Chips	~20-25% annually	India Semiconductor Association, Ernst & Young
Consumer Electronics and Electrical Goods	~15% annually	Consumer Electronics and Appliances Manufacturers Association (CEAMA), PwC
BPO, KPO, and GCC (Global Capability Centres)	BPO/KPO: ~7-10%, GCC: ~15-20% annually	NASSCOM, Zinnov
Make in India and China+1	Variable, potentially high	Government of India, Various market analyses

These expected growth rates are based on current and futuristic sentiments and trends of users, investment interests, policies, external factors and industry analysis. Growth rates may be higher or lower than stated here depending on the fluctuations in the underlying factors affecting the overall growth.

Macro Trend 4

Bio Innovation and Wellness

AI in Diagnostics and Drug Discovery

The integration of Artificial Intelligence (AI) in diagnostics and drug discovery represents a transformative trend in healthcare and pharmaceuticals. AI's capabilities in handling vast amounts of data, recognizing patterns, predicting outcomes, and learning from new data are being leveraged to enhance the accuracy of medical diagnoses, personalize treatment plans, and accelerate the drug discovery process. In diagnostics, AI algorithms assist in interpreting complex medical imaging, identifying diseases from scans earlier than traditional methods, and even predicting disease progression.

In drug discovery, AI is used for target identification, drug design, understanding drug interactions, and repurposing existing drugs for new uses, significantly reducing the time and cost associated with bringing new drugs to market. This trend is fuelled by advancements in machine learning, deep learning, big data analytics, and computational power, making AI an indispensable tool in modern healthcare.

The integration of AI into healthcare, particularly in drug discovery and diagnostics, is propelled by several critical growth drivers. The explosion of data from EHRs, medical imaging, and genomics provides AI with vast datasets to learn from. The traditional drug discovery process's inefficiencies in terms of time and cost are mitigated by AI's ability to analyse data at scale, speeding up candidate identification and increasing success rates.

AI's role in personalized medicine allows for treatments tailored to individual genetic profiles, improving outcomes. Moreover, AI's potential to enhance diagnostic accuracy, reduce costs by optimizing drug development, and leverage advanced computing capabilities are significant. Collaborative efforts across sectors and the urgent need for solutions during global health emergencies further catalyse AI's adoption in healthcare.

Handling sensitive medical data with AI raises critical concerns about privacy, security, and the ethical use of patient information. Bias in AI algorithms, stemming from incomplete or skewed datasets, risks perpetuating healthcare disparities, undermining trust, and outcomes. Regulatory approval for AI-designed drugs or diagnostics is another hurdle, as current frameworks are not fully equipped to address the complexities of AI in medicine.

The interpretability of AI models, especially deep learning systems, is a key issue. These "black box" systems often lack transparency, making it difficult to validate their recommendations—a crucial factor in medical decision-making. Over-reliance on AI could erode essential human skills and judgment in healthcare, posing risks to patient care.

Technical integration into existing healthcare systems is challenging and requires significant investment, while legal and liability concerns remain unresolved, particularly when AI errors lead to adverse outcomes. Intellectual property issues also arise, particularly regarding the ownership of AI-generated insights in drug discovery. Resistance to change among traditional healthcare providers, fuelled by cultural inertia or fear of obsolescence, adds to the barriers.

Telehealth and Remote Monitoring

Telehealth and remote patient monitoring (RPM) have emerged as pivotal trends in healthcare, transforming how medical services are delivered. Telehealth involves providing healthcare remotely through telecommunications technology, allowing patients to consult with healthcare providers via video calls, phone, or messaging. Remote patient monitoring extends this by using digital technologies to collect health data from individuals in one location and transmit it to healthcare professionals in another for assessment and recommendations.

This trend has been accelerated by technological advancements, consumer acceptance, regulatory changes, and the need for cost-effective healthcare solutions. It encompasses everything from routine check-ups and chronic disease management to post-hospital care and mental health services.

The expansion of telehealth is driven by multiple factors that address both technological and societal needs. Advancements in technology like broadband, mobile devices, AI, and IoT have made remote healthcare more accessible and efficient. An aging global population increases the demand for healthcare services that can be delivered at home, supporting aging in place.

The management of chronic diseases through continuous monitoring is better facilitated by telehealth, enhancing patient care while also considering convenience and cost efficiency. Telehealth significantly improves access to care, especially in underserved or remote areas, and has proven invaluable during health crises by allowing healthcare to continue when physical distancing is necessary. Furthermore, the integration of data analytics in telehealth systems provides insights for better health management and predictive care, further solidifying its growth trajectory.

The digital divide remains a critical issue, as not all patients have access to the required technology or high-speed internet, potentially widening healthcare disparities. The transmission and storage of sensitive health data on digital platforms introduce significant risks of breaches or misuse, raising concerns about data privacy and security.

Ensuring quality of care in virtual consultations is another hurdle, as the lack of physical examinations can lead to misdiagnoses or incomplete treatment plans if not effectively managed. The regulatory and reimbursement landscape for telehealth is evolving, with uncertainties around long-term support for various telehealth services. Technical issues, such as connectivity problems, can disrupt care and cause delays in treatment.

Legal and liability concerns also arise, particularly in providing care across jurisdictions with differing licensure requirements and patient rights. Over-reliance on telehealth could lead to the neglect of nuances that in-person consultations often capture. Building trust and rapport in a virtual setting can be more challenging, potentially affecting patient satisfaction and adherence to care plans.

Gene Editing and Personalized Medicine

Gene Editing and Personalized Medicine represent a convergence of biotechnology and healthcare, aiming to tailor medical treatment to the individual characteristics of each patient. Gene editing technologies, most notably CRISPR-Cas9, offer the ability to make precise changes to DNA within living organisms, potentially correcting genetic defects, enhancing disease resistance, or even altering physical traits.

Personalized medicine uses genetic profiling along with other data like lifestyle, environment, and microbiome to craft treatments that are specifically designed for each patient, which could lead to treatments that are more effective and with fewer side effects. This trend is part of a broader movement towards precision medicine, where the focus is on customizing healthcare by considering individual variability in genes, environment, and lifestyle.

The field of gene therapy is experiencing rapid growth, fuelled by significant advancements in gene editing technologies like CRISPR-Cas9, which have become more precise and accessible. The massive increase in genomic data, thanks to cheaper sequencing and projects like the Human Genome Project, lays the groundwork for personalized medicine.

Successful clinical trials, especially for treating rare genetic disorders and cancers, have not only proven the efficacy of these therapies but also attracted substantial investment. The growing burden of chronic and genetic diseases worldwide further propels the demand for targeted treatments. Pharmacogenomics plays a crucial role by tailoring drug responses to individual genetics. Meanwhile, evolving regulatory frameworks are smoothing the transition from research to clinical use. Patient advocacy for new treatment options and the integration of AI in genetic analysis are also key drivers, enhancing the prediction of treatment outcomes and accelerating the development of gene therapies.

Germline editing, which affects future generations, raises significant moral questions about consent, equality, and the potential misuse of technology for creating "designer babies." Tools like CRISPR, while revolutionary, pose risks of off-target effects that may cause unintended genetic changes with unknown long-term consequences. Ensuring the safety and efficacy of gene therapies remains a critical hurdle, with challenges such as immune responses and unintended side effects.

Access to these treatments is another concern, as their excessive costs could create a healthcare divide where only the wealthy benefit from such innovations. Regulatory frameworks, while evolving, are complex and struggle to keep pace with the novel nature of gene therapies. Public apprehension about genetic manipulation adds to the barriers, potentially slowing acceptance and adoption. Intellectual property disputes over gene-editing technologies could stifle innovation and delay progress.

Releasing genetically modified organisms into the environment, if not carefully managed, poses ecological risks, while the long-term effects of gene editing on human health remain largely unknown, necessitating ongoing research and monitoring. Data privacy is critical, as the collection and use of genetic data must be protected to prevent misuse. Scaling personalized medicine also presents logistical challenges in terms of data management, cost, and time.

3D Printing in Healthcare

The trend of 3D Printing in Healthcare has been gaining momentum as an innovative technology that offers personalized solutions in medical care. Also known as additive manufacturing, 3D printing in healthcare ranges from producing patient-specific anatomical models for surgical planning to creating custom implants, prosthetics, and even bio-printed organs. This technology allows for the creation of complex and precise structures that are difficult or impossible to achieve with traditional manufacturing methods.

Its applications are diverse, impacting areas like orthopaedics, dentistry, reconstructive surgery, and regenerative medicine. The customization capability of 3D printing can lead to better patient outcomes, improved surgical planning, and potentially reduced costs in the long term.

The adoption of 3D printing in medicine is driven by its ability to provide highly customized solutions, from patient-specific medical devices to complex anatomical models. The technology excels in creating intricate shapes that align perfectly with human anatomy, significantly reducing the time and cost associated with bringing new medical devices to market. It is particularly beneficial for small-scale or bespoke manufacturing. In surgical contexts, 3D printing aids in detailed planning through tangible models, while in regenerative medicine, it opens the frontier of bioprinting organs and tissues.

Dental care benefits from precise custom implants, and drug delivery is revolutionized with tailored medications. Additionally, 3D printing serves as an educational tool for medical training, offering hands-on experience with realistic models. The continuous innovation in biocompatible materials further supports the growth of 3D printing in healthcare applications.

Regulatory challenges are a significant barrier, as the framework for 3D-printed medical devices is still evolving, creating uncertainty for manufacturers and healthcare providers. Ensuring consistent quality across various 3D printing technologies and materials is critical, as inconsistencies can lead to device failure or patient harm.

Intellectual property concerns, such as disputes over design and patent rights, complicate the legal landscape. Material limitations also pose a challenge, as not all biocompatible materials can be effectively 3D printed. While the technology promises cost-effective solutions for custom medical devices, the initial investment in 3D printers and materials remains high.

Sterilization is another hurdle, as 3D-printed parts must withstand sterilization processes without degrading their material properties. Patient safety is paramount, as any inconsistency in the printing process can result in device failure or rejection by the body.

Reimbursement issues add complexity, as insurance and healthcare systems may not have policies in place to cover 3D-printed medical products. Using patient-specific data to create 3D models also raises data privacy and security concerns. A skill and knowledge gap exists, with healthcare professionals requiring specialized training to use and interpret 3D-printed models effectively.

Supply chain vulnerabilities emerge as reliance on specific printers and materials grows, and legal liability issues complicate accountability if a 3D-printed device fails or causes harm, particularly when produced at the point of care.

Health Gadgets and Health Wearable Technology

The trend towards Health Gadgets and Wearable Technology is reshaping personal health management by integrating technology directly into our daily lives. This sector includes devices like fitness trackers, smartwatches, health monitoring patches, smart clothing, and even implantable sensors. These gadgets are designed to monitor various health metrics—from steps taken and calories burned to heart rate, sleep patterns, blood oxygen levels, and more advanced metrics like glucose levels or ECG. The integration of AI and machine learning allows these devices to provide personalized health insights, predict potential health issues, and recommend lifestyle adjustments.

The wearables market is expanding due to a confluence of health trends and technological advancements. A shift towards preventive healthcare and heightened consumer health awareness has significantly increased the demand for devices that monitor health metrics. Technological improvements in sensors, battery life, and data processing have made these devices more reliable and user-friendly. Their integration with smartphones for data sharing broadens their appeal, while AI and machine learning offer personalized health insights.

Wearables support remote patient monitoring, aligning with telehealth trends, and some insurance providers encourage their use for health benefits. An aging population looking to manage chronic conditions, coupled with a pervasive fitness culture, further drives demand. Additionally, these devices are gaining traction in clinical settings with regulatory support, and their design evolution has made them fashionable, blending health with style. Data privacy is a critical concern, as wearables collect sensitive health information that could be misused by third parties if security measures are inadequate. Accuracy remains an issue for some devices, particularly when used for medical purposes, leading to potential misinterpretation of data or reliance on inaccurate readings without professional consultation.

The convenience of wearables also raises the risk of over-reliance, where users might neglect other essential health assessments or over-medicalize normal activities. Ethical concerns include issues around data ownership, consent for data sharing, and the potential for discrimination or profiling based on health data. Social pressures, driven by constant health monitoring, can create unrealistic fitness expectations.

Navigating the regulatory landscape is another challenge as wearables increasingly cross into medical territory, requiring compliance with safety and efficacy standards. Cybersecurity threats loom large, as connected devices are vulnerable to hacking, potentially compromising personal health data.

Mental Wellness Apps

The trend towards Mental Wellness Apps has seen significant growth, particularly in response to increasing awareness of mental health issues and the demand for accessible, immediate support. These apps offer a range of services from meditation and mindfulness to cognitive behavioural therapy (CBT) techniques, mood tracking, stress reduction, and even AI-assisted therapy sessions. The proliferation of mental wellness apps is driven by the need for mental health support that is convenient, affordable, and can be accessed privately on personal devices. This trend spans across different user demographics, including those seeking to improve overall well-being, manage stress, or cope with conditions like anxiety, depression, PTSD, and insomnia.

The surge in mental health apps is fuelled by several key drivers. Increased societal awareness of mental health issues has destigmatized seeking help, making apps a convenient option for those with busy schedules. Technological advancements enable these apps to offer personalized, interactive experiences using AI and machine learning. They are often more cost-effective than traditional therapy, providing privacy and anonymity which are crucial for many users.

Customization ensures that support is tailored to individual needs, while data tracking offers insights into one's mental health. Their global accessibility means even remote or underserved populations can benefit. Integration with other health platforms and corporate wellness programs further extends their reach. Additionally, the sector sees significant investment, fostering innovation, and many apps include community features that help combat isolation by connecting users with peers.

A primary concern is the wide variance in the quality, scientific backing, and efficacy of these apps, which can lead to inconsistent user experiences and outcomes. Privacy and data security are critical, as these apps handle sensitive personal information that could be misused if not securely managed.

There is a risk that users might perceive mental health apps as replacements for professional care rather than supplemental tools, potentially delaying necessary interventions. Apps offering diagnostic-like feedback could lead to inaccurate self-diagnoses, exacerbating mental health issues rather than alleviating them. Additionally, AI-driven recommendations may suffer from algorithmic bias, failing to address the diverse needs of users and leading to unequal outcomes.

Sustaining user engagement over time is challenging, especially if the app fails to meet user expectations or lacks sufficient personalization. Regulatory oversight for mental health apps remains less robust compared to pharmaceuticals or medical devices, creating gaps in quality assurance. Furthermore, while these apps can bridge gaps, they do not address the systemic shortage of mental health professionals.

Monetization models also raise concerns, as free apps might prioritize user engagement metrics over actual mental health outcomes to drive revenue. Cultural sensitivity is another issue, as apps developed in one cultural context may not resonate with or appropriately address the needs of users from diverse backgrounds.

Adoption of Natural Ingredients

The Adoption of Natural Ingredients in food, clothing, and home chemicals is a pronounced trend reflecting a broader consumer shift towards health, sustainability, and environmental consciousness. In food, there is an increasing demand for products free from artificial preservatives, colours, and Flavors, with a preference for organic, non-GMO, and locally sourced ingredients. In clothing, the trend is towards natural fibres like cotton, wool, silk, and linen, often sourced from environmentally friendly practices or certified organic materials. Home chemicals, including cleaning products, personal care items, and cosmetics, are seeing a rise in formulations using plant-based, biodegradable, and non-toxic ingredients.

The growth in demand for natural products across food, clothing, and home chemicals is driven by a collective shift towards health, sustainability, and transparency. In the food sector, health consciousness and the clean label movement are key, with consumers favouring products that are transparently labelled and naturally sourced. In clothing, the push for sustainability, comfort, and health benefits of natural fibres like cotton or wool over synthetics is notable, supported by certifications like GOTS. For home chemicals, there is a clear trend towards eco-friendly options due to health and environmental concerns, with innovation in natural chemistry providing effective alternatives. This shift is further propelled by regulatory trends that Favor natural over synthetic, and an overall increase in consumer education and demand for product transparency.

The use of natural ingredients in food, home products, and chemicals offers an appealing alternative to synthetic counterparts, but it also comes with notable challenges. One primary concern is efficacy, as natural ingredients may lack the same preservative or cleaning power as synthetic options, leading to shorter shelf life or less effective products. Additionally, sourcing and processing natural ingredients often incur higher costs, making these products more expensive for consumers and potentially limiting market accessibility.

Scalability is another challenge, as sustainably sourcing enough natural ingredients becomes increasingly difficult as demand grows. This issue is compounded by the potential for overuse of natural resources, which could disrupt ecological balance and strain supply chains. While "natural" products are often marketed as environmentally friendly, their overall production processes may still leave a significant environmental footprint.

The lack of legal definitions and uniform international standards for "natural" products creates regulatory ambiguity. Ensuring consistent quality across batches is more complex with natural ingredients, while potential allergens and sensitivities can pose risks to certain consumers. Furthermore, supply chain transparency remains a challenge, as global sourcing makes it difficult to ensure adherence to ethical and sustainable practices.

Consumer education is essential to help distinguish between truly natural products and those marketed as such, but perceptions often outpace reality, leading to misconceptions about the benefits of natural ingredients.

Supplements and Nutraceuticals

The trend in Supplements, and Nutraceuticals has been on an upward trajectory, reflecting a growing consumer interest in health and wellness. Supplements might include vitamins, minerals, amino acids, fatty acids, and other substances to augment the diet. Nutraceuticals are a broader category, encompassing not just vitamins but also functional foods and dietary supplements that have health benefits beyond basic nutrition.

The dietary supplement market is experiencing growth due to a variety of factors. Preventive healthcare has become a priority for many, leading to the use of supplements for overall well-being and disease prevention. An aging demographic is particularly interested in supplements that support areas like bone health and cognitive function. Lifestyle and dietary trends, including restrictive diets, necessitate supplementation to address nutritional deficiencies. Increased health consciousness, backed by scientific research, validates the use of supplements for specific health benefits.

The trend towards personalization in nutrition means supplements are being tailored to individual needs, while the ease of access via e-commerce platforms expands market reach. The sports and fitness community continues to drive demand for performance-enhancing supplements. Additionally, a preference for natural and organic products, coupled with celebrity endorsements, further propels market growth, alongside the need for supplements targeting specific health conditions in a relatively permissive regulatory environment.

A key issue is regulatory oversight, as supplements often bypass the rigorous testing and approval processes that pharmaceuticals undergo. This lack of stringent regulation can result in variability in product quality, including contamination, inconsistent potency, or stability issues.

Misinformation is prevalent in the industry, with exaggerated or unsupported health claims misleading consumers and fostering false expectations. Additionally, supplements can interact with medications or have contraindications, which are not always well-communicated, posing risks to users. Over-supplementation, particularly with fat-soluble vitamins like A, D, E, and K, can lead to toxicity, emphasizing the need for clear dosage guidelines.

A false sense of security is another concern, as consumers might overly rely on supplements while neglecting essential lifestyle changes or a balanced diet. For many products, especially newer or trendy supplements, the lack of long-term scientific studies raises questions about their efficacy and safety. Market saturation further complicates consumer choices, making it difficult to distinguish between credible, scientifically backed products and those with less substantiated claims.

Economic factors also play a role, as the cumulative cost of supplements can be significant, often placing them out of reach for lower-income populations. Cultural dietary differences add another layer of complexity, as supplements may not align with the nutritional needs or habits of diverse populations.

Conclusion

As the global population ages, substantial focus will shift toward both preventive healthcare and advanced treatments. Innovations in the healthcare sector are likely to receive accelerated adoption as the demand for solutions grows in an expanding market. The desire to stay healthy, youthful, and active will open numerous opportunities within the healthcare space, driving advancements and creating significant potential for growth.

Trend	Expected Growth Rate (2025-2030)	Source
AI in Diagnostics and Drug Discovery	~25-30% annually	Nasscom, Deloitte India
Telehealth and Remote Monitoring	~30-35% annually	PwC, India Brand Equity Foundation (IBEF)
Gene Editing and Personalized Medicine	Variable, high potential for growth	Biotech Industry Reports, Government of India's DBT
3D Printing in Healthcare	~20-25% annually	MarketsandMarkets, Frost & Sullivan
Health Gadgets and Wearable Technology	~20-25% annually	IDC, Counterpoint Research
Mental Wellness Apps	~30-35% annually	Market research, startup ecosystem reports
Adoption of Natural Ingredients	~15% annually	FICCI, India's Wellness Market Analysis
Supplements and Nutraceuticals	~15-20% annually	Assocham, Frost & Sullivan

These expected growth rates are based on current and futuristic sentiments and trends of users, investment interests, policies, external factors and industry analysis. Growth rates may be higher or lower than stated here depending on the fluctuations in the underlying factors affecting the overall growth.

Macro Trend 5

Smart Home Gadgets and Home Solutions

Smart Entertainment

The trend in Smart Entertainment, Gaming, and Over-The-Top (OTT) Devices revolves around the integration of advanced technology into consumer electronics to enhance home entertainment. This includes smart TVs with built-in streaming services, gaming consoles that double as media centres, portable gaming devices with streaming capabilities, and specialized OTT devices like Roku, Fire TV Stick, and Chromecast. These devices offer seamless access to content, interactive gaming experiences, and a convergence of entertainment options, reflecting a shift towards more personalized, on-demand, and immersive entertainment experiences.

The market for entertainment devices is expanding due to several key trends. Consumer demand for on-demand content has shifted the focus towards streaming platforms, necessitating devices that can handle multiple services seamlessly. Technological advancements have improved visual and gaming experiences, with high-resolution displays and VR technology becoming more mainstream.

The expansion of the gaming industry, including esports and cloud gaming, has broadened the appeal of gaming devices. Integration into smart home systems provides added convenience and connectivity. However, as subscription fatigue sets in due to content fragmentation across numerous platforms, there is a push for devices that can simplify this by aggregating content. Lastly, the trend towards mobile and portable entertainment continues to drive demand for devices that support high-quality entertainment experiences on the go.

OTT devices face challenges such as content saturation, where the abundance of options can lead to choice fatigue for users. Privacy concerns arise from extensive data collection for personalization, while interoperability issues among devices can fragment the user experience. Excessive costs of entry for feature-rich devices may exclude certain market segments, and technical issues, like connectivity or latency, further impact user satisfaction. Additionally, content licensing restrictions limit access in different regions, reducing the global appeal of these platforms.

AI-Enhanced Home Devices

AI-enhanced home devices with voice and gesture control are becoming integral components of modern smart homes. These devices leverage artificial intelligence to understand and respond to natural language and human gestures, allowing for intuitive control of home automation systems, entertainment devices, and even household appliances. This trend signifies a shift towards more seamless human-device interaction, reducing the need for manual input and enhancing accessibility.

There is a growing preference for hands-free and touchless interactions, especially post-pandemic, where health and hygiene have become more significant concerns. Improvements in AI, particularly in natural language processing (NLP) and computer vision, have made voice and gesture recognition more accurate and responsive, driving the adoption of these technologies in consumer products.

The proliferation of IoT devices and the development of standards like Matter facilitate integration between devices, making voice and gesture control more practical across various ecosystems. These technologies offer solutions for individuals with disabilities, providing a more inclusive environment by allowing control of devices without physical interaction.

One of the most pressing concerns is privacy and security, as these systems often require constant listening or visual monitoring, raising fears about potential data breaches or unauthorized surveillance. Accuracy and reliability also remain issues; misinterpretation of commands or gestures can frustrate users and undermine trust in the technology.

Additionally, many of these systems are heavily dependent on internet connectivity, relying on cloud-based processing to function effectively. This dependence makes them vulnerable to connectivity issues, which could render the devices unusable offline. For many users, the complexity of setup and use can also be a barrier. While the technology aims to simplify everyday tasks, the initial installation and calibration can be daunting for less tech-savvy individuals, potentially limiting adoption.

The market for voice and gesture control devices is at risk of saturation and fragmentation. An influx of related products may confuse consumers with too many choices, while a lack of universal standards could create interoperability issues, preventing seamless integration across devices. Addressing these challenges is essential for the technology to achieve widespread acceptance and trust.

Home Energy Conservation

Home energy conservation has become a pivotal trend, driven by environmental concerns, escalating energy costs, and technological advancements. It includes a range of strategies and technologies aimed at reducing energy consumption in residential settings, promoting sustainability, and lowering utility bills. This trend aligns with broader movements towards green living and smart home technologies, where energy efficiency is not just about cost-saving but also about reducing one's carbon footprint.

Increased public consciousness about climate change and the desire to reduce personal environmental impact are significant motivators. Rising energy prices and potential savings from energy-efficient technologies encourage homeowners to invest in conservation measures. Government incentives and rebates further stimulate this trend.

Smart thermostats, LED lighting, energy-efficient appliances, and home energy management systems make energy conservation more accessible and effective. Policies promoting energy efficiency, like building codes that require energy-efficient standards, and regulations like the UK's Warm Homes Plan, drive consumer and industry behaviour. Energy-efficient homes are increasingly seen as more valuable, both in terms of resale value and appeal to environmentally conscious buyers.

One of the most significant barriers is the high initial cost of installation or retrofitting homes with energy-efficient systems. For many homeowners, this upfront expense can deter investment, even when long-term savings are evident. Additionally, return on investment (ROI) uncertainty is a concern. Homeowners may doubt the financial benefits of these upgrades, especially if energy prices fluctuate, potentially delaying the payoff period.

The rebound effect poses another challenge, where increased energy efficiency leads to higher overall consumption due to the perception of reduced energy costs. This unintended consequence can undermine the very goal of reducing energy usage. Technological obsolescence also plays a role; with rapid advancements in energy-efficient technologies, systems installed today could become outdated in just a few years, leaving homeowners with suboptimal solutions. Lastly, privacy concerns arise from smart devices that monitor and optimize energy usage.

Robotic Assistants

The trend towards robotics for household use signifies a burgeoning market focused on automating domestic chores and providing assistance within the home. These robots range from cleaning devices like robotic vacuums to more sophisticated machines that can perform tasks like lawn mowing, window cleaning, or even offering companionship. This trend is part of a broader shift towards smart homes where technology integrates seamlessly into daily life, enhancing convenience, efficiency, and potentially improving quality of life.

Improvements in AI, machine learning, and sensor technology have made household robots more capable, efficient, and user-friendly. In countries with an aging demographic, like Japan, there is a growing need for robots that can assist with daily tasks, providing both practical help and companionship. Modern consumers expect technology to simplify life, driving demand for devices that handle mundane tasks autonomously. As work hours increase, there is a greater desire for home automation to free up time for hobbies, family, or leisure. Post-pandemic, the push for touchless cleaning solutions has accelerated the adoption of robotic cleaning devices.

Household robots, while offering convenience and automation, face several challenges that could hinder widespread adoption. Excessive costs make these devices accessible primarily to affluent consumers, limiting market penetration. Additionally, reliability and maintenance issues can result in costly repairs or disruptions in functionality.

Privacy and security concerns arise from robots equipped with cameras, microphones, or internet connectivity, which could lead to data breaches or hacking risks. Beyond technical challenges, the emotional and social impact of over-reliance on robots—especially as companions for children or the elderly—raises concerns about social isolation or diminished interpersonal skills. Lastly, ethical, and regulatory questions around autonomy, safety, and accountability highlight the need for clear standards and guidelines as household robotics continue to evolve.

Smart Home Security

Smart home security represents a trend where traditional home security systems are being augmented or replaced by smart devices and technologies. This includes not only surveillance cameras and smart locks but also integrated systems that utilize AI, IoT, and cloud computing for more comprehensive protection. These systems offer real-time monitoring, remote access, and intelligent threat detection, making home security more proactive, accessible, and integrated with other smart home functionalities.

Rising crime rates in some areas have heightened the demand for more effective home security solutions.

Innovations in AI, machine learning, and IoT have enabled smarter, more intuitive security systems that can learn behaviour patterns, recognize faces, and predict potential security breaches. The ability to monitor and control home security from anywhere via smartphones or other devices is a significant driver. Consumers desire a seamless smart home experience where security integrates with lighting, climate control, entertainment, and more, making comprehensive home management platforms attractive. The availability of easy-to-install, DIY security systems has expanded the market to include tech-savvy homeowners who prefer to set up their own systems.

Smart home security systems bring innovative solutions but face notable challenges. Privacy concerns arise as devices like cameras and voice assistants collect and potentially share sensitive data. Their vulnerability to hacks makes them potential targets for cyberattacks, compromising the very security they promise. Issues like false alarms from AI misinterpretations can be frustrating and diminish trust in the systems. Furthermore, dependency on technology might lead to neglect of traditional security practices. Despite standards like Matter, compatibility and interoperability between devices remain problematic, and the complexity of setup and maintenance can deter less tech-savvy users. These factors highlight the balance needed between convenience and robust security.

Readymade and DIY Furniture and Modular Homes

The trend of readymade and DIY furniture and modular homes reflects a growing interest in personalizing living spaces, reducing costs, and embracing sustainability. Readymade furniture provides convenience to choose as per personalized décor need and are ready to consume. DIY furniture involves individuals crafting or assembling their own furniture, often using kits, plans, or recycled materials. Modular homes, on the other hand, are prefabricated units that can be customized and easily assembled on-site, offering flexibility in design and construction. Together, these trends cater to a desire for unique, personalized, functional, and cost-effective solutions in home design and furnishing.

Consumers seek unique home environments that reflect personal style, which readymade and DIY furniture allows, while modular homes offer customizable layouts. Both DIY furniture and modular homes can be less expensive than buying custom or high-end furniture or building a traditional home from scratch.

There is an increased focus on using eco-friendly materials, reducing waste, and repurposing, which aligns with DIY and modular construction practices. Modular homes can be expanded or altered with relative ease, and DIY furniture can be adapted or rebuilt as needs change. The DIY movement encourages learning new skills, giving a sense of accomplishment and ownership over one's living space. In urban settings where space is at a premium, modular homes and space-saving DIY furniture solutions become particularly appealing.

Readymade furniture may restrict the customization approach and sometimes be quite expensive. Quality control can be a concern, as DIY projects may lack professional durability. Time and effort are significant for DIY furniture, while modular homes might face delivery or assembly delays. Design limitations exist in modular homes compared to custom builds, and regulatory hurdles can complicate compliance with local building codes. Resale value may also be impacted if DIY modifications lack professional quality. Additionally, the absence of warranties and support for DIY furniture can deter consumers seeking long-term assurance.

Augmented and Virtual Reality for Home Design

The trend of using Augmented Reality (AR) and Virtual Reality (VR) for home design is transforming how individuals and professionals visualize, plan, and execute home decor and architectural projects. AR overlays digital information on the real world, allowing users to see how furniture or decor would look in their space. VR, on the other hand, immerses users in a fully virtual environment, where they can walk through their home design before it is built or furnished. This technology fosters a more interactive and intuitive design process, reducing guesswork and enhancing the decision-making phase.

AR and VR provide a tangible way to preview designs, aiding in better decision-making and reducing costly mistakes. These technologies offer an engaging and interactive experience for clients, potentially increasing satisfaction, and confidence in their design choices. Designers can work with clients remotely, making it easier to collaborate across distances or during times like the global health crisis when in-person meetings are not feasible.

By allowing multiple design iterations in a virtual space, AR and VR can save time and reduce the need for physical prototypes or samples. Improvements in AR and VR technology have made devices more affordable and their applications more user-friendly and accessible. With a growing interest in personalized spaces, AR and VR offer tools to tailor designs to specific tastes without the need for physical alterations.

AR/VR in home design offers immersive visualization but comes with challenges. High initial costs for advanced setups can limit adoption, and a learning curve may deter less tech-savvy users. Accuracy issues in scale or lighting representation could lead to discrepancies between virtual designs and real outcomes. Over-reliance on technology might overlook practical considerations, while privacy concerns arise from sharing designs in virtual environments. Additionally, physical interaction limitations prevent users from experiencing materials and spaces as they would in real life, posing a drawback for tactile design elements.

Advanced Cookware

Advanced cookware is an evolving trend where traditional kitchen items are enhanced with innovative technology to improve cooking efficiency, health benefits, sustainability, and design. This includes cookware with smart features like Wi-Fi connectivity for remote cooking, materials developed for superior heat distribution and retention, non-stick surfaces free from harmful chemicals, and ergonomic designs that align with modern kitchen aesthetics. These advancements aim to make cooking more precise, enjoyable, and aligned with contemporary lifestyle needs.

The push towards smart homes extends to the kitchen, with consumers looking for cookware that can connect with other devices for control and monitoring. With a growing focus on health, there's demand for cookware that supports cooking methods that preserve nutrients, minimize oil use, or offer non-toxic cooking surfaces.

Cooks of all levels desire tools that offer precise temperature control and even heat distribution, which can significantly affect cooking outcomes. Environmentally conscious consumers seek out cookware made from sustainable materials or designed for reduced energy use. The cookware not only needs to function well but also to complement the modern, often minimalist design trends in kitchens. As global cuisines become more accessible, there is a need for versatile cookware that can handle diverse cooking techniques.

Smart cookware brings innovation to kitchens but faces challenges. Higher costs for advanced features may limit accessibility, while added complexity could deter less tech-savvy users. Concerns about durability and repairability arise with integrated technology, along with data privacy risks for devices collecting user data. Material innovation raises safety questions over long-term use under heat, and dependence on technology means malfunctions could disrupt cooking, unlike traditional, reliable cookware.

Conclusion

As technology integrates deeper into daily life, the demand for smart home gadgets and solutions is poised to surge. From enhancing convenience and energy efficiency to improving security and lifestyle personalization, smart home innovations are becoming essential. The shift toward connected, automated living spaces opens vast opportunities for growth, as consumers increasingly seek intelligent solutions to simplify and elevate their home environments.

Trends	Expected Growth Rate (2025-2030)	Source
Smart Entertainment	~20-25% annually	Statista, PwC India
AI-Enhanced Home Devices	~30-35% annually	Deloitte, Frost & Sullivan
Home Energy Conservation	~15-20% annually	IBEF, McKinsey & Company
Robotic Assistants	~25-30% annually	Nasscom, TechSci Research
Smart Home Security	~20-25% annually	MarketsandMarkets, India Smart Security Association
Readymade and DIY Furniture and Modular Homes	~15-20% annually	Research and Markets, Wood Magazine
Augmented and Virtual Reality for Home Design	~30-35% annually	IDC, Gartner
Advanced Cookware	~10-15% annually	Euromonitor, Market Research Future

These expected growth rates are based on current and futuristic sentiments and trends of users, investment interests, policies, external factors and industry analysis. Growth rates may be higher or lower than stated here depending on the fluctuations in the underlying factors affecting the overall growth.

Macro Trend 6

Digital Education and Skill Development

K-12 and Higher Education Platforms

The trend towards K-12 and Higher Education Platforms involves the increasing use of digital platforms to deliver educational content, manage student engagement, and facilitate learning both in traditional classrooms and in remote settings. These platforms range from Learning Management Systems (LMS) like Canvas and Blackboard, to specialized educational apps and tools for coding, language learning, virtual labs, and more. The shift has been accelerated by the need for remote learning during global events like pandemics, but it is also driven by the desire for more personalized, flexible, and interactive educational experiences.

Improvements in AI, cloud computing, and mobile technology have made educational platforms more robust, accessible, and user-friendly. There is a push for education tailored to individual student needs, with platforms offering adaptive learning paths and personalized content.

Digital platforms can reach students in remote areas, offer language support, and include features for students with disabilities, broadening educational access. Platforms can collect data on student performance, allowing for better-informed teaching strategies and institutional decision-making. Online platforms facilitate international education, enabling students to learn from global educators and resources.

Digital education platforms face several challenges. The digital divide highlights unequal access to technology and reliable internet, exacerbating educational disparities. Data privacy concerns arise over how student information is handled, while questions about the quality of education remain, particularly for social and practical skills. Cheating and academic integrity in online assessments demand novel solutions, and teacher training is essential for effective integration but often lacking. An over-reliance on technology risks diminishing traditional teaching skills and the interpersonal connections crucial for holistic education.

Vocational Training and Upskilling

The trend towards vocational training and upskilling represents a shift in education and workforce development, focusing on equipping individuals with specific skills for immediate job readiness or career advancement. This includes traditional vocational education, apprenticeships, online courses, and micro-credentials that cater to the evolving job market. As industries change due to technology, automation, and new economic models, there is a growing need for specialized skills that can be quickly acquired and updated, leading to a boom in vocational training programs and continuous professional development.

Rapid technological changes necessitate new skills, from coding to managing AI systems, in virtually every sector. Globalization and changes in industry structures mean job roles evolve, requiring workers to upskill or reskill to remain competitive or transition careers. An aging workforce retiring, coupled with a young generation entering the job market, creates a dual need for upskilling existing workers and training new entrants.

Many industries face skill gaps, leading companies to invest in training rather than just hiring from the external market. There is a societal shift towards viewing education as a lifelong journey rather than a one-time event, supported by the availability of online learning platforms. Many governments incentivize vocational training to boost employment, economic growth, and address unemployment.

Training programs, while expanding opportunities, face challenges like quality and accreditation, with some courses lacking legitimacy or recognition. Access and equity remain concerns due to digital divides and cost barriers. There is a risk of misalignment with job market needs, rendering skills outdated or redundant. Employer recognition of micro-credentials varies, impacting their value. Over-specialization can limit adaptability if market demands shift, while employee retention post-training poses ROI risks for companies investing in upskilling.

Corporate Training Platforms

Corporate Training Platforms are becoming increasingly sophisticated, moving beyond traditional e-learning to include advanced technologies like AI, VR, AR, microlearning, and personalized learning paths. These platforms aim to enhance employee development, facilitate compliance training, promote continuous learning, and adapt to the specific needs of companies. The trend reflects a shift towards more dynamic, engaging, and effective training methods to keep up with the fast pace of industry changes and skill demands.

AI and machine learning allow for personalized training experiences, while VR/AR offers immersive learning scenarios. The shift to remote and hybrid work models has necessitated robust online training solutions that can reach employees globally.

As industries face more regulations, there is a need for scalable, trackable training solutions to ensure compliance. With rapid technological changes, companies need platforms that can quickly adapt training content to address emerging skill requirements. Effective training platforms can improve employee satisfaction, engagement, and retention by fostering a culture of learning and development. Digital platforms reduce the need for physical training materials and travel, offering cost savings over traditional methods.

Corporate training platforms face key challenges, including data privacy and security, requiring robust measures to protect sensitive employee information. Adoption resistance can occur if platforms are not user-friendly or perceived as unnecessary. An over-reliance on technology risks losing the human touch crucial for certain skills. System integration with existing HR tools can be complex, while content quality varies, potentially leading to ineffective training. Additionally, measuring training effectiveness remains challenging, particularly for soft skills and nuanced tasks.

Lifelong Learning Platforms

Lifelong Learning Platforms have emerged as a pivotal trend in education, catering to the need for continuous personal and professional development throughout one's life. These platforms offer a broad spectrum of learning opportunities, from formal education to informal learning, including courses, microlearning modules, certifications, and community-driven learning experiences. They aim to make education accessible, flexible, and tailored to individual needs, supporting career progression, personal enrichment, and adaptability in a rapidly changing world.

The fast pace of technological advancement and globalization requires individuals to constantly update their skills. Online platforms provide learning opportunities that fit into busy lifestyles, allowing for self-paced education anytime, anywhere. There is an increasing cultural acceptance and expectation of continuous learning for personal growth and career advancement.

Employers and learners value short, targeted courses that offer specific skills or certifications, which these platforms readily provide. Advances in AI enable platforms to offer personalized learning experiences based on the learner's progress, interests, and career goals. Aging populations need to upskill or reskill, while younger generations enter the workforce with a learning mindset.

The rise of lifelong learning platforms brings challenges such as ensuring quality assurance and credibility amidst a proliferation of options. The digital divide limits access for those lacking technology, connectivity, or digital skills. Learning fatigue can overwhelm users with endless choices, while privacy and data security concerns arise from the extensive data collected for personalized learning. Ensuring career relevance of skills amidst evolving job markets is critical, and low motivation and completion rates remain obstacles for self-directed learners.

Conclusion

As the digital revolution transforms how knowledge is delivered, digital education and skill development have emerged as key drivers of growth. From K-12 and higher education platforms to vocational training, corporate upskilling, and lifelong learning, the demand for accessible, flexible, and personalized learning solutions is accelerating. In a world where continuous learning is vital, these micro-trends cater to diverse needs, fostering innovation and adaptability in education for individuals and organizations alike.

Trends	Expected Growth Rate Over (2025-2030)	Source
K-12 and Higher Education Platforms	~20-25% annually	HolonIQ, KPMG
Vocational Training and Upskilling	~25-30% annually	NSDC, PwC India
Corporate Training Platforms	~15-20% annually	Deloitte, Training Industry India
Lifelong Learning Platforms	~20-25% annually	Coursera, edX, Udemy market reports

These expected growth rates are based on current and futuristic sentiments and trends of users, investment interests, policies, external factors and industry analysis. Growth rates may be higher or lower than stated here depending on the fluctuations in the underlying factors affecting the overall growth.

Macro Trend 7

Urbanization and Real Estate Transformation

Affordable and Co-Living Spaces

The trend towards Affordable and Co-Living Spaces addresses the challenges of urbanization, high living costs, and the desire for community in housing. Affordable housing focuses on providing cost-effective living options for low to middle-income individuals, often through public-private partnerships, government initiatives, or innovative design solutions. Co-living spaces, on the other hand, offer shared living arrangements where residents have private bedrooms but share common areas like kitchens, lounges, and sometimes workspaces, fostering a community environment. These trends reflect broader shifts in lifestyle choices, economic necessities, and urban planning strategies.

As urban rents soar, affordable housing becomes essential, and co-living provides a viable alternative for cost-sharing. With more people moving to cities, there is a higher demand for affordable housing solutions and environments that combat loneliness. Co-living appeals to those seeking a sense of community, networking opportunities, and shared experiences.

Both affordable and co-living spaces cater to the needs of gig workers, freelancers, and those with non-traditional work schedules. Shared spaces can be more environmentally friendly, with reduced resource consumption per capita. Young professionals, students, and older individuals looking for companionship or downsizing are key demographics for co-living.

Co-living and affordable housing face challenges such as privacy and space limitations, which may deter individuals preferring private accommodations. Ensuring quality and maintenance within budget constraints is complex, and regulatory hurdles like zoning laws can delay development. Market saturation in certain regions can impact occupancy and profitability, while cultural fit remains critical, as not everyone embraces communal living. Balancing affordability and investor returns is delicate, requiring innovative financial and operational strategies.

Senior Living and Assisted Living

The Senior Living and Assisted Living trend reflects the growing demand for specialized housing and care services tailored for the elderly. This sector is evolving to meet the needs of an aging population, with a focus on creating environments that support independence, health, wellness, and community engagement. The trend encompasses various living arrangements, from independent living communities to assisted living facilities, continuing care retirement communities (CCRCs), and memory care units, each designed to cater to diverse levels of care and lifestyle preferences.

The global population is aging, with projections indicating a significant increase in the number of seniors, especially those over eighty. As people live longer, there is a need for facilities that can support them through various stages of aging. Many seniors desire to maintain independence for as long as possible, which has led to innovations in assisted living that offer more autonomy.

There is a shift towards incorporating wellness programs, nutritional support, and preventive healthcare into senior living facilities. Smart home technologies, health monitoring devices, and telehealth services are becoming integral for enhancing care and safety. Senior living is increasingly viewed as a lifestyle choice offering community, amenities, and care, rather than just a necessity for those unable to live independently.

Senior and assisted living faces challenges such as affordability, with excessive costs limiting accessibility for many. Quality of care is a persistent issue, requiring consistent staffing and facility standards, while regulatory oversight adds complexity for operators. Despite community living, some residents may experience isolation or mental health issues, highlighting the need for holistic care. Rapid expansion risks oversupply in some regions, impacting occupancy and profitability, and cultural integration within facilities requires sensitivity to ensure inclusivity and social harmony.

Digital Governance and Smart City Solutions

Digital Governance and Smart City Solutions represent a trend where technology is leveraged to enhance urban living, governance, and public services through data-driven decision-making, IoT (Internet of Things), AI (Artificial Intelligence), and digital platforms. This includes everything from smart traffic management and energy-efficient infrastructures to e-governance, where services like tax payments, public consultations, and civic engagement are digitized. This trend aims at creating cities that are more efficient, sustainable, inclusive, and responsive to the needs of their citizens.

The growth of smart cities is propelled by several key drivers, primarily urbanization, which necessitates innovative approaches to manage increasing population densities, congestion, and resource allocation. Technological advancements in areas like the Internet of Things (IoT), Artificial Intelligence (AI), big data analytics, and blockchain have transformed urban management into a real-time, data-driven process, enhancing efficiency and responsiveness. Sustainability is another major driver, with smart cities playing a crucial role in combatting climate change through reduced carbon emissions and fostering sustainable urban development.

Citizen engagement has also evolved, with digital platforms enabling more participatory forms of governance, where residents can contribute to decision-making processes, increasing transparency and democratic participation. Economically, smart cities promise to streamline operations, leading to cost savings in public services like energy management and waste disposal, while also improving health and safety through real-time monitoring and response systems.

However, the journey towards smart cities is not without its risks and concerns. Privacy and data security emerge as significant issues, as the extensive data collection required for smart city functionalities could lead to surveillance concerns, data breaches, and violations of personal privacy.

There is also the risk of exacerbating the digital divide, where not everyone has equal access or ability to engage with smart technologies, potentially deepening social inequalities. Over-reliance on technology poses its own threats, particularly in terms of system reliability; a failure or a cyber-attack could disrupt essential services. Interoperability among various smart city solutions is another hurdle, where lack of standardization might result in fragmented services or vendor lock-in, limiting flexibility and innovation.

Ethical considerations around the use of AI and data must be addressed to prevent biased outcomes or discriminatory practices. Finally, the substantial cost of implementing smart city infrastructure raises questions about funding and the return on investment, especially given the rapid pace of technological change which could render today's solutions obsolete tomorrow.

Co-Working Spaces

Co-working Spaces have become a significant trend in the modern workspace landscape, offering flexible, shared working environments. These spaces cater to freelancers, startups, remote workers, and even large corporations looking for flexible office solutions. They provide amenities like high-speed internet, meeting rooms, communal areas, and sometimes additional services like event hosting or networking opportunities. The trend reflects a shift towards flexible work arrangements, community-focused work environments, and cost-effective alternatives to traditional office leases.

The rise of co-working spaces is driven by several factors, with the changing landscape of work culture at the forefront, where remote work, freelancing, and flexible hours are becoming the norm. These spaces offer cost-effective solutions compared to traditional office leases, which is particularly appealing for startups and small businesses looking to minimize overhead.

The community aspect of co-working spaces also acts as a significant draw, promoting networking and collaboration among diverse professionals, which can lead to innovation and business growth. Urbanization adds to this demand by necessitating flexible, accessible workspace options in densely populated areas. Moreover, large corporations are increasingly adopting co-working spaces for satellite offices or to provide flexible work environments for employees. The integration of technology in these spaces, from smart booking systems to security, further enhances their appeal by simplifying management and access.

However, this growth is not without risks. There is a concern about market saturation, where an oversupply could lead to lower occupancy rates and financial strain for operators. Privacy and security in shared environments are ongoing challenges, especially for businesses handling sensitive information.

The reliance on long-term real estate leases poses significant risk if the co-working trend reverses or during economic downturns, which could reduce demand as companies cut costs. Managing the community within these spaces is another critical aspect; the atmosphere can make or break a co-working space, requiring constant attention to maintain. Finally, in the post-COVID era, ensuring health and safety, including adherence to new sanitation and social distancing norms, has become a paramount concern for co-working space operators.

Alternative and Pre-engineered Building Materials

The trend towards Alternative and Pre-Engineered Building Materials is driven by the need for more sustainable, cost-effective, and innovative construction solutions. Alternative materials refer to those that are eco-friendly, recycled, or have a lower environmental impact than traditional materials like concrete and brick. Pre-engineered building materials involve components that are designed and manufactured off-site for assembly on-site, often using steel or other modular systems to speed up construction while reducing waste. This trend is reshaping the construction industry by offering quicker, greener, and more adaptable building practices.

With climate change at the forefront of global concerns, there is an increasing demand for materials with a reduced environmental impact, including those that are recyclable or have a lower carbon footprint. This trend is supported by cost and time efficiencies offered by pre-engineered materials, which can dramatically cut down construction timelines and labour costs, making projects more financially feasible.

Technological innovation in material science is also playing a significant role, introducing materials like recycled plastics, bio-based composites, and advanced polymers that offer high performance. Regulatory frameworks are further pushing this shift by favouring or even mandating the use of sustainable materials in construction. Rapid urbanization globally necessitates quick, scalable building solutions, while the need for disaster-resilient infrastructure underscores the value of durable, lightweight materials.

Quality assurance remains a challenge, as the performance and longevity of newer or less conventional materials need thorough testing and validation. Market acceptance can be slow, given the long-standing trust in traditional construction materials. Standardization issues could lead to quality inconsistencies or challenges in integrating these materials into existing construction practices.

The cost of innovation, particularly in the research and development phase, can be prohibitive, although it might pay off in the long run. Supply chain complexities for alternative materials might disrupt construction schedules, and there is the cultural dimension where these materials might not fit with local architectural aesthetics or preferences, potentially limiting their adoption.

Digital Twins

Digital Twins are virtual models of physical objects, systems, or processes that simulate their real-world counterparts in real-time. This trend spans across industries, from manufacturing where digital twins of factories optimize production, to healthcare where they model human organs for surgery planning, and urban planning for simulating city development. Digital twins leverage IoT, AI, and data analytics to provide insights, predict outcomes, and facilitate decision-making, enhancing efficiency, maintenance, and innovation.

The expansion of the Internet of Things (IoT) has generated a wealth of data, enabling the creation of more precise digital representations of physical assets. AI and machine learning further enhance these models by allowing them to predict outcomes, learn from operational data, and optimize performance in real-time, aligning perfectly with the industry 4.0 paradigm where smart manufacturing is central. Sustainability benefits from digital twins as they facilitate simulations that lead to better resource management and reduced environmental impact. In healthcare, digital twins offer the potential for personalized medicine through virtual patient models or organ simulations. For urban planning, they provide a tool to model and manage city growth, traffic, and infrastructure development efficiently.

However, the implementation of digital twins comes with its set of risks and concerns. Data privacy and security are paramount, given the extensive data collection required, posing risks of breaches or misuse. The complexity and cost involved in developing and maintaining these detailed models can be prohibitive, requiring significant investment in technology and specialized skills.

Ensuring the accuracy and reliability of a digital twin against its physical counterpart over time is another hurdle, as is achieving interoperability among various systems and software to make the digital twin universally applicable. Ethical considerations, particularly in sensitive applications like healthcare, involve managing consent and protecting individual privacy. Finally, scaling digital twins to cover expansive or complex systems like entire cities presents significant technical challenges, potentially limiting their widespread adoption and effectiveness.

Facade and Glass-Based Buildings

The trend in Facade and Glass-Based Buildings reflects a move towards using glass and advanced facade systems in architecture for both aesthetic and functional benefits. This includes skyscrapers with glass curtain walls, buildings with double or triple glazing for energy efficiency, and structures using smart glass that can change transparency or tint. The trend emphasizes transparency, natural light, environmental sustainability, and the integration of technology into building skins for enhanced performance, aesthetics, and user comfort.

The aesthetic appeal of glass facades aligns with the contemporary demand for sleek, modern designs in urban environments. An increased focus on natural light not only enhances the well-being of building occupants but also contributes to energy savings by reducing the need for artificial lighting. Advancements in energy-efficient glazing technologies, such as low-emissivity (low-E) coatings and triple glazing, have made glass a viable option for maintaining thermal comfort while minimizing energy use.

The integration of smart building technologies like smart glass adds another layer of functionality, allowing for dynamic control over light, heat, and privacy. Sustainability benefits from glass when it is part of systems designed to reduce overall energy consumption, and in densely populated urban areas, glass can create a sense of openness and space.

However, employing glass in architecture is not without its risks and concerns. The primary challenge is managing heat gain and loss, which can lead to energy inefficiencies if not addressed with the right technologies. Maintenance of glass facades can be both costly and frequent due to the need for cleaning and potential for damage. There is also the environmental impact of bird collisions with glass, pushing for bird-safe designs.

Privacy can become an issue, requiring careful design or the use of special glass types. Ensuring the safety and durability of glass structures against natural forces like wind or earthquakes is another critical consideration. Finally, while glass contributes to sustainability in use, its production carries a high carbon footprint, though this is being mitigated through recycling and new manufacturing processes.

Multistorey Buildings and Elevators

The trend in Multistorey Buildings and Elevators involves the continuous growth of vertical urban development driven by population density, land scarcity, and the desire for efficient land use. Elevators are crucial to this trend, not just for their functional necessity in accessing higher floors but also for their increasing integration with smart building technologies, sustainability, and safety innovations. This includes the evolution from traditional elevators to high-tech, energy-efficient systems, and the introduction of novel elevator concepts like multi-car systems or horizontal movement within buildings.

The growth in the elevator industry is closely tied to the dynamics of urbanization and land scarcity, where vertical expansion becomes the most viable option for accommodating growing populations in densely populated areas. Technological advancements have transformed elevators into smart, energy-efficient systems that not only enhance user experience through features like IoT for predictive maintenance but also contribute to building sustainability.

Elevators are now equipped with numerous safety features and designed to be accessible, ensuring they cater to a diverse user base. Moreover, they have become an integral part of architectural design, adding to the aesthetic appeal of buildings.

However, this growth comes with its share of risks and concerns. The maintenance and reliability of elevators are paramount, especially in high-rises where any breakdown can disrupt daily life or pose safety risks. The financial aspect is significant, with both installation and maintenance costs being high, which can influence the overall economics of property development.

Safety during emergencies is a critical issue, requiring comprehensive evacuation plans and fail-safes like backup power systems. Despite efforts towards sustainability, the environmental impact of producing and operating elevators remains a concern. Lastly, in extremely tall buildings, managing elevator traffic to avoid long waits and congestion presents a logistical challenge, requiring sophisticated traffic management systems.

Centralized Air Conditioning, Heating and Ventilation

The trend towards Centralized Air Conditioning, Heating and Ventilation systems combines the benefits of large-scale cooling, heating with integrated air quality management. These systems are designed not just for temperature control but also for maintaining optimal indoor air quality through effective ventilation strategies. They are increasingly seen in large commercial, institutional, and multi-unit residential buildings, where they offer benefits like energy efficiency, centralized control, and uniform comfort and air quality across extensive spaces. The trend is further propelled by a growing focus on indoor environmental health, especially post-global health crises. Cooling systems are being increasingly used for data centres and premises with heavy energy consumption to cool down through liquid pipping solutions as well as air cooling.

An increased awareness of the health implications of indoor air quality has underscored the need for systems that not only cool but also ventilate spaces effectively. Energy efficiency is another key driver, with innovations like HRVs and ERVs allowing these systems to operate with less energy while still providing fresh air.

Integration into smart building technologies offers the advantage of automation and optimization based on real-time data from sensors. Regulatory pressures to meet new building standards for ventilation and energy efficiency further encourage the use of centralized systems. Aesthetically, these systems offer a cleaner look and save space by eliminating the need for multiple units. For large-scale or multi-story buildings, the scalability of centralized systems makes them a practical choice.

However, there are significant risks and concerns associated with these systems. The complexity of installation, particularly in retrofitting scenarios, can be daunting, requiring extensive modifications like ductwork installation. The initial cost for such systems is high, which can be a barrier to adoption. Maintenance and operational costs over time are also substantial, and any failure in the system can have a widespread impact on the building's occupants.

There is also the risk of efficiency losses if the system is not well-designed or maintained, leading to energy waste. Environmental concerns persist, particularly with the use of refrigerants, though efforts are being made to reduce this impact through more eco-friendly options.

Waste Management Approach in Buildings

The trend in Waste Management Approaches in Buildings is shifting towards more sustainable, efficient, and integrated systems. This includes not only the reduction of waste at the source through design and material choices but also the implementation of sophisticated sorting, recycling, trend disposal facilities within buildings. This trend is driven by environmental regulations, corporate sustainability goals, and increased public awareness about waste's impact. It encompasses everything from residential complexes to commercial high-rises, with a focus on reducing landfill contributions, enhancing recycling rates, and even turning waste into energy or other resources.

Stricter laws and building codes are compelling property managers to implement more effective waste handling practices. The pursuit of green building certifications like LEED or BREEAM is another significant driver, as these standards emphasize waste reduction and recycling. Technological innovations such as IoT for real-time monitoring, automated sorting, and waste-to-energy solutions are making waste management more efficient and environmentally friendly.

Consumer and tenant expectations are also shifting, with a growing demand for buildings that facilitate responsible waste disposal. The broader adoption of circular economy principles encourages buildings to minimize waste and maximize material reuse. Urbanization further amplifies the need for sophisticated waste management to cope with the sheer volume of waste generated in cities.

However, there are notable risks and concerns associated with this transition. The cost of implementing such systems can be high, encompassing both the initial investment in technology and infrastructure as well as the ongoing operational expenses. Space within buildings, particularly older ones, can be a limiting factor when trying to incorporate recycling or composting facilities.

The success of these systems also hinges on behavioural changes among occupants, requiring ongoing education and incentives to ensure participation. Contamination of recyclables is a practical concern that can undermine the effectiveness of waste sorting efforts. There is also the issue of technology reliability; any system downtime can lead to inefficiencies or mismanagement. Additionally, navigating the variability in local waste management regulations can pose challenges for buildings operating or expanding across different jurisdictions.

Conclusion

As urbanization reshapes the world's demographics, the real estate landscape is undergoing a profound transformation. Rapid urban growth fuels demand for innovative housing solutions, smart city infrastructure, and sustainable real estate developments.

Trend	Expected Growth (2025-2030)	Source
Affordable and Co-Living Spaces	~15-20% annually	JLL, Knight Frank India
Senior Living and Assisted Living	~25-30% annually	PwC, Elder Care India Reports
Digital Governance and Smart City Solutions	~20-25% annually	Government of India, Smart Cities Mission, Gartner
Co-Working Spaces	~15-20% annually	CBRE, Colliers International India
Alternative and Pre-engineered Building Materials	~15-20% annually	MarketsandMarkets, Research and Markets
Digital Twins	~30-35% annually	Gartner, Deloitte Insights
Facade and Glass-Based Buildings	~10-15% annually	Transparency Market Research, Glass Magazine
Multistorey Buildings and Elevators	~10-15% annually	Elevator World, Statista
Centralized Air Conditioning, Heating, and Ventilation	~15-20% annually	MarketsandMarkets, Frost & Sullivan
Waste Management Approach in Buildings	~10-15% annually	World Bank, Urban Development Reports

These expected growth rates are based on current and futuristic sentiments and trends of users, investment interests, policies, external factors and industry analysis. Growth rates may be higher or lower than stated here depending on the fluctuations in the underlying factors affecting the overall growth.

Macro Trend 8

Technology and Artificial Intelligence (AI) Adoption

AI-Driven Customer Services

The trend of AI-Driven Customer Service represents a significant shift towards automation and personalization in customer interactions. AI chatbots, powered by natural language processing, machine learning, and sometimes generative AI, are being integrated into customer service platforms to provide instant, 24/7 support, handle routine inquiries, and even offer personalized recommendations or solutions. This trend is driven by the need for cost-effective, scalable customer service solutions that can adapt to individual customer needs while reducing the burden on human agents.

The ability to offer 24/7 availability caters to the modern consumer's expectation for immediate service. Cost efficiency plays a significant role, as chatbots can handle numerous customer interactions simultaneously, reducing the need for a large customer service team. This scalability also means that businesses can manage high volumes of interactions during peak times without additional human resources.

Personalization through AI allows for tailored customer experiences based on past interactions and data analysis, improving customer satisfaction. The data collected through these interactions offers businesses insights into customer needs and behaviours, which can be leveraged for service enhancements. Finally, AI can manage routine inquiries swiftly, allowing human agents to focus on more complex customer service issues, thereby enhancing the overall quality of customer experience.

However, implementing AI chatbots comes with its set of risks and concerns. Privacy and data security are paramount, as the personalization of services requires handling potentially sensitive customer data. Accuracy and reliability of AI responses are crucial; any misinterpretation or incorrect information can lead to customer frustration. There is also the issue of the lack of human touch; some customers value the empathy and nuanced understanding only a human can provide, which AI might not replicate effectively.

An overemphasis on automation could lead to customer dissatisfaction if human support is not readily available for more intricate problems. Integration with existing systems can be complex, requiring significant technical effort to ensure a seamless customer service experience. Lastly, there are ethical considerations, particularly around AI biases, which could manifest in customer service if the algorithms are not designed with fairness and inclusivity in mind.

Predictive Analytics and Big Data

The trend of Predictive Analytics and Big Data involves using vast amounts of data to forecast future trends, behaviours, and outcomes across various industries. Big Data refers to the large volume of structured and unstructured data that businesses collect, while Predictive Analytics applies statistical, machine learning, and AI techniques to analyse this data for predictive insights. This trend is pivotal in areas like marketing, healthcare, finance, and logistics, where anticipating future events can significantly enhance decision-making, efficiency, and strategic planning.

An explosion in data from myriad sources like digital transactions, IoT devices, and social media provides the foundational material for sophisticated analysis. Technological advancements, particularly in AI, machine learning, and cloud computing, have democratized access to big data analysis, making it both feasible and cost-effective. Businesses leverage predictive analytics to gain insights into customer behaviour, market dynamics, and operational efficiencies, thereby securing a competitive edge.

Personalization of services and products is another driver, directly contributing to enhanced customer engagement and satisfaction. In sectors like finance and manufacturing, predictive analytics plays a critical role in risk management, from detecting fraud to anticipating equipment maintenance needs. In healthcare, it is instrumental in predicting patient outcomes and optimizing medical resources.

However, this growth is not without its challenges and risks. Data privacy and security are major concerns given the sensitive nature of the information involved, with potential for data breaches or misuse of personal data. The accuracy of predictive models can be compromised by biases in the data or outdated models, leading to erroneous predictions.

The complexity of big data analytics demands a high level of technical expertise, which can be a barrier for many organizations. There is also the risk of over-reliance on data-driven decisions, potentially sidelining human intuition or qualitative insights. The costs associated with setting up the necessary infrastructure and hiring or training staff can be significant, particularly for smaller businesses. Lastly, navigating the regulatory landscape, especially with laws like GDPR or CCPA, adds another layer of complexity to ensure compliance in data usage.

Automation in Manufacturing and Robotics

The trend of Automation in Manufacturing and Robotics is reshaping industrial processes by integrating advanced technologies like AI, machine learning, IoT, and robotics to enhance productivity, quality, and efficiency. This includes the use of industrial robots for repetitive tasks, Cobots (collaborative robots) that work alongside human workers, and automation systems that manage everything from assembly to quality control. The focus is on creating flexible, smart manufacturing environments that are responsive to market changes, improve safety, and reduce operational costs.

Labour shortages, particularly in areas with aging populations, have made automation an attractive solution for maintaining productivity. Cost reduction is another major driver, as robots can operate continuously without the need for breaks, overtime, or benefits, thereby lowering operational costs while boosting production efficiency. Automation also enhances product quality and consistency by minimizing human error, which is crucial in industries where precision is paramount.

Technological advancements have made robotics more versatile and accessible, with enhancements in sensory capabilities, AI integration, and simpler programming. The demand for product customization in modern manufacturing is well-served by flexible automation systems that can quickly adapt to new production requirements. Finally, in a global market, automation helps companies maintain competitiveness by improving speed and reducing costs.

However, this trend towards automation comes with significant risks and concerns. Job displacement is a primary worry, as automation can replace many traditional manufacturing jobs, pushing for retraining programs and new employment strategies.

The high initial investment required for advanced automation systems can be a barrier, particularly for smaller businesses.

There is also a growing need for technical skills in robotics and programming, highlighting a skills gap that could slow adoption. The reliability of automated systems is another concern; maintenance is necessary, and any downtime can lead to substantial financial losses. Integrating new technology with existing infrastructure presents its own set of challenges, requiring careful planning and sometimes significant system overhauls. Lastly, the ethical and social implications of widespread automation, including potential increases in economic inequality, spark debates about how society should adapt to these changes.

Blockchain and Distributed Ledgers

Blockchain and Distributed Ledgers represent a transformative trend in technology, finance, and data management, focusing on creating secure, transparent, and decentralized systems for recording transactions and data. Blockchain, a specific type of distributed ledger, is best known for underpinning cryptocurrencies like Bitcoin but has expanded into various applications including supply chain management, identity verification, smart contracts, and more. This trend leverages the principles of decentralization, cryptographic security, and immutability to foster trust in digital transactions and data storage without the need for a central authority.

Its core feature of providing transparency and security through an immutable ledger reduces fraud and increases trust in transactions. The decentralized nature of blockchain removes the need for intermediaries, cutting costs and accelerating processes in industries like finance, logistics, and beyond.

Smart contracts automate and enforce agreements without human intervention, offering significant efficiencies in sectors like legal services and real estate. The rise of cryptocurrencies and decentralized finance (DeFi) platforms has significantly increased interest and demand for blockchain infrastructure. In supply chains, blockchain enables full transparency from product origin to end consumer, enhancing traceability and accountability. Additionally, some governments are beginning to explore blockchain for enhancing public services, suggesting regulatory support for the technology's broader application.

However, there are notable risks and concerns associated with blockchain implementation. Scalability remains a significant issue for many blockchain networks, as they often struggle with the speed and capacity to handle high transaction volumes, which is crucial for widespread adoption. The energy consumption associated with some blockchain consensus mechanisms, particularly Proof of Work, has led to environmental criticisms due to the high electricity usage.

Regulatory uncertainty across different regions can hinder development and adoption, as the legal framework for blockchain and cryptocurrencies is still evolving. Privacy is another concern; while the technology offers anonymity in transactions, there is a risk of personal data being deduced through complex data analysis. The complexity of integrating blockchain into existing systems can be a barrier to adoption, requiring significant technical knowledge and organizational change. Finally, while blockchain is secure by design, it is not invulnerable; smart contract bugs or other cyber vulnerabilities can be exploited.

Generative AI and Content Creation

The trend towards Generative AI in Content Creation is revolutionizing how content is produced across various media, including text, images, videos, and music. Generative AI, powered by large language models (like those behind ChatGPT), AI-driven image generators (like DALL-E), and other creative AI tools, allows for the automated or semi-automated creation of content that can mimic human creativity. This technology is being adopted for marketing, journalism, entertainment, education, and personal use, providing unprecedented speed, scalability, and personalization in content generation.

Its ability to generate content with incredible efficiency and speed is particularly valuable for tasks that are repetitive or require high output. Personalization through AI allows for content that resonates more deeply with specific audiences, increasing engagement. From a business perspective, generative AI significantly reduces the cost of content production by automating various aspects of the creative process.

It also pushes the boundaries of creativity, offering novel approaches to art, music, and narrative that can sometimes go beyond what humans might produce alone. The incessant demand for fresh content in digital spaces like social media, advertising, and journalism further propels the adoption of AI tools. Moreover, AI democratizes content creation, empowering those without formal training to produce high-quality materials.

However, this technological advancement comes with its set of risks and concerns. The quality and authenticity of AI-generated content can be questionable, potentially lacking the nuanced understanding or emotional depth humans bring to their work. Copyright and plagiarism become significant issues since AI might reproduce or closely mimic existing content without clear legal precedents for ownership.

Ethically, there are worries about job displacement in creative fields, biases within AI that could skew content, and the broader implications of using AI in artistic expression. An over-reliance on

AI might lead to a lack of diversity in content, risking a homogenized cultural landscape. Data privacy is another critical concern, as AI models need vast datasets, which raises questions about data acquisition and usage. Finally, the regulatory landscape must evolve to tackle new challenges like deepfakes and the spread of misinformation through AI-generated content.

Augmented Reality (AR), Virtual Reality (VR), and Mixed Reality (MR)

The trend of Augmented Reality (AR), Virtual Reality (VR), and Mixed Reality (MR) involves immersive technologies that alter or enhance our perception of reality. AR overlays digital information on the real world, VR creates a completely virtual environment, and MR blends aspects of both, allowing for real-time interaction between digital and physical elements. These technologies are becoming integral across industries like gaming, education, healthcare, retail, and manufacturing, offering new ways to interact, learn, work, and entertain.

The proliferation of consumer electronics, including specialized devices like VR headsets and AR-enabled smartphones, has made these technologies more accessible to the public. In gaming and entertainment, AR/VR/MR offer unparalleled immersive experiences, significantly enhancing user engagement in games, movies, and live events. Education benefits from these technologies by providing experiential learning opportunities that can range from virtual field trips to hands-on simulations in professional training. In healthcare, AR and VR are transforming patient care through applications like therapy, surgical navigation, and complex medical visualization. The shift towards remote work has seen VR and AR being utilized for virtual collaboration, allowing for a sense of presence despite physical distances. Businesses across industries are adopting these technologies for various applications, from design visualization to remote troubleshooting, which boosts efficiency and customer interaction.

However, there are several risks and concerns associated with the expansion of AR/VR/MR. Health implications, such as motion sickness or eye strain from prolonged use, are significant, with the long-term effects still not fully understood. Privacy and security are major concerns, as these devices can collect extensive environmental and personal data, necessitating robust data protection measures.

The cost of entry for high-quality AR/VR/MR hardware remains a barrier, potentially slowing down widespread adoption. Technical limitations like latency, battery life, and the need for powerful computing resources can detract from the user experience. Creating compelling content for these platforms requires new skills and significant investment, posing challenges for content developers. Lastly, there is a social aspect to consider; while these technologies can enhance virtual interaction, there is a risk they might diminish real-world social engagements, leading to concerns about social isolation.

Robots and Cobots

The trend towards Robots and Cobots (Collaborative Robots) in various industries is fundamentally altering how tasks are performed by combining the capabilities of automation with human interaction. Robots are increasingly integrated into manufacturing, logistics, healthcare, and even domestic settings, performing tasks ranging from heavy lifting to precision assembly. Cobots, specifically, are designed to work safely alongside humans, enhancing productivity while providing flexibility and safety. This trend is driven by advancements in AI, machine learning, sensor technology, and the need for more efficient, adaptable work environments.

The adoption of collaborative robots, or Cobots, is driven by several key factors. Labour shortages across various industries make Cobots an appealing option for tasks that are repetitive, require high precision, or are hazardous. They enhance productivity by working tirelessly, thereby increasing output while maintaining consistent quality.

Safety is another significant driver; Cobots are designed with sensors to work alongside humans without risk of collision, significantly reducing workplace accidents. Technological advancements in AI and machine vision have made these robots more adept at performing complex tasks, easier to program, and thus more versatile. Over time, the cost efficiency of using Cobots can lead to substantial savings in labour and improve operational efficiencies. Additionally, the flexibility of Cobots to be reprogrammed for different tasks supports businesses in meeting demands for customization without the need for extensive retooling.

However, implementing Cobots technology is not without its challenges and concerns. One of the primary risks is job displacement, as automation might reduce the need for human labour in certain roles, pushing for workforce retraining or career shifts. The high initial cost of purchasing, setting up, and integrating robotics solutions can deter smaller businesses.

The complexity of integrating these systems into existing workflows can be significant, often requiring considerable time and resources. Maintenance of robots is another concern; any downtime can lead to productivity losses, and there is a growing need for skilled technicians to handle repairs and updates. Even with safety features, there remains a risk if these are not properly maintained or if safety procedures are overlooked. Lastly, public perception can be a hurdle, with some sectors of society expressing concerns or resistance towards replacing human workers with robots.

Quantum Technologies

Quantum Technologies represent a frontier in computing, communications, sensing, and cryptography, leveraging the principles of quantum mechanics to perform tasks unattainable by classical technologies. This includes quantum computing, which uses quantum bits (qubits) to solve complex problems exponentially faster than classical computers in certain areas; quantum sensors for ultra-precise measurements; quantum communication for secure data transmission; and quantum cryptography for encryption that is theoretically unbreakable. This trend signifies a potential paradigm shift in technology, with implications for numerous industries.

Quantum computers could perform complex calculations, such as optimization problems or molecular simulations, at speeds unattainable by classical computers. This potential extends to secure communication through quantum key distribution (QKD), which could provide unbreakable encryption. In sensing, quantum technologies offer precision that could transform medical diagnostics, environmental monitoring, and navigation systems.

The field is seeing sizable investment from both public and private sectors, pushing the boundaries of research and development. The interdisciplinary nature of quantum tech means it has applications in diverse fields, from pharmaceuticals to finance. As quantum systems move towards fault tolerance, they edge closer to practical, commercial applications, marking a significant technological maturation.

However, this advancement is not without its challenges and risks. The technical difficulties in maintaining qubit coherence due to environmental noise are substantial, leading to errors that can undermine quantum operations. Scalability remains a critical issue, as increasing the number of qubits while ensuring system stability and effective error correction is still a daunting task.

The excessive costs associated with quantum technology development and maintenance make it an elite field, not yet accessible for broad commercial use. There is an ongoing debate about quantum supremacy, questioning the real-world benefits versus the current capabilities of quantum computers. Security is a double-edged sword; while quantum tech can bolster security measures, it also threatens existing encryption systems, pushing for the development of quantum-resistant algorithms. Finally, there is a pronounced talent gap in quantum-related fields, requiring a significant investment in education and training to build the workforce needed for this emerging technology.

Enterprise Tech and SaaS Solutions

The trend in Enterprise Tech and SaaS (Software as a Service) Solutions points to a significant shift towards cloud-based software for business operations, management, and analytics. Enterprises are increasingly adopting SaaS for its scalability, flexibility, and cost-effectiveness over traditional on-premises software. This trend encompasses a wide range of solutions, from CRM (Customer Relationship Management) and ERP (Enterprise Resource Planning) to specialized applications for HR, finance, supply chain, and cybersecurity. The move to SaaS is driven by the need for real-time data access, remote collaboration, and the ability to quickly adapt to market changes.

The widespread adoption of cloud computing has businesses seeking the scalability, cost savings on infrastructure, and global data access that SaaS provides. The shift towards remote work has further increased the demand for SaaS solutions that facilitate collaboration, communication, and project management across distributed teams.

Many SaaS platforms now incorporate advanced data analytics and AI, offering businesses valuable insights for strategic decision-making and operational improvements. The subscription-based model of SaaS shifts expenses from capital to operational, offering cost efficiency and flexibility. The ability to integrate and customize through APIs allows businesses to adapt SaaS solutions to their specific needs. Additionally, with rising cybersecurity threats, SaaS providers are often able to offer security measures and compliance with regulations that are beyond the reach of many individual companies.

However, there are significant risks and concerns associated with this model. Data privacy and security are paramount, as sensitive information is hosted on third-party servers, raising issues about data breaches and regulatory compliance, like GDPR or HIPAA. Vendor lock-in is another concern, where businesses might find it challenging to switch providers due to deep integration or data migration complexities. Service reliability depends on both internet connectivity and the provider's infrastructure; any disruptions can significantly impact business operations.

While customization is possible with SaaS, there is a ceiling on how much tailoring can be done compared to on-premises solutions. Over time, the cumulative cost of subscriptions might exceed what a company would spend on traditional software, particularly for long-term or large-scale users. Finally, as businesses increase their use of multiple SaaS applications, the complexity of ensuring these systems work together seamlessly can grow, sometimes necessitating additional integration tools or services.

5G Technology

The trend of 5G technology represents a significant leap in mobile networking, offering unprecedented speed, lower latency, and the ability to connect a massive number of devices simultaneously.

5G is not just an evolution of 4G/LTE but a foundational change that enables new applications and services, from enhanced mobile broadband (eMBB) to massive machine-type communications (mMTC) and ultra-reliable low-latency communications (URLLC).

It is pivotal for the Internet of Things (IoT), smart cities, autonomous vehicles, remote healthcare, and advanced industrial applications, fundamentally changing how we interact with technology. Days are not far when we see 6G technology emerging.

The rollout of 5G technology is driven by its transformative capabilities. Its promise of speed and capacity, offering data rates dramatically higher than 4G, supports emerging technologies like high-definition streaming, augmented reality, and real-time data processing. The exceptionally low latency of 5G opens up applications requiring immediate responsiveness, such as autonomous vehicles and telehealth services.

The proliferation of the Internet of Things (IoT) is significantly bolstered by 5G's capacity to connect a massive number of devices, facilitating smart homes, cities, and industrial applications. In the context of Industry 4.0, 5G enables smart manufacturing with real-time data analytics and machine-to-machine communication. Economically, 5G is seen as a catalyst for growth, with investments aimed at fostering innovation and maintaining competitive edges. Technological advancements like beamforming, MIMO (Multiple Input Multiple Output), and network slicing further enhance the functionality and efficiency of 5G networks.

However, this rapid advancement comes with its set of risks and concerns. The infrastructure costs for deploying 5G are high, involving extensive new installations like small cells and fibre optics. Public health concerns about radiation from 5G networks, though largely unfounded by current scientific standards, still pose challenges for public acceptance. Security is a heightened concern as the expanded network increases potential vulnerabilities, particularly when critical infrastructure is involved.

There is also the risk of widening the digital divide, as 5G deployment might not be uniform, leaving some areas, especially rural ones, behind. Interoperability across various 5G networks and devices globally presents technical challenges. Lastly, managing spectrum efficiently, particularly in the higher frequency bands where 5G operates, is crucial for performance but can be complex, involving regulatory and technical issues.

Platform Businesses

Platform Businesses represent a paradigm shift in how companies operate, focusing on creating value by facilitating interactions between different user groups rather than by directly producing products or services. These businesses leverage digital platforms to connect producers, consumers, or both, enabling transactions, information exchange, or collaboration.

Examples include marketplaces like Amazon, service platforms like Uber or Airbnb, and social networks like LinkedIn or Instagram. The trend towards platform businesses is driven by the digital economy's growth, offering scalability, network effects, and new revenue models like subscription fees or transaction commissions.

The growth of digital platforms is fuelled by several key drivers. The network effect is central, where the platform's value increases with each additional user, encouraging more to join. The ongoing digital transformation, driven by higher digital literacy and better connectivity, has facilitated the widespread adoption of platform business models across various sectors. Modern consumer expectations for convenience, variety, and instant access are well-served by platforms, enhancing their appeal.

The ability to leverage data collected from users for personalization, service improvement, and innovation adds to the platform's attractiveness. The relatively low capital intensity of digital platforms compared to traditional businesses lowers entry barriers and supports rapid scaling. Additionally, the global reach of these platforms allows even small businesses to access international markets.

However, this growth model is not without its risks and concerns. Regulatory challenges are significant, with platforms often under scrutiny for antitrust issues, data privacy violations, and labour practices, which could lead to new regulations or penalties. As the market becomes saturated with platforms, differentiation becomes more challenging, leading to intense competition. Security and privacy concerns are paramount, as platforms are lucrative targets for cybercriminals due to the vast amounts of data they hold.

The business model's reliance on user engagement means that any decline in user activity can threaten sustainability. Managing platform governance, including content moderation, and preventing fraud, is inherently complex and resource intensive. Lastly, there are ethical considerations, especially in how platforms treat gig economy workers, raising questions about the fairness of platform economics.

Voice and Intent Recognition

Voice and Intent Recognition technologies are at the forefront of enhancing human-computer interaction by allowing devices to understand and respond to spoken commands with context and intent. This trend includes advancements in natural language processing (NLP), speech recognition, and machine learning to interpret not just what is said but the underlying intent of the speaker. Applications range from smart home devices, customer service bots, to accessibility aids, transforming how we interact with technology by making it more intuitive and human-like.

The surge in voice recognition technology is driven by several compelling factors. Consumers increasingly seek convenience, favouring natural, hands-free interaction with their devices, particularly in situations where multitasking is necessary. Advances in AI and machine learning have dramatically improved the accuracy and functionality of voice recognition, enabling more complex command interpretations.

The expansion of smart home ecosystems requires a unified control method, where voice commands offer a seamless way to manage various IoT devices. The trend towards smaller, more ubiquitous mobile and wearable technologies further underscores the utility of voice as an interface. Voice recognition also plays a crucial role in enhancing accessibility, making technology more inclusive for those with disabilities. In business contexts, voice bots streamline customer service interactions, enhancing efficiency and reducing costs.

However, this technology is not without its risks and concerns. Privacy and security issues are at the forefront, with continuous voice data collection posing significant risks regarding how this data is managed, stored, and potentially exploited. Accuracy remains a challenge; voice systems can misinterpret commands due to accents, background noise, or ambiguous queries, leading to user dissatisfaction. The ethical use of AI in voice recognition must be vigilantly monitored to avoid biases and ensure privacy.

Many voice services depend on internet connectivity for cloud-based processing, making them susceptible to disruptions or slower performance in areas with poor internet service. Cultural and linguistic diversity poses another hurdle, as systems might not adequately support all languages or dialects, limiting their global reach. Lastly, building and maintaining user trust is critical, especially when voice interactions involve personal or sensitive information.

Cloud Computing and Data Storage

Cloud computing and data storage have become foundational technologies in the digital era, offering scalable, flexible, and cost-effective solutions for data management and computational needs. This trend involves moving away from traditional on-premises data centres to cloud-based infrastructures where data and applications are hosted on remote servers accessible over the internet. It encompasses various service models like Infrastructure as a Service (IaaS), Platform as a Service (PaaS), and Software as a Service (SaaS), catering to diverse needs from raw computing power to fully managed applications. The trend is driven by the need for agility, cost reduction, and the ability to handle the exponential growth of data.

Scalability is at the forefront, allowing businesses to adjust their computing resources dynamically according to demand without the burden of significant initial investments in infrastructure. This scalability is paired with cost efficiency through pay-as-you-go models, which shift from capital expenditure to operational expenditure, reducing hardware and maintenance costs. The exponential growth in data, from business operations to IoT and digital interactions, necessitates scalable, flexible storage solutions, which cloud computing provides.

The shift towards remote work has further accelerated the adoption of cloud services for collaboration and data access. Cloud platforms also foster innovation by enabling quick service deployment and experimentation with new technologies. Moreover, cloud storage enhances business continuity through effective disaster recovery and data backup solutions.

However, the transition to cloud computing comes with its own set of risks and concerns. Security and privacy top the list, with the potential for data breaches being a major worry, especially when sensitive information is involved. Data sovereignty issues arise when dealing with international data laws, requiring businesses to navigate complex legal landscapes. Vendor lock-in is another concern, where companies might find it challenging to move away from a provider due to integration with proprietary systems or data formats. Performance issues, including latency, can affect applications requiring real-time processing or high computational power.

Cost management is crucial; while cloud services can be initially cost-effective, without proper oversight, expenses can escalate due to "cloud sprawl" or inefficient resource use. Lastly, the complexity of managing multiple or hybrid cloud environments demands a high level of expertise, potentially straining internal resources.

Conclusion

Technology and Artificial Intelligence (AI) Adoption is revolutionizing the way the world operates, with an unmatched potential to disrupt and transform industries in ways that often surpass imagination. The global spotlight is firmly fixed on this space, as nations and industries race to harness its power. With advancements in machine learning, natural language processing, and predictive analytics, AI is not only reshaping current paradigms but also creating new opportunities in sectors we are yet to envision, making it a cornerstone of the future.

Trend	Expected Growth Rate (2025-2030)	Source
AI-Driven Customer Services	~30-35% annually	NASSCOM, Deloitte AI Index
Predictive Analytics and Big Data	~25-30% annually	Forrester Research, IBEF
Automation in Manufacturing and Robotics	~20-25% annually	Make in India, PwC
Blockchain and Distributed Ledgers	~30-40% annually	IBM, Deloitte
Generative AI and Content Creation	~25-30% annually	McKinsey, Adobe
Augmented Reality (AR), Virtual Reality (VR), and Mixed Reality (MR)	~25-30% annually	IDC, PwC
Robotics and Cobots	~20-25% annually	IFR, McKinsey
Quantum Technologies	Variable, potentially high; specifics unclear	Nature, IBM Research
Enterprise Tech and SaaS Solutions	~20-25% annually	NASSCOM, Gartner
5G Technology	~25-30% annually	Deloitte, IBEF
Platform Businesses	~15-20% annually	BCG, McKinsey
Voice and Intent Recognition	~25-30% annually	Voicebot.ai, Juniper Research
Cloud Computing and Data Storage	~20-25% annually	Gartner, NASSCOM

These expected growth rates are based on current and futuristic sentiments and trends of users, investment interests, policies, external factors and industry analysis. Growth rates may be higher or lower than stated here depending on the fluctuations in the underlying factors affecting the overall growth.

Macro Trend 9

Agri-Tech and Sustainable Agriculture

Precision Farming and IoT in Agriculture

Precision Farming and IoT (Internet of Things) in Agriculture represent a significant trend where technology is used to make farming more accurate and efficient. Precision farming involves applying agricultural inputs like water, fertilizers, and pesticides at the right time and in the right amounts, tailored to specific field conditions. IoT in agriculture integrates sensors, drones, GPS technology, and data analytics to collect real-time data on crop health, soil conditions, weather, and equipment performance. This convergence aims to increase yield, reduce waste, lower costs, and promote sustainable farming practices.

The integration of IoT in agriculture, often referred to as precision farming, is driven by several key growth factors. Resource efficiency is significantly enhanced as IoT technologies allow for precise application of water, fertilizers, and energy, reducing waste and environmental impact while cutting costs. The availability of real-time data empowers farmers to make data-driven decisions, enhancing crop management, yield prediction, and overall farm planning. In the face of climate change, IoT offers tools for adaptation through predictive analytics, helping farmers anticipate and respond to adverse weather conditions.

Labour shortages in agriculture can be mitigated by automation and remote monitoring capabilities. There is also a growing consumer demand for high-quality, sustainably produced food, which precision farming can help meet. Additionally, many governments are providing incentives and support for adopting these technologies to bolster food security and promote sustainable farming practices.

However, the adoption of IoT in agriculture is not without its challenges and concerns. The initial investment required for IoT devices, sensors, and related systems can be substantial, posing a barrier for small-scale farmers. Data privacy and security become critical as farming data, which can be quite proprietary, is collected and analysed, opening up possibilities for data breaches or misuse.

There is a risk of becoming overly dependent on technology, where system failures or a lack of technical skills could disrupt operations. Connectivity is another practical issue, as IoT effectiveness relies on stable internet access, which might not be readily available in remote or rural agricultural areas. The fragmentation of IoT technology can lead to compatibility issues, making integration across different systems or platforms complex. Lastly, there is an environmental concern if precision farming leads to overuse of resources in some contexts, potentially harming local ecosystems.

Agri Digital Supply Chain and E-Marketplace

The trend towards an Agri Digital Supply Chain and E-marketplace signifies the integration of digital technologies into the agriculture industry to improve efficiency, transparency, and connectivity in the supply chain from farm to fork. This involves the use of IoT, blockchain, AI, and big data analytics to track, manage, and optimize the movement of agricultural products. E-marketplaces or digital platforms connect farmers directly with buyers, reducing intermediaries, speeding up transactions, and offering better price transparency. This trend aims to modernize agriculture, making it more responsive to market demands and sustainable.

Transparency and traceability, often facilitated by technologies like blockchain, provide consumers with confidence in food safety and origin, building trust. Digital platforms and e-marketplaces open up new market opportunities for small producers by connecting them directly with consumers or larger markets without the traditional middlemen.

Efficiency gains from automation and digitalization not only reduce waste but also lower logistical costs, making supply chains more cost-effective. Data-driven insights from real-time analytics aid in better forecasting, planning, and inventory control, which can lead to more responsive and efficient agricultural operations. Sustainability is enhanced as digital tools help in optimizing resource use and minimizing food waste. Additionally, consumer demand for transparency regarding food sourcing and quality further accelerates the adoption of digital supply chains.

However, this digital transformation comes with its set of risks and concerns. The digital divide is a significant issue, where access to technology and the knowledge to use it might not be uniform, potentially leaving some farmers behind. Data privacy becomes a concern as detailed agricultural data is collected, which could reveal proprietary farming techniques or personal information. The cybersecurity of digital supply chains is crucial; any breach could disrupt operations or compromise sensitive data.

The excessive costs associated with implementing these technologies can be a barrier, particularly for smaller producers. Regulatory challenges also arise, especially when dealing with cross-border trade or compliance with different regional laws. Lastly, there is an inherent risk in relying heavily on technology;

any breakdown or failure in digital infrastructure could have significant operational impacts.

Sustainable and Organic Farming

The trend towards Sustainable and Organic Farming reflects a growing movement to address environmental concerns, consumer health, and ethical farming practices. Sustainable farming focuses on methods that maintain or enhance the health of the land while providing for current food needs without compromising future generations' ability to do the same. Organic farming, a subset of sustainable practices, avoids synthetic pesticides and fertilizers, genetically modified organisms (GMOs), and irradiation, instead relying on natural processes, biodiversity, and soil health. This trend is gaining momentum through consumer demand, environmental awareness, and supportive policies.

Consumer awareness is at the forefront, with a rising interest in health, food safety, and the environmental impact of food production pushing demand for products that are grown with these considerations in mind. Environmental concerns about conventional agriculture's impact on soil, water, and biodiversity are also significant motivators for adopting more sustainable practices.

Policy and regulatory support from governments through incentives, organic certifications, and environmental laws further encourage this transition. Technological advances in areas like organic pest control, soil management, and water conservation have made sustainable farming more practical and effective. The market potential is another driver, as organic products can fetch higher prices, offering economic benefits to farmers willing to adapt. Moreover, sustainable practices can enhance agricultural resilience to climate change by fostering healthier soils and ecosystems.

However, this shift is not without its challenges and risks. The higher costs associated with organic and sustainable farming, including labour and certification, can make these products more expensive, which might limit market penetration. There is also the issue of yield variability; although not universally true, there is a perception that organic farming might produce less per acre than conventional methods. The transition period from conventional to organic farming can be financially strenuous for farmers, as they might not immediately benefit from organic premiums. Scaling up these practices while maintaining their environmental integrity poses another challenge, especially in large operations.

Consumer education remains critical, as not everyone fully grasps the benefits and differences of organic versus conventional farming. Finally, dealing with various regulatory frameworks and certification processes can be complex, particularly for those looking to export their produce to different countries with varying standards.

Controlled Environment and Inhouse Agriculture

Controlled Environment Agriculture (CEA) and Inhouse Agriculture are trends that involve growing crops in controlled, often indoor, environments where conditions like light, temperature, humidity, and nutrient delivery are precisely managed. This includes technologies like hydroponics, aeroponics, aquaponics, and vertical farming, which aim to maximize yield, quality, and consistency while minimizing resource use. These methods are seen as solutions to the challenges of traditional farming, such as climate variability, water scarcity, and the need for year-round production. Inhouse agriculture often refers to urban farming setups where food is produced close to where it will be consumed, reducing transportation needs and enhancing food security in urban areas.

Urbanization has led to a demand for local food production to minimize transport-related carbon emissions and provide fresh produce to city dwellers. Climate change adds to the appeal of CEA by offering a buffer against variable weather, ensuring stable food production. Resource efficiency is another key driver, with CEA systems using significantly less water and land while recycling nutrients, addressing both sustainability and resource scarcity issues.

The ability to produce year-round in controlled settings meets the consumer demand for constant availability of fresh produce. Technological advancements, including efficient LED lighting, automation, and data analytics, further enhance the productivity and management of these systems. There is also a notable consumer demand for locally sourced, pesticide-free, and potentially organic produce, which CEA can cater to effectively.

However, the adoption of CEA is accompanied by several risks and concerns. The high initial costs for setting up facilities with the necessary technology and infrastructure can be prohibitive. Energy consumption, especially for lighting in indoor setups, remains a challenge; unless powered by renewable energy, this could undermine the environmental benefits. The economics of scale can be tricky, as the high operational costs might not be offset by the price consumers are willing to pay, particularly for staple crops.

Operating CEA systems successfully requires a blend of agricultural and technological expertise, which might not be widely available, thus limiting adoption. There is also the risk of market saturation, where an influx of producers could lead to an oversupply of certain crops, affecting prices and profitability. Lastly, the environmental impact of CEA heavily depends on the energy source; reliance on fossil fuels could negate some of the sustainability advantages.

Biological and Hybrid Crop Seed and Protection

The trend in Biological and Hybrid Crop Seed and Protection involves the development and adoption of seeds with enhanced genetic traits and the use of biological methods for pest and disease management. Hybrid seeds, which combine the desirable traits from two parent varieties, aim to improve yield, disease resistance, and other agronomic characteristics. Biological crop protection, on the other hand, refers to the use of natural organisms like beneficial bacteria, fungi, and insects to control pests and diseases, offering a more sustainable alternative to chemical pesticides. This trend is driven by the push for sustainability, food security, and the need to reduce the environmental impact of agriculture.

There is a strong push towards sustainability in agriculture, with a global trend to reduce chemical inputs for environmental benefits, favouring biological solutions. Hybrid seeds are designed for resilience, resisting climate changes, pests, and diseases, which contributes to more predictable and stable crop yields. Consumer demand is shifting towards organic and sustainably produced foods, boosting the market for biological protection methods.

Regulatory environments are also evolving, with stricter controls on chemical pesticides encouraging the use of biological alternatives. Innovations in biotechnology have enabled the development of superior hybrid seeds through advanced genetic engineering and breeding techniques. Furthermore, biological controls align well with Integrated Pest Management (IPM) strategies, promoting a more holistic approach to crop protection.

However, this shift is not without its challenges and concerns. The efficacy and consistency of biological products can vary, being more dependent on environmental conditions than chemical counterparts. The cost of high-quality hybrid seeds and biological controls can be prohibitive, and their availability might not match that of conventional products. Intellectual property issues around hybrid seeds, particularly related to patents, raise questions about seed saving and farmer autonomy. The market for hybrid seeds is often concentrated in the hands of a few large corporations, which could stifle competition and limit innovation.

There is also a risk of genetic uniformity if the same few varieties are sed extensively, potentially making crops more susceptible to widespread failure. Regulatory hurdles can delay the market entry of new biological products due to the time and complexity involved in getting approvals and establishing standards.

Circular Agriculture

Circular Agriculture represents a transformative approach to farming that focuses on sustainability by closing resource loops, minimizing waste, and using natural processes to regenerate the environment. This trend involves integrating practices like crop rotation, composting, agroforestry, and the use of renewable energy, alongside reducing external inputs like synthetic fertilizers and pesticides. The aim is to create a self-sustaining agricultural system that mimics natural ecosystems, where waste from one process becomes the resource for another, thus reducing the environmental footprint of farming and enhancing soil health, biodiversity, and community resilience.

Environmental sustainability is key, as circular practices aim to mitigate issues like soil degradation, water scarcity, and biodiversity loss, fitting well with global sustainability objectives. Resource efficiency is enhanced by the reuse and recycling of materials within the system, decreasing reliance on external inputs, which can lower both costs and environmental footprints.

Consumer demand for products from sustainable and regenerative farming is on the rise, driven by greater public awareness. Policy support from governments and international organizations further encourages these practices through various incentives and regulatory frameworks. Circular agriculture also offers resilience against climate change through its emphasis on soil health and biodiversity, potentially leading to more stable agricultural systems. Economically, there are long-term benefits, including cost savings and potentially higher yields due to enhanced soil fertility.

However, the transition to circular agriculture comes with its set of challenges and concerns. The initial shift can involve significant costs and complexities, requiring farmers to learn new methods and sometimes change cultural practices. Scalability can be an issue, particularly when trying to apply these principles to large-scale, monoculture farming systems which might need substantial redesign to become truly circular. There is also the economic viability to consider; in the short term, circular practices might not yield immediate financial returns comparable to conventional farming.

A knowledge and skills gap exists, as not all farmers have access to or are trained in these newer methods. Market acceptance is not guaranteed, with potential resistance or misunderstanding from both consumers and traditional agricultural markets about the value of circular products. Lastly, the adoption of circular agriculture often necessitates new technologies or infrastructural changes, which might not be readily available or affordable in all areas.

Conclusion

Agriculture, as a fundamental pillar of human survival, is poised to embrace technologies and innovative methods that drive efficiency and sustainability. With a long-term vision of eradicating hunger globally, the sector is evolving to meet the growing demand for food while addressing challenges such as resource scarcity and environmental impact. Through advancements in precision farming, biotechnology, and sustainable practices, agriculture is set to play a transformative role in ensuring food security for future generations.

Trend	Expected Growth Rate (2025-2030)	Source
Precision Farming and IoT in Agriculture	~20-25% annually	India Electronics and Semiconductor Association (IESA), PwC
Agri Digital Supply Chain and E-Marketplace	~15-20% annually	IBEF, McKinsey & Company
Sustainable and Organic Farming	~15-20% annually	FSSAI, APEDA
Controlled Environment and Inhouse Agriculture	~20-25% annually	TechSci Research, MarketsandMarkets
Biological and Hybrid Crop Seed and Protection	~10-15% annually	Indian Council of Agricultural Research (ICAR), AgriFutures Australia
Circular Agriculture	Variable, potentially high; specifics unclear	World Bank, FAO

These expected growth rates are based on current and futuristic sentiments and trends of users, investment interests, policies, external factors and industry analysis. Growth rates may be higher or lower than stated here depending on the fluctuations in the underlying factors affecting the overall growth.

Macro Trend 10

Financial and Wealth Management

Personal Financial Planning & Advisory

Holistic Financial Planning & Advisory has emerged as a significant trend where financial advisors provide comprehensive, integrated advice that goes beyond traditional investment management to encompass an individual's or family's entire financial picture. This approach considers all aspects of a client's financial life, including but not limited to investments, tax planning, estate planning, insurance, retirement, and even lifestyle goals. The trend reflects a shift towards personalized, life-centric advice that aligns financial strategies with personal values, long-term objectives, and unexpected life events, fostering a deeper advisor-client relationship.

There is an increasing client demand for personalized financial advice that considers individual circumstances, rather than generic recommendations. The complexity of modern financial products necessitates advisors who can provide a holistic view, integrating various aspects of a client's financial life. Life stage transitions, such as marriage, having children, or approaching retirement, underscore the need for comprehensive financial strategies that adapt to changing personal circumstances.

A regulatory environment that emphasizes a fiduciary duty to act in the client's best interest encourages advisors to adopt a more thorough, all-encompassing approach. Technological advancements have provided tools that facilitate a more integrated analysis of financial health, making holistic planning more practical. Moreover, market volatility and economic uncertainties have shown the value of having a robust, holistic financial strategy.

However, this shift towards holistic financial planning also brings forth several risks and concerns. The delivery of such comprehensive advice demands a wide-ranging knowledge and can be resource-intensive, potentially stretching an advisor's capabilities. The cost of providing these extensive services might make them less accessible to some client segments, creating a barrier. There is also the risk of overwhelming clients with too much information or too many strategic options, leading to inaction or poor decision-making.

Handling extensive personal financial data raises significant privacy and data security issues. As the market sees an influx of advisors offering holistic services, standing out becomes more difficult, potentially leading to market saturation. Finally, ensuring regulatory compliance across the broad spectrum of financial planning services can be complex, particularly when dealing with different regulations in various jurisdictions.

IPO, Equity, Mutual Funds and Wealth Management

IPO, Equity Investing, mutual funds, and wealth management in India has been experiencing significant growth, driven by increasing financial literacy, rising disposable incomes, savings, wealth creation and a burgeoning middle class. This sector includes investing and managing investments in stocks, bonds, several types of mutual funds, and alternative assets for clients, aiming for wealth creation and preservation. As equity awareness has risen, IPO market has remained buoyant in India especially with regulatory reforms and SEBI framework. That has enabled SMEs and Small companies to raise capital through primary market easier and efficient.

Equity investing involves investing in stocks directly or through equity mutual funds to potentially achieve higher returns, with strategies tailored to market conditions, investor profiles, and economic forecasts. Wealth Management extends beyond equity to include estate planning, tax management, retirement planning, and personalized investment advice.

As India's economy grows, so does the number of high-net-worth individuals (HNWI) and ultra-high-net-worth individuals (UHNWIs), increasing the demand for sophisticated wealth management services. The rise of fintech, mobile penetration, internet and digital platforms has made IPO filling, equity investing more accessible for masses. As equity investing, mutual fund penetration is showing growth, businesses like depository participants, management services, demat service providers are also flourishing.

Regulatory reforms have opened the market, encouraging more participation in financial markets through easier access to mutual funds, demat accounts, and other investment vehicles. Increased awareness and education about investment options are driving more people to engage actively in equity markets, systematic Investment planning though mutual funds (SIP) and seek professional wealth management advice.

The Indian wealth management sector is navigating through several challenges including market volatility, which can lead to significant portfolio losses without proper diversification. The trend of speculative activities, particularly among the youth, increases risk exposure through derivatives and IPOs. Regulatory changes demand constant adaptation for compliance, while cybersecurity threats have escalated with digitalization, risking client data and trust.

Inflation and economic downturns challenge wealth preservation, and the competitive landscape is intensifying with both local and international players, impacting profitability. Retaining skilled talent is difficult amid high job mobility, and there is a risk of mis-selling due to sales pressure, potentially damaging reputations. Global economic influences affect local market performance, and with clients now better informed, expectations for higher returns, personalization, and transparency are pressuring firms to excel in service delivery.

Alternative Investments

The trend towards Alternative Investments involves diversifying investment portfolios beyond traditional stocks, bonds, and cash to include assets like real estate, private equity, hedge funds, commodities, art, cryptocurrencies, and more. These investments often aim at achieving higher returns, diversification benefits, and lower correlation with traditional markets, thus offering potential protection against market volatility. The democratization of access through platforms and funds has made alternative investments more approachable to retail investors, not just institutional ones.

The growth in alternative investments in India is driven by several factors. In an environment where traditional investments might offer lower yields, especially during periods of low interest rates, investors are increasingly seeking out higher yield opportunities through alternatives. Diversification is another key driver, as these investments often do not correlate directly with stock or bond markets, potentially reducing overall portfolio risk.

Technological advancements have made alternative investments more accessible, with platforms now offering fractional ownership in assets like real estate or art, broadening the investor base. Regulatory changes have sometimes made it easier for retail investors to engage with these markets. During times of market volatility, alternative investments can offer stability or even capitalize on conditions that challenge conventional investments. Moreover, there is a growing educational push, with more resources and media coverage increasing investor awareness and understanding of these options.

However, this trend comes with its set of risks and concerns. Liquidity is a major issue; many alternative investments might not be easily sold or converted to cash, posing challenges in times of financial need. The complexity of these investments necessitates thorough due diligence, which can be daunting for less experienced investors.

Management fees in some alternative sectors, like private equity or hedge funds, can be considerably higher than those for traditional investments. Transparency can also be a concern, as there might be less public information available on the performance or valuation of these assets. With potentially less regulatory oversight, there is an increased risk of fraud or mismanagement. Finally, even though alternatives are often promoted for their low correlation with traditional markets, they can still be influenced by broader economic factors, affecting their performance.

Financial Literacy and Education

The trend towards Financial Literacy Programs reflects a growing recognition of the importance of financial education in nurturing personal financial well-being and economic stability. These programs aim to equip individuals with the knowledge and skills necessary to make informed decisions about money management, including budgeting, saving, investing, trading, debt management, and understanding financial products. They are increasingly being integrated into school curriculums, offered by workplaces, offered by private players, individuals as courses, promoted by governments, and facilitated by non-profit organizations to address the widespread lack of financial understanding.

A buoyant capital market, with rising indices, returns from small caps, and increased participation from the youth through direct investing, trading, or Systematic Investment Plans (SIPs), has highlighted the need for financial knowledge. Economic crises, like the 2008 financial downturn, have underscored the importance of financial education to mitigate future instability. Rising debt levels, particularly among the younger demographic, necessitate education on debt management and credit understanding.

Technological advancements have made financial education more accessible through digital platforms, offering interactive and engaging learning experiences. Policy and legislative changes are increasingly recognizing financial literacy's importance, with mandates for incorporating it in educational curriculums. In the workplace, there is a growing recognition of the benefits of financially educated employees, leading to better decision-making, reduced stress, and higher productivity. An aging population also demands more knowledge on retirement planning, investments, and estate management.

However, there are significant challenges and risks associated with this push for financial literacy. Implementation can be complex, requiring tailored programs for diverse groups. There is a risk that not all educational initiatives will be of high quality, missing practical, up-to-date financial knowledge. Cultural and language barriers can hinder effective learning if not addressed properly.

Even with education, changing ingrained financial behaviours is tough, needing continuous support. Resource allocation for these programs might be insufficient, affecting both the scope and quality of education provided. Finally, the spread of misinformation through online channels poses a risk, where individuals might fall prey to financial frauds like pump and dump schemes or be misled by inaccurate advice.

Microinsurance and Affordable Coverage

Microinsurance and Affordable Coverage have become significant trends in the insurance landscape, focusing on providing low-cost, accessible insurance solutions to low-income populations or those traditionally underserved by conventional insurance markets. Microinsurance products are tailored to cover small risks with small premiums, often dealing with life, health, agriculture, and property insurance. The aim is to offer financial protection that is both affordable and relevant to the needs of the economically disadvantaged, thereby promoting financial inclusion, resilience, and empowerment.

The growth of microinsurance in India is propelled by several significant drivers. There is a strong global movement towards financial inclusion, where microinsurance serves as a critical tool to bring more people into the formal financial sector. Regulatory support from both national governments and international organizations encourages the expansion of insurance to underserved populations.

Technological advancements, particularly the widespread use of mobile phones, have made it easier to distribute and manage microinsurance products, even in remote areas. Awareness about the benefits of insurance is on the rise, thanks to concerted educational efforts. Strategic partnerships between insurers, NGOs, microfinance institutions, and telecom companies facilitate broader distribution networks. Additionally, increasing climate and health risks due to global phenomena like climate change or pandemics necessitate affordable insurance options to protect vulnerable populations.

However, this expansion is not without its risks and concerns. One of the primary challenges is balancing affordability with meaningful coverage; low premiums might mean limited benefits, potentially leaving consumers underinsured. Distribution to

208

remote or low-literacy areas requires innovative approaches, as traditional sales channels might not be effective. Sustainability of microinsurance schemes is a concern, ensuring they are financially viable while still serving the low-income market effectively. Regulatory compliance can be complex, with different regions having different standards. There is also a significant need for consumer education to ensure understanding and proper utilization of insurance products. Lastly, the risk of fraud or mis-selling increases in environments with less regulatory oversight or where consumer awareness is low, which could undermine trust in microinsurance.

Conclusion

With increasing financial literacy and a growing range of options to invest savings in businesses and financial instruments, we are entering an era where individuals can build significant, sustainable wealth through financial products. This shift not only empowers people to secure their futures but also strengthens the nation's economic fabric by channelling resources into productive avenues.

Trend	Expected Growth Rate (2025-2030)	Source
Personal Financial Planning & Advisory	~15-20% annually	PwC, Deloitte
IPO, Equity, Mutual Funds & Wealth Management	~20-25% annually	SEBI, AMFI, IBEF
Alternative Investments	~20-25% annually	Preqin, Bain & Company
Financial Literacy and Education	Variable, potentially high.	RBI, NCFE, Various market analyses
Microinsurance and Affordable Coverage	~15-20% annually	IRDAI, Microinsurance Network

These expected growth rates are based on current and futuristic sentiments and trends of users, investment interests, policies, external factors and industry analysis. Growth rates may be higher or lower than stated here depending on the fluctuations in the underlying factors affecting the overall growth.

Macro Trend 11

Cybersecurity and Data Protection

Cyber Threat Prevention Solutions

The trend in Cyber Threat Prevention Solutions is driven by the escalating sophistication and frequency of cyber-attacks across all sectors. This includes the development and deployment of advanced security technologies like AI-driven threat detection, zero trust architectures, endpoint protection, cloud security solutions, and more. The aim is not just to react to cyber threats but to predict, prevent, and mitigate them proactively. This trend reflects the growing necessity to safeguard digital assets, personal data, and business continuity in an increasingly interconnected world.

The cybersecurity sector in India is experiencing growth driven by several critical factors. An increase in cyber threats, ranging from ransomware to sophisticated state-sponsored attacks, has heightened the demand for advanced prevention strategies. The integration of AI and machine learning into cybersecurity tools allows for more dynamic threat detection and prediction, enhancing security measures.

Regulatory compliance is another major driver, with global data protection laws compelling businesses to adopt more comprehensive security frameworks. The shift towards remote work has broadened the potential attack surfaces, necessitating more robust security solutions for remote environments.

The expansion of IoT devices and cloud services further complicates the security landscape, requiring specialized protection for these new frontiers. Additionally, consumer expectations for security are rising, pushing both B2B and B2C sectors to prioritize cyber threat prevention.

However, this growth comes with its own set of risks and concerns. The complexity of managing numerous security tools can lead to an overload for cybersecurity teams, potentially reducing efficiency. There is also the delicate balance between security and privacy; overly aggressive security measures might encroach on personal privacy. The issue of false positives, where normal activities are flagged as threats, can lead to alert fatigue, diminishing the effectiveness of security systems.

The financial aspect is significant, as high-quality cybersecurity solutions can be costly, posing a challenge for smaller enterprises. There exists a notable skills gap in the cybersecurity field, with a shortage of qualified professionals to manage these advanced systems. Lastly, cyber threats are constantly evolving, often at a pace that challenges the ability of organizations to keep their defences up to date.

Data Protection and Privacy Solutions

Data Protection and Privacy Solutions are crucial trends in response to the increasing volume of data breaches, privacy concerns, and stringent regulatory environments like GDPR, CCPA, and others. These solutions encompass a broad range of technologies and practices aimed at securing personal and corporate data, ensuring compliance with privacy laws, and protecting user privacy. This includes encryption, data anonymization, privacy-enhancing technologies (PETs), secure data storage, access control, and privacy by design in software development.

The growth in data protection and privacy solutions in India is driven by several compelling factors. Regulatory compliance has become a significant driver with the introduction of privacy laws like GDPR, CCPA, and local regulations, pushing companies to implement robust privacy measures. The escalation in cybersecurity threats, including high-profile data breaches, has made data protection an urgent priority. Consumer awareness and demand for privacy are also on the rise, reflecting a broader societal shift towards valuing personal data control.

Technological advancements, such as AI, blockchain, and quantum cryptography, provide new tools to enhance privacy and security. As part of digital transformation, more businesses are operating online, exponentially increasing the data that needs protection. Additionally, privacy has emerged as a competitive differentiator, where companies can attract more customers by showcasing their commitment to data protection.

However, this growth is accompanied by various risks and concerns. The complexity of complying with a mosaic of global privacy laws requires significant resources for legal and technical expertise. The costs associated with implementing comprehensive data protection can be prohibitive, especially for small and medium-sized enterprises (SMEs). There is a delicate balance between protecting privacy and fostering innovation, particularly in fields like AI where data is crucial.

Data sovereignty issues arise with international data handling, where different countries have varying regulations about data storage and processing. Managing user consent in a transparent and user-friendly manner is essential but challenging. Lastly, there is the risk of privacy fatigue where consumers might become desensitized to privacy notices, leading to less engagement with privacy settings, which could undermine the effectiveness of privacy controls.

Business and Governance Cybersecurity

The trend in Business and Governance Cybersecurity reflects the increasing recognition of cybersecurity as a critical aspect of organizational risk management and governance. This involves integrating cybersecurity strategies into business operations and decision-making processes at the highest levels, including board oversight, policy development, and compliance with evolving cyber laws and standards. The trend encompasses not only protecting against cyber threats but also ensuring resilience, managing cyber risks, and fostering a culture of security awareness across all levels of an organization.

The growth in cybersecurity governance in India is propelled by several key drivers. Regulatory pressures, including mandates from bodies like the SEC in the U.S., are compelling companies globally, including those in India, to adopt stringent cybersecurity governance practices. The sophistication of cyber-attacks, such as ransomware and state-sponsored cyber operations, has escalated the need for robust defence mechanisms.

Digital transformation across industries has expanded the cyber-attack surface, making integrated governance critical. There is an increasing expectation for corporate boards to take accountability for cybersecurity risks, understanding and overseeing these threats. The requirements of cyber insurance and compliance with various regulations further drive organizations towards better cybersecurity practices. Lastly, maintaining consumer and stakeholder trust necessitates strong data protection, which in turn influences governance structures to prioritize cybersecurity.

However, there are significant risks and concerns associated with this shift. One major issue is the skill gap at governance levels, where many organizations lack the specialized knowledge to manage cybersecurity effectively. The cost of establishing comprehensive cybersecurity governance can be considerable, potentially straining the budgets of smaller firms. There is also the ongoing challenge of balancing privacy with security needs, ensuring that data protection does not impede operational efficiency or infringe on privacy rights.

The rapid evolution of technology means that cybersecurity measures can quickly become outdated, necessitating continuous updates and adaptation. Interoperability of cybersecurity systems, especially with third-party vendors, adds another layer of complexity. Finally, cultural resistance within organizations can hinder the adoption of new cybersecurity practices, as changing the mindset to prioritize security might not be straightforward.

Identity Verification and Fraud Detection

The trend in Identity Verification and Fraud Detection involves leveraging advanced technologies to authenticate individuals and prevent fraudulent activities in an increasingly digital world. This encompasses methods like biometric verification (facial recognition, fingerprint scanning), AI-driven analysis of behaviour patterns, document verification, and the use of blockchain for secure identity management. The goal is to enhance security in online transactions, compliance with regulations (like KYC - Know Your Customer), and protect against identity theft and financial fraud in sectors like finance, healthcare, and e-commerce.

The surge in digital transactions necessitates secure methods to verify identities, ensuring the safety of online interactions. Regulatory requirements, including GDPR, AML, and KYC, compel businesses to adopt stringent identity verification processes. The rise in fraud, especially sophisticated forms like synthetic identity theft, underscores the need for advanced detection capabilities.

Technological advancements, particularly in AI, machine learning, and biometrics, are enhancing the efficiency and accuracy of these systems. Consumer demand for security has grown as awareness of cyber threats increases, pushing companies to invest in identity verification. Moreover, the interconnected nature of modern digital services requires seamless identity management across different platforms.

However, this expansion comes with its set of risks and concerns. Privacy is a significant issue; the need for security must be balanced with respect for personal data rights. There is also the risk of accuracy and bias in AI-driven systems, which might not perform equally across diverse populations if not professionally trained. The cost of implementing and maintaining these advanced verification systems can be substantial, posing challenges for smaller organizations.

An overly complex verification process might degrade user experience, potentially leading to customer drop-off. As fraud techniques evolve, verification systems must continuously adapt, adding to the operational burden. Finally, ensuring compliance with a myriad of global regulations can complicate the deployment of identity verification solutions across different markets.

Conclusion

As the digital age advances, the importance of cybersecurity and data protection has become paramount. With increasing reliance on technology and the exponential growth of data, the need to safeguard sensitive information has never been greater. This era presents an opportunity for individuals, businesses, and nations to invest in robust cybersecurity measures, ensuring trust and resilience in the digital ecosystem. As threats evolve, so do the innovations in this space, making it a critical pillar for a secure and prosperous future.

Trend	Expected Growth Rate (2025-2030)	Source
Cyber Threat Prevention Solutions	~25-30% annually	Gartner, NASSCOM
Data Protection and Privacy Solutions	~20-25% annually	Deloitte, PwC
Business and Governance Cybersecurity	~20-25% annually	Accenture, Frost & Sullivan
Identity Verification and Fraud Detection	~25-30% annually	MarketsandMarkets, Juniper Research

These expected growth rates are based on current and futuristic sentiments and trends of users, investment interests, policies, external factors and industry analysis. Growth rates may be higher or lower than stated here depending on the fluctuations in the underlying factors affecting the overall growth.

Macro Trend 12

Tourism and Experience Consumption

Aviation Regional and International Connectivity

The trend in Aviation Regional and International Connectivity focuses on enhancing air travel networks to better connect cities, regions, and countries, thereby improving economic, cultural, and social links. This includes expanding routes, increasing flight frequencies, developing new airport infrastructure, and leveraging technology to streamline operations and passenger experiences. The trend is driven by globalization, tourism growth, trade, and the need for efficient transportation in an increasingly interconnected world. It also encompasses the challenges of balancing growth with sustainability, regulatory compliance, and technological integration.

The growth in air connectivity in India is propelled by several significant drivers. Economic growth naturally necessitates improved air links to support trade, tourism, and business travel. Globalization has increased the demand for more direct and frequent flights as businesses and cultural exchanges expand globally. The tourism sector's growth also plays a crucial role, with travellers seeking more destinations and experiences, thus requiring a broader network of flight options.

Technological advancements in aviation, including fuel-efficient aircraft and digital enhancements, enable airlines to expand their networks efficiently. Liberalization of air services through open skies policies and airline alliances has opened numerous new routes, fostering competition and connectivity. Urbanization further fuels this demand, as burgeoning cities require enhanced air connectivity to manage both population and business flows.

However, this growth is not without its risks and concerns. The environmental impact of increased air travel, particularly the rise in carbon emissions, is a major concern, urging the aviation industry towards sustainability. Infrastructure at airports can become a bottleneck; without adequate investment, overcrowding can lead to delays and diminish passenger experience.

Navigating the complex web of aviation regulations across different countries can be challenging for international route planning. Economic volatility can directly influence airline profitability, affecting route sustainability. Security and safety issues globally might result in route changes or restrictions. Lastly, there is the risk of market saturation in some regions, where an oversupply of flights could lead to intense competition, possibly resulting in route cancellations or consolidations.

Domestic and International Tourism

The trend in Domestic and International Tourism in India reflects a significant growth in the tourism sector, driven by both domestic travel within the country and an increasing influx of international visitors. India's rich cultural heritage, diverse landscapes, and historical sites attract tourists globally, while domestic tourism is fuelled by India's large and increasingly affluent population, better infrastructure, and promotional campaigns like "Dekho Apna Desh" for domestic tourism and "Incredible India" internationally. The sector has seen a rebound post-COVID, with a focus on sustainable tourism, wellness tourism, adventure, and cultural experiences.

The growth of tourism in India is driven by a combination of economic and cultural factors. Economic growth has led to increased disposable incomes, particularly among the burgeoning middle class, boosting domestic travel. India's rich cultural heritage, historical landmarks, and diverse natural landscapes continue to attract tourists from around the globe. Infrastructure development, such as new airports and improved road networks, has made travel within the country more accessible.

Government initiatives, including streamlined e-visa processes, tourism development projects, and promotional campaigns, have further enhanced India's appeal as a travel destination. The rise of digital booking platforms has made planning and booking trips more convenient, contributing to both domestic and international tourism. Additionally, there is a growing interest in sustainable and wellness tourism, with travellers seeking experiences in eco-tourism, yoga, and Ayurveda.

However, this growth comes with its set of risks and concerns. Over-tourism at iconic sites like the Taj Mahal poses a threat to both the site's integrity and visitor experience. In some areas, infrastructure still lags the demand for tourism, which can hinder sustainable growth. Security and safety issues, ranging from personal safety to health and hygiene standards, can negatively impact tourist numbers.

The environmental impact of tourism necessitates sustainable practices to conserve natural resources. Economic benefits from tourism might not be evenly spread, leading to social disparities or community tensions. Political stability is also crucial; any unrest or political events can quickly alter international perceptions and affect tourism.

Multi-Dimensional and Advanced Cinema

The trend towards Multi-dimensional Cinema encompasses the evolution of movie-going experiences that go beyond traditional 2D and even 3D formats to engage audiences through multiple sensory dimensions. This includes technologies like 4DX, which adds motion, environmental effects (like wind, water, scent), and Dolby Cinema or IMAX Laser, which provide enhanced visuals and sound for a more immersive experience. Additionally, VR cinemas and interactive screenings where the audience can influence the narrative are part of this trend, aiming to make movie-watching an experience that stimulates more than just sight and sound.

There is an increasing audience demand for immersive experiences that transcend traditional viewing, akin to the engagement levels found in video games. Technological advancements in areas like projection, sound systems, and sensory effects are making these experiences more accessible and impactful. As home viewing options become more sophisticated, cinemas are compelled to provide unique experiences that cannot be replicated at home, thus justifying the cinema-going experience.

Film studios use these advanced formats as a marketing tool to promote high-budget films, enhancing their appeal and potentially increasing box office returns. The global expansion of multi-dimensional cinemas into both established and emerging markets is broadening the audience base. Additionally, there is a cultural shift towards valuing experiences over material possessions, which supports the growth of experiential entertainment like multi-dimensional cinema.

However, this trend also brings forth several risks and concerns. The excessive costs associated with installing and maintaining these sophisticated systems can be prohibitive for both cinemas and consumers, who pay a premium for the experience. There is also the issue of niche appeal; not every film benefits from or even necessitates multi-dimensional effects, which can limit the number of screenings that truly leverage this technology.

Some viewers might find the sensory overload uncomfortable or even distressing. The complex machinery requires ongoing maintenance, and technical failures can disrupt screenings or degrade the experience. Creating content that genuinely enhances the film through additional dimensions without turning into a gimmick is a significant creative challenge. Lastly, cultural fit can be an issue; not all markets or audiences might be interested or culturally accustomed to these highly technological cinema experiences, potentially affecting adoption rates.

Events and Related Services

The trend in Events and Related Services is a dynamic area where the entertainment, hospitality, and marketing industries intersect to create memorable, engaging experiences. This includes live music events, stand-up comedy, weddings with unique entertainment elements, and corporate marketing events that leverage music or humour for impact. The trend reflects a move towards personalization, experiential marketing, and the integration of technology to enhance event experiences. Services involved range from event planning and management to specialized entertainment like bands or DJs, lighting, sound, and even VR/AR for immersive experiences.

There is a noticeable shift in consumer preferences towards experiences rather than material possessions, boosting demand for diverse and engaging events. Technology plays a pivotal role, with digital tools enhancing planning, marketing, and the execution of events, from interactive apps to virtual reality experiences.

Social media has a noteworthy influence, where events that offer unique, shareable moments gain more visibility, thus amplifying their reach and impact. Customization is becoming increasingly important, with both weddings and corporate events seeking personalized, memorable experiences. The economic recovery post-COVID has led to a surge in events, as people are eager to reconnect and celebrate. Additionally, cross-industry collaborations are creating innovative event formats, blending music, technology, and branding in novel ways.

However, this growth is not without its challenges and concerns. Market saturation can occur when too many similar events compete for attention, potentially reducing the perceived value of each event. The excessive costs associated with creating distinctive experiences might limit accessibility or affect the profitability of events.

There is a risk of technological dependence, where any technical glitch could disrupt the event experience. Privacy concerns arise with the increasing personalization of events, as data collection practices must respect individual privacy. Event fatigue could set in if consumers are overwhelmed by the frequency or similarity of events, leading to decreased engagement. Finally, navigating the complex landscape of regulatory compliance, including health, safety, and copyright laws, adds another layer of challenge to event management.

Luxury Tech Vehicles

The trend towards Luxury Tech Vehicles represents the intersection of high-end automotive design with innovative technology. These vehicles are not only about luxury in terms of materials and comfort but also incorporate advanced tech features like autonomous driving capabilities, sophisticated infotainment systems, augmented reality interfaces, and unparalleled connectivity options. Luxury brands are pushing the boundaries of what vehicles can do, aiming to offer an experience that blends luxury with the future of mobility. This includes electric luxury cars that offer both performance and eco-friendliness, alongside innovative interior designs that turn the car into a mobile living space.

The integration of advanced technologies in luxury vehicles in India is driven by several key factors. Consumer expectations are evolving, with luxury buyers now seeking vehicles that not only offer traditional luxury but also incorporate innovative technology. The automotive industry is witnessing a significant shift towards electric vehicles (EVs) and autonomy, with luxury brands leading the charge in these areas.

There is a high demand for connectivity and personalization, where vehicles act as extensions of one's digital life, offering tailored experiences. Luxury car manufacturers leverage advanced technology to differentiate their brands in a highly competitive market. Environmental awareness among luxury consumers is pushing for more sustainable options, encouraging brands to develop eco-friendly vehicle technologies. Additionally, vehicles are increasingly seen as mobile platforms for work, entertainment, and relaxation, necessitating sophisticated tech integration.

However, this push towards technological sophistication in luxury cars comes with its set of risks and concerns. The cost of integrating these advanced features can drive up prices, potentially limiting the market to only the wealthiest consumers. There is also the issue of technology obsolescence; the fast pace of technological change means that features considered luxurious today might become standard or outdated shortly. Privacy and security are major concerns, as connected cars gather extensive data, posing risks of data breaches or misuse.

Regulatory challenges, especially concerning autonomous driving and electric powertrains, could delay or complicate the rollout of these technologies. The complexity of new systems can lead to reliability issues and require specialized maintenance, increasing ownership costs. Lastly, not all luxury car buyers might be eager or able to adapt to highly advanced, tech-heavy vehicle interfaces, potentially alienating traditional luxury consumers.

Railway and Yacht Luxury Experience

The trend towards luxury experiences in both the railway and yacht sectors reflects a growing demand for exclusive, high-end travel experiences where the journey itself is as significant as the destination. Luxury Rail experiences include fine dining, private cabins, and scenic routes through some of the world's most beautiful landscapes. Luxury Yachting, on the other hand, provides an intimate, bespoke experience on the water, with yachts equipped with state-of-the-art amenities, personalized services, and the ability to explore remote or exclusive destinations. Both trends cater to a niche market seeking adventure, privacy, and unparalleled luxury.

The growth in luxury yachting and train travel in India is fuelled by several compelling drivers. An increase in the number of high-net-worth individuals globally has spurred demand for unique, experiential luxury travel, where both yachts and luxury trains offer unparalleled experiences. There is a noticeable shift towards slower, more mindful travel, where luxury trains, with their nostalgic appeal, provide an unhurried journey through scenic or culturally rich landscapes.

Yachts offer exclusive access to secluded destinations or coastal areas not easily reachable by conventional travel, while luxury trains can journey through off-the-beaten-path routes, providing an intimate view of diverse regions. Both sectors emphasize personalization, allowing for tailored itineraries and onboard experiences. Additionally, these forms of travel immerse passengers in the culture, history, and cuisine of the areas they traverse, all within a luxurious setting.

However, this niche market faces several risks and concerns. The excessive costs associated with these experiences can make them accessible only to a small segment of the population, potentially limiting market size. Environmental concerns, particularly the carbon footprint of yacht travel, are significant, although both sectors are attempting to adopt more sustainable practices.

The capacity constraints of both yachts and luxury trains mean they serve an exclusive clientele, which can enhance the luxury appeal but also restrict revenue if demand outstrips supply. Regulatory and safety issues are complex, especially when dealing with international waters or cross-border rail travel, involving compliance with diverse laws and safety standards. As the market for these luxury services grows, there is a risk of saturation, making it harder for operators to maintain uniqueness or competitive edge. Lastly, managing privacy and security for high-profile clients is logistically challenging, requiring sophisticated measures to protect passenger identity and safety.

Conclusion

People are prioritizing unique, immersive experiences over material possessions, fuelling demand for niche travel, experiences, adventure tourism, and cultural exploration. With advancements in infrastructure, technology, and accessibility, the tourism and experience sectors are evolving rapidly, offering tailored experiences that cater to diverse preferences. This shift represents an excellent opportunity for investors to bet on businesses which can innovate and create lasting memories for consumers while contributing to the global economy.

Trend	Expected Growth Rate (2025-2030)	Source
Aviation (Regional and International Connectivity)	~10-15% annually	IATA, CAPA India
Domestic and International Tourism	~15-20% annually	WTTC, Ministry of Tourism, India
Multi-Dimensional and Advanced Cinema	~15-20% annually	PwC, FICCI Frames
Events and Related Services	~10-15% annually	Eventbrite, UFI
Luxury Tech Vehicles	~20-25% annually	Deloitte, Statista
Railway and Yacht Luxury Experiences	Railway Luxury: ~10-15%, Yacht Luxury: Variable	IRCTC, Superyacht Times

These expected growth rates are based on current and futuristic sentiments and trends of users, investment interests, policies, external factors and industry analysis. Growth rates may be higher or lower than stated here depending on the fluctuations in the underlying factors affecting the overall growth.

Macro Trend 13

New-Age Logistics

Real-Time Tracking and Warehouse Automation

The trend in Real-Time Tracking and Warehouse Automation involves the integration of technologies to enhance the efficiency, accuracy, and responsiveness of warehouse operations. Real-time tracking uses RFID (Radio-Frequency Identification), IoT (Internet of Things) sensors, GPS, and other technologies to monitor the location and status of goods, equipment, and personnel within a warehouse or across a supply chain. Warehouse automation leverages robotics, automated storage, and retrieval systems (AS/RS), autonomous guided vehicles (AGVs), and sophisticated software solutions like warehouse management systems (WMS) to streamline processes from receiving to shipping. This trend is driven by the need for speed, precision, and cost-efficiency in fulfilment, especially with the growth of e-commerce.

The growth in tracking and automation technologies within warehouse operations in India is driven by several key factors. The surge in e-commerce has created a demand for faster and more precise order fulfilment, pushing for the adoption of tracking systems to monitor goods from storage to shipment and automation to streamline processes. Labour shortages, particularly for repetitive or strenuous tasks, are addressed through automation, enhancing efficiency.

The integration of IoT and enhanced connectivity allows for real-time data sharing among devices, improving both tracking accuracy and automated operations. This data is crucial for data-driven decision-making, optimizing inventory, and operational strategies. Automation also offers substantial cost reductions by minimizing labour costs and increasing throughput. Additionally, customer expectations for swift and accurate delivery are pushing warehouses to leverage these technologies for better service.

However, implementing these technologies comes with its set of risks and concerns. The high initial investment required for adopting advanced tracking and automation can be a barrier for smaller businesses or those with limited budgets. The technical complexity of these systems necessitates skilled workers for management and maintenance, which might not be readily available. Integration of multiple technologies for a cohesive operation can be challenging, often requiring custom solutions.

Data security becomes a significant concern as the volume of data collected increases, risking breaches or misuse. There is also the issue of dependence on technology; any system failure or transition can disrupt operations. Lastly, the automation of warehousing tasks can lead to job displacement, highlighting the need for workforce retraining programs to transition workers into new roles or industries.

Last Mile Delivery Innovation

The trend of Last Mile Delivery Innovation is cantered on optimizing the final leg of delivery from a distribution centre or store to the consumer's doorstep. Innovations in this area include the use of Micro Fulfilment Centres (MFCs), drones, and autonomous vehicles. MFCs are smaller, strategically located warehouses that allow for quicker order processing and delivery in urban areas. Drones offer the potential for rapid, traffic-avoiding delivery of small parcels, while autonomous vehicles, including robots and self-driving delivery vans, aim to make deliveries more efficient, safe, and cost-effective. This trend is spurred by the growth of e-commerce, consumer demand for speed, and the need for sustainable delivery solutions.

The expansion of e-commerce has created an urgent need for last-mile delivery solutions that are both quick and efficient. Urban congestion makes traditional delivery methods less effective, thus MFCs and drones offer a way to circumvent traffic, reducing delivery times and potentially lowering environmental impact. Consumer expectations are evolving, with a demand for near-instantaneous delivery options like same-day or next-day services, which these technologies can fulfil.

Technological advancements in AI, robotics, and battery life are making these solutions more practical and cost-effective. The strategic placement of MFCs can lead to cost efficiencies by reducing the distance goods need to travel, while drones and electric autonomous vehicles present greener alternatives to fossil fuel-powered delivery methods.

However, this innovation comes with its set of risks and concerns. Regulatory hurdles are significant; drone operations require navigation through complex airspace regulations, and autonomous vehicles must comply with road safety laws. Finding suitable locations for MFCs in urban environments is challenging due to space and cost constraints. The reliability of these technologies in diverse and sometimes harsh conditions remains a concern, necessitating advanced maintenance and troubleshooting capabilities.

Privacy issues arise with drone usage, alongside cybersecurity risks for autonomous systems, which must be protected against potential hacking attempts. Public acceptance is not guaranteed; there's often resistance due to concerns about noise, safety, or the visual impact of these new delivery methods. Lastly, the high initial investment required for these technologies poses a risk, as the return on investment might not be immediate or certain for all businesses.

Forecasting, Route Optimization, and Predictive Analysis

The trend in Forecasting, Route Optimization, and Predictive Analysis within logistics, supply chain management, and related sectors is about leveraging data and technology to make more informed decisions. Forecasting uses historical data and predictive models to anticipate future demand or trends. Route Optimization employs algorithms to find the most efficient paths for delivery or transportation, minimizing costs and time while maximizing resource use. Predictive Analysis covers a broader scope, using data mining, machine learning, and statistical methods to predict outcomes, optimize operations, and manage risks. These trends are increasingly integrated with IoT, AI, and big data technologies to provide real-time insights and dynamic adjustments.

The exponential growth of e-commerce has necessitated more efficient management of shipping volumes, fuelling the demand for sophisticated logistics solutions. These technologies offer cost efficiency by optimizing planning and resource use, reducing operational expenses. Consumer expectations for fast, reliable deliveries are pushing logistics providers to leverage these tools for faster turnaround times. The availability of vast amounts of data from various logistics touchpoints enables more accurate analysis and decision-making.

Advances in AI and machine learning have made it possible to employ predictive models that can anticipate demand, optimize routes, and make real-time decisions. Additionally, there is an environmental benefit as route optimization helps in reducing carbon emissions by cutting down unnecessary travel.

However, this adoption is not without its challenges and concerns. The quality and security of data are paramount; inaccurate or compromised data can undermine the effectiveness of analytics and tracking systems. Integrating these technologies into existing logistics operations can be complex, requiring significant technical know-how and resources. While AI can make predictions, these models are not always perfect, necessitating ongoing refinement to account for unpredictable external factors.

There is also a risk of over-reliance on technology, potentially reducing the human element in decision-making which might miss nuanced insights. The cost of adopting and maintaining these advanced systems can be prohibitive for smaller logistics players. Finally, ensuring that these technologies comply with stringent data protection regulations across different regions adds another layer of complexity.

Elastic and Collaborative Logistics

Elastic and Collaborative Logistics is an emerging trend that focuses on creating supply chain systems that are both flexible and cooperative. Elastic logistics refers to the adaptability of logistics operations to scale up or down in response to fluctuating demand or supply conditions, leveraging technologies like cloud computing, IoT, and AI for real-time adjustments. Collaborative logistics emphasizes partnerships between different stakeholders within the supply chain, such as suppliers, manufacturers, logistics providers, and even competitors, to share resources, data, and capabilities for mutual benefit. This can involve shared warehousing, transport pooling, or integrated IT systems for better visibility and efficiency.

Volatile market conditions push companies to adopt strategies that allow for quick adaptation to changes in demand or supply. Technological advancements, including AI for demand forecasting, IoT for real-time tracking, and blockchain for enhanced transparency, facilitate these dynamic approaches. Both collaborative and elastic logistics offer cost efficiencies by sharing resources or optimizing them based on actual needs. There is also an environmental benefit; collaborative logistics can lead to sustainability through optimized transport routes and reduced waste. Consumer expectations for faster and more reliable delivery services are met more effectively with these strategies. In the context of globalization, managing complex international supply chains necessitates greater integration and cooperation among different parties.

However, implementing these strategies comes with its set of risks and concerns. The complexity in coordinating with multiple partners or scaling operations up or down can lead to inefficiencies or miscommunications. Data sharing, crucial for collaboration, brings up issues of data security, privacy, and the potential risk to competitive advantage. There is a dependency risk when companies rely heavily on partners; any failure or conflict can disrupt operations.

Navigating different regulatory environments across regions adds another layer of complexity to collaborative logistics, particularly when dealing with international shipments. The initial investment in technology for elastic logistics can be significant, with uncertain returns for some. Lastly, there might be cultural resistance within organizations accustomed to traditional, competitive business models, making the shift to a collaborative mindset challenging.

Cold Chain and Logistic Parks

The trend towards Cold Chain and Logistic Parks reflects the growing need for specialized logistics solutions to handle temperature-sensitive goods like perishables, pharmaceuticals, and chemicals. Cold chain logistics involves maintaining a specific temperature range from production to consumption to preserve product quality, safety, and efficacy. Logistic Parks, on the other hand, are large-scale facilities that combine warehousing, distribution, and sometimes manufacturing under one roof, designed to optimize logistics operations.

The integration of cold chain capabilities within logistic parks is becoming crucial, especially with the rise in demand for fresh produce, vaccines, and other time and temperature-sensitive products. This trend is supported by technological advancements, sustainability goals, and the push for more efficient supply chains.

The growth in cold chain logistics within logistic parks in India is driven by several key factors. There is an increased demand for fresh and perishable goods due to globalization, a consumer preference for fresh products, and the expansion of the pharmaceutical industry, which requires precise temperature control, particularly evident with the distribution of vaccines post-COVID. The surge in e-commerce, especially in groceries and pharmaceuticals, necessitates a robust cold chain for last-mile delivery to ensure product integrity. Sustainability efforts are also pushing for better cold chain management to reduce food waste through improved storage and transportation conditions. Technological advancements, including IoT, AI for real-time monitoring, and automation, are enhancing the efficiency and reliability of cold chain operations. Additionally, urbanization and infrastructure development are leading to the creation of more strategic logistic parks to cater to growing urban centres.

However, this growth comes with its set of risks and concerns. The high capital investment required for setting up and maintaining cold chain facilities within these parks can be a significant barrier. Energy consumption for maintaining cold environments is both costly and environmentally challenging, pushing for sustainable energy solutions. Regulatory compliance, particularly in the pharmaceutical sector, demands strict adherence to temperature control standards, which can be operationally demanding.

The last mile of delivery remains a complex challenge, where maintaining the cold chain can be difficult. There is also the risk of market saturation if the development of cold chain facilities outpaces actual demand, leading to overcapacity in some regions. Lastly, the reliability of technology used for monitoring and control is crucial, with any system failure potentially leading to product spoilage or loss.

Conclusion

As global commerce evolves, new-age logistics is at the forefront of revolutionizing supply chains. With the integration of advanced technologies, logistics is becoming faster, smarter, and more transparent. The rise of e-commerce, coupled with the demand for real-time delivery and optimized operations, is driving innovation in warehousing, transportation, and last-mile delivery. This sector not only enhances efficiency but also opens opportunities for sustainable practices, ensuring the seamless flow of goods in an increasingly interconnected world.

Trend	Expected Growth Rate (2025-2030)	Source
Real-Time Tracking and Warehouse Automation	~20-25% annually	Deloitte, PwC
Last Mile Delivery Innovation	~25-30% annually	McKinsey, Mordor Intelligence
Forecasting, Route Optimization, and Predictive Analysis	~15-20% annually	Gartner, EY
Elastic and Collaborative Logistics	Variable, high potential; specifics unclear	Accenture, World Economic Forum
Cold Chain and Logistic Parks	~15-20% annually	IBEF, Research And Markets

These expected growth rates are based on current and futuristic sentiments and trends of users, investment interests, policies, external factors and industry analysis. Growth rates may be higher or lower than stated here depending on the fluctuations in the underlying factors affecting the overall growth.

Macro Trend 14

Youth and Lifestyle

Dating and Friendship Apps/Platforms

The trend in Dating and Friendship apps/platforms is moving towards platforms that emphasize exploration, combating loneliness, and fostering connections that are not solely focused on marriage or long-term relationships. This shift reflects changing societal values, particularly among younger generations who are prioritizing personal development, casual connections, and authentic experiences over traditional relationship milestones. Apps are now incorporating features that facilitate friendships, networking, and various forms of companionship, acknowledging the diverse needs for human connection beyond romance.

The evolution of dating apps in India towards platforms that facilitate both romantic and platonic relationships is driven by several growth factors. There is a noticeable shift in relationship dynamics, particularly among Gen Z, who are more focused on personal growth and experiencing diverse life stages before considering long-term commitments like marriage. The recognized epidemic of loneliness, now seen as a public health issue, has increased the demand for apps that can connect people for companionship beyond romance.

Technological advancements in AI and machine learning are enhancing the capabilities of these apps to match users based on shared interests and values, not just for dating but for friendship. The user base of dating apps has expanded to include a wide range of demographics, including those looking for non-romantic connections or members of the LGBTQ+ community seeking both friends and partners. The rise of remote work has also contributed, as individuals seek new ways to meet people in a digital environment.

However, this expansion brings its own set of risks and concerns. User fatigue from the constant swiping or browsing can extend to friendship-seeking, possibly leading to disengagement. Ensuring authenticity and user safety on these platforms is challenging, with risks of encountering fraud, harassment, or unwanted advances. Privacy issues arise from the increased data collection needed for personalized matching, questioning how this data is managed.

Market saturation with numerous apps offering similar services might degrade the quality of connections or the overall user experience. There is also the potential for misalignment in user expectations, where some seek friendship while others might expect more, leading to mismatched interactions. Lastly, cultural resistance in some areas of India might view the use of apps for seeking friendships as unconventional or stigmatized, potentially limiting adoption.

Fast Fashion

The trend in fast fashion continues to be a significant aspect of the global apparel industry, characterized by quickly producing low-cost clothing to keep pace with the latest fashion trends. Fast fashion brands like Zara, H&M, Shein, and others have mastered the art of rapid production cycles, often releasing new collections weekly or bi-weekly. However, this model faces increasing scrutiny due to its environmental impact, labour practices, and the broader implications for sustainability and consumer culture. The industry is seeing a push towards more sustainable practices even as fast fashion remains popular for its affordability and trendiness.

The growth of fast fashion in India is propelled by several key drivers. There is a significant consumer demand for keeping up with the latest fashion trends, which fast fashion brands cater to by quickly producing and delivering new styles. Affordability is a major factor, as these brands offer clothing at low prices, broadening their market to include consumers who might not have previously considered fashion a priority due to cost.

Globalization has enabled efficient supply chains and manufacturing in low-cost countries, which supports the fast-paced production necessary for this model. Digital influence, through social media and fashion influencers, has accelerated the trend cycle, making fast fashion an attractive option for those wanting to stay current. The ease of access, whether through online platforms or numerous retail outlets, further facilitates consumer engagement. Fast fashion companies also excel in marketing and branding, keeping their products in the public eye.

However, this growth is not without significant risks and concerns. The environmental impact of fast fashion is profound, contributing to high levels of pollution, excessive water use, and enormous textile waste. Labor exploitation in the manufacturing sector raises ethical issues concerning working conditions, wages, and worker rights. The emphasis on producing vast quantities often results in lower quality products that do not last, perpetuating a cycle of overconsumption.

There is a growing sustainability backlash as consumers become more aware and critical of these practices, pushing for more ethical and environmental considerations in fashion. Market saturation with similar fast fashion products can lead to consumer fatigue and reduced brand loyalty. Finally, regulatory pressures are increasing, with more stringent rules on environmental protection and labour rights potentially affecting how fast fashion companies operate or their profitability.

Beauty Enhancement and Alterations

The trend in Beauty Enhancement and Alterations continues to evolve, driven by technological advancements, changing societal norms, and the democratization of procedures through social media and more accessible pricing. This trend encompasses a wide range of treatments from non-invasive options like artificial hair, fillers, Botox, and laser treatments to surgical interventions like rhinoplasty, liposuction, and breast augmentation. There is also a significant push towards natural-looking results, personalized treatments, and combining traditional beauty practices with modern science. The rise of at-home beauty devices and the influence of beauty influencers on platforms like TikTok further shape consumer expectations and preferences.

Social media platforms have a significant impact, setting beauty standards and trends that push individuals towards cosmetic procedures to align with these ideals. Technological advancements have made treatments safer, more effective, and with less downtime, encouraging more people to consider enhancements.

The increased accessibility of these procedures, through a growing number of clinics, reduced costs in some areas, and the emergence of at-home beauty technologies, has democratized cosmetic enhancements. There is also a cultural shift where these procedures are increasingly viewed as an aspect of self-care or personal enhancement, diminishing the stigma once associated with them. An aging population is seeking anti-aging solutions to maintain their appearance, while personalization in treatments allows for tailored results to individual needs and desires.

However, this trend comes with notable risks and concerns. Health risks, although reduced, are still present with any procedure, ranging from minor complications to significant health issues. There is the danger of over-enhancement, where individuals might chase an idealized look, leading to unnatural outcomes or a cycle of dependency on treatments.

The influence of beauty standards can negatively impact mental health, potentially leading to or exacerbating conditions like body dysmorphia. Regulatory variances across regions can compromise the safety, quality, and ethical conduct of procedures. The cost, although becoming more accessible, can accumulate, especially with the need for ongoing maintenance or multiple treatments. Lastly, the personalization of treatments involves handling sensitive personal data, which raises privacy concerns regarding how this information is used and protected.

Influencer Marketing

Influencer Marketing has evolved from a niche strategy into a cornerstone of digital marketing, where brands collaborate with individuals who have a significant following on social media platforms to promote products, services, or messages. This trend continues to grow, diversifying from macro-influencers to micro and nano-influencers, who often have high engagement rates due to their perceived authenticity and niche audiences. The integration of AI, the rise of video content, and the focus on long-term partnerships rather than one-off campaigns are notable developments. Additionally, there is a shift towards more transparent, ethical, and value-driven collaborations.

Consumers often find influencer recommendations more trustworthy than traditional ads due to the perceived authenticity and relatability of the influencers themselves. This trust allows for highly targeted marketing, as influencers have specific audiences aligned with certain demographics or interests, enabling brands to reach their ideal consumers more effectively. Influencers also serve as content creators, producing engaging, platform-specific content that blends naturally into users' social media experiences.

The expansion of social media platforms like TikTok, Instagram, and YouTube has created diverse ecosystems where influencers can thrive, offering various avenues for brands to engage with audiences. The ability to measure return on investment (ROI) through advanced analytics tools has made influencer marketing's impact more quantifiable. Additionally, consumer behaviour, with more time spent on social media, especially by younger generations, has increased the demand for influencer engagement.

However, this growth is accompanied by risks and concerns. As influencer marketing becomes more commercial, maintaining authenticity can be challenging, potentially alienating followers who value genuine connections. Regulatory issues have arisen around transparency, with mandates for clear disclosure of sponsored content to combat consumer scepticism.

Market saturation with numerous influencers vying for attention can dilute the effectiveness of individual campaigns. The volatile nature of an influencer's reputation means brands can face risks if associated with someone whose public image changes negatively. Data privacy is another concern, as influencers and brands handle consumer data, sometimes without clear consent or protection mechanisms. Finally, while there are metrics for tracking engagement, attributing direct sales or long-term brand value to influencer efforts remains a complex task.

Healthy Diet and Workout

The trend towards gym, workout, yoga, and healthy diets reflects a broader societal shift towards health and wellness, driven by increased awareness of the benefits of physical fitness and nutrition. This movement encompasses traditional gym workouts, specialized fitness classes, the resurgence of yoga for both physical and mental health, and a focus on diets that are not just about weight loss but about overall health, sustainability, and sometimes ethical considerations like plant-based or organic eating. Technology, from fitness apps to smart home gym equipment, plays a significant role in personalizing and gamifying health routines.

Increased health awareness has educated individuals on how physical activity and diet directly relate to health outcomes, pushing interest in practices like yoga and mindful eating. There is also a heightened focus on mental health, where these practices are not only valued for physical benefits but also for their potential to alleviate stress, anxiety, and depression. The integration of technology, through fitness wearables, health apps, and virtual classes, has made these practices more accessible, personalized, and engaging than ever before.

Cultural shifts are moving away from extreme diets towards sustainable, balanced lifestyles that emphasize enjoyment in health practices. Social media platforms have become a powerful force, with fitness influencers and wellness communities inspiring and educating people on these subjects. An aging population further drives demand for activities that support long-term mobility, strength, and quality of life.

However, this trend comes with its set of risks and concerns. The abundance of health information can lead to confusion or the adoption of potentially harmful trends due to misinformation. The pursuit of idealized body images propagated through these movements can foster unhealthy behaviours or contribute to body dysmorphia. Commercialization within the wellness sector sometimes prioritizes profit, potentially leading to products or practices that lack scientific backing or true health benefits.

Accessibility remains an issue, with not all individuals having equal access to the resources or knowledge needed for these practices. Sustainability concerns arise, especially with the environmental impact of producing certain health foods or superfoods. Lastly, the drive for constant improvement in fitness can result in over-exercise, where individuals might neglect the importance of rest and recovery, crucial elements for maintaining health.

Conclusion

As the youth shape cultural and economic dynamics, the lifestyle sector is experiencing a transformation like never before. This sector mirrors the aspirations of a generation eager to redefine norms, blending convenience, aesthetics, and health into everyday life. Investors and businesses alike are poised to benefit from this vibrant and ever-adaptive market.

Trend	Expected Growth Rate (2025-2030)	Source
Dating and Friendship Apps/Platforms	~20-25% annually	Statista, App Annie
Fast Fashion	~10-15% annually	McKinsey, Euromonitor
Beauty Enhancement and Alterations	~15-20% annually	Grand View Research, TechNavio
Influencer Marketing	~25-30% annually	Influencer Marketing Hub, Deloitte
Healthy Diet and Workout	~20-25% annually	IBEF, Research And Markets

These expected growth rates are based on current and futuristic sentiments and trends of users, investment interests, policies, external factors and industry analysis. Growth rates may be higher or lower than stated here depending on the fluctuations in the underlying factors affecting the overall growth.

Uncharted Territory: Unseen, Experimental Trends in Their Infancy

Unseen and Experimental trends often captivate our imagination with the promise of transformative change. Concepts like quantum internet, and artificial photosynthesis hold the potential to redefine industries and solve critical global challenges. However, actively investing in these trends today may not yield meaningful returns and comes with significant risks due to the highly probabilistic nature of their success.

Most unseen and experimental trends are still in the initial stages of innovation, often confined to the minds of visionary researchers or the controlled environments of laboratories. These trends lack commercial viability, established markets, or proven demand, making them speculative at best. Even with groundbreaking potential, many of these ideas fail to transition from concept to scalable product due to technical challenges, regulatory hurdles, or a lack of infrastructure to support their growth.

Investors should recognize that the timeline for these trends to materialize is often uncertain, and initial attempts may lead to failure before achieving success. Betting on such trends too early can result in tying up capital in ventures that may never reach fruition. Instead, tracking the movement of these trends—monitoring breakthroughs in research, emerging patents, or early-stage prototypes—can offer a clearer picture of their feasibility and market potential.

Knowledge of unseen trends is particularly valuable for innovators, researchers, and policymakers. For them, understanding these trends can guide efforts toward addressing societal needs and technological gaps. For investors, the focus should be on observing signals of progress—funding rounds, pilot programs, or successful case studies. This measured approach ensures readiness to capitalize when these trends move closer to commercialization.

In essence, while unseen and futuristic trends represent the frontier of possibility, they are better suited for curiosity, observation, and preparation rather than immediate investment action.

Health and Biotechnology

Health and biotechnology are rapidly transforming how we understand, diagnose, and treat diseases. Advances like CRISPR gene-editing are paving the way for targeted evolution, enabling scientists to precisely modify DNA to address genetic disorders and enhance agricultural resilience. Beyond healthcare, CRISPR's applications in conservation and biofuel production highlight its versatility.

Neuroprosthetics with direct brain-computer interfaces are revolutionizing sensory and motor function restoration. These brain-controlled devices are offering new hope for individuals with paralysis or limb loss, merging advanced robotics with neural integration to create seamless, life-enhancing solutions.

Personalized medicine is also gaining momentum, with epigenetics playing a pivotal role. By analysing how environmental factors influence gene expression, treatments can be tailored to individuals, leading to more effective and less invasive therapies. This approach is particularly impactful for chronic conditions and rare diseases.

Antibiotic resistance poses a significant global threat, but biotechnology is providing innovative solutions such as phage therapy and gene-editing techniques to combat superbugs. Additionally, advances in synthetic biology and genomics are expanding the possibilities for designing personalized medicine and sustainable biological systems.

Human Augmentation and Assistive Technologies encompass a broad category of innovations aimed at enhancing human capabilities beyond their natural limits or compensating for deficiencies.

Quantum Technology and Computing

Technology and computing are entering an era of groundbreaking possibilities. The quantum internet promises ultra-secure communications through quantum entanglement, revolutionizing how sensitive data is transmitted. It could redefine cybersecurity, scientific collaboration, and financial systems, creating a leap in secure, interconnected networks.

Neuromorphic computing is bringing brain-like efficiency to everyday devices. By mimicking neural networks, it enables ultra-low power consumption and high-speed processing, making devices smarter and more adaptable. Holographic data storage, with its potential to store vast amounts of data in 3D media, is set to meet the surging demand for information storage while optimizing space and energy use.

AI ethics consulting is becoming essential as artificial intelligence integrates into critical decision-making processes. Frameworks and audits are helping ensure responsible use, reducing bias, and fostering public trust. Additionally, digital twins for personal health are enabling predictive management of medical conditions by simulating individual health digitally, paving the way for personalized healthcare solutions.

Energy and Environment

Energy and environmental innovations are at the forefront of addressing climate challenges. Artificial photosynthesis is leading efforts to produce fuel or electricity by mimicking nature's process but with greater efficiency, providing a sustainable alternative to fossil fuels. Similarly, thermoacoustic refrigeration is introducing sound waves as a clean, eco-friendly solution for cooling, eliminating harmful refrigerants.

Bio-photovoltaics is turning living plants and algae into electricity generators, offering a green energy source for buildings and small devices. Alongside these, sustainable manufacturing innovations, such as lab-grown leather and renewable plastics, are minimizing environmental impact and aligning with consumer demand for eco-friendly products.

These technologies are creating pathways to reduce carbon footprints while ensuring economic viability. The future of energy and environmental sustainability lies in the balance of innovation, cost efficiency, and large-scale adoption, heralding a greener, more efficient world.

Materials Science

Materials science is redefining durability, adaptability, and functionality. Self-healing materials, like polymers and concrete, can repair damage autonomously, extending product lifespans and reducing maintenance costs. This innovation is especially impactful in construction and transportation industries.

4D printing takes traditional 3D printing further by enabling materials to change shape or properties over time, responding to environmental stimuli like heat or water. Applications range from adaptive clothing to self-assembling structures.

Sustainable materials, including biodegradable fabrics and renewable-source plastics, are addressing global environmental concerns. Smart textiles with integrated health-monitoring capabilities are also emerging as a key trend in healthcare and lifestyle products.

These advancements are shaping industries with materials that are not only high-performing but also sustainable and versatile, meeting the demands of a rapidly evolving world.

Transportation

Transportation is on the brink of transformation. Hyperloop subsystems are reimagining high-speed travel with decentralized pods that integrate into urban environments, promising efficiency, and sustainability. Personal Air Vehicles (PAVs), including eVTOL designs, may bring the dream of flying cars closer to reality, offering solutions to urban congestion and reducing travel time.

Driverless mobility would be advancing with autonomous vehicles and logistics systems, improving safety, efficiency, and accessibility. These technologies are set to redefine commuting, logistics, and urban planning by enabling seamless, eco-friendly mobility solutions.

Together, these innovations will be creating a future where transportation is faster, smarter, and more sustainable, fundamentally changing how we move within cities and across continents.

Economic and Social

The metaverse is creating immersive virtual spaces for work, commerce, and entertainment, opening new economic opportunities in virtual goods and services. Universal Basic Income (UBI) trials are experimenting with blockchain-based systems to distribute funds equitably, addressing economic disparity and automation-driven job displacement.

Decoupling of economies, driven by nationalism and protectionism, is forcing a re-evaluation of global supply chains and business strategies. This shift presents opportunities for regional manufacturing and localized economic resilience.

These trends are reshaping societal and economic frameworks, encouraging inclusivity, and fostering innovation to meet the challenges of an interconnected yet fragmented world.

Space Industry

Space technologies are expanding beyond exploration to practical applications like satellite broadband, which enhances global internet access, and asteroid mining, which offers access to rare resources. Lunar resource utilization focuses on mining the moon for Helium-3 and water ice, with potential applications in energy production and space exploration.

In-orbit manufacturing is emerging as a key trend, leveraging low-gravity environments to produce pharmaceuticals, high-purity crystals, and other valuable products. These advancements are creating an entirely new economy beyond Earth, positioning space as the next frontier for business innovation and collaboration.

Agriculture and Food

Agriculture is undergoing a revolution. Regenerative agriculture and soil health solutions are enhancing sustainability and productivity. Genetically engineered pollinators are addressing the decline in bee populations, ensuring crop pollination and food security.

Food from air, using microbial fermentation to produce protein from CO_2, will be reducing dependency on traditional agriculture, while plant-based and cultivated meat alternatives would be gaining popularity for their environmental and ethical benefits.

These innovations would transform food production to be more sustainable and resilient, addressing global challenges like climate change and population growth.

Experiential and Entertainment

Immersive reality for education and training is leveraging sensory feedback and virtual environments to create lifelike simulations, improving learning outcomes in industries from healthcare to engineering.

Mindfulness and digital detox solutions are addressing the growing need for mental well-being, offering products and services that help individuals disconnect and recharge. These trends are redefining how people learn, connect, and find balance in an increasingly digital world, emphasizing experiences that enrich lives.

As we conclude two chapters on trends, we have made every effort to compile a comprehensive list of major, unseen, and forward-looking trends that we believe are shaping industries and consumption patterns. These insights are drawn from extensive research and multiple reliable sources. However, we understand that the world of trends is dynamic, and some emerging opportunities may not yet be fully visible. If you feel we have missed a significant trend or have insights into other emerging opportunities, we would love to hear from you.

Please feel free to reach out to us at lifenivesh.com. Your contributions will help us refine our understanding and foster a broader conversation on the future of trends.

Additionally, as we receive suggestions, we plan to compile and share them with our readers and community on our X (Twitter) @darshaninvestor, keeping you updated on new and exciting opportunities. Join the discussion and stay informed as we continue to explore the evolving world of trends together.

The Practical Side of Trend-Investing

Identifying micro-trends starts with a thorough analysis of macro trends. By breaking down these broader trends, investors and businesses can uncover specific niches, sub-categories, or emerging needs within a larger movement. This section provides strategies for dissecting macro trends to pinpoint high-potential micro-trends.

1. Breaking Down a Macro Trend

To identify micro-trends within a macro trend, start by understanding the core components and drivers of the broader trend. Here is how:

- Identify Key Drivers: Determine what is fuelling the macro trend. Drivers might include technological advancements, regulatory changes, consumer demands, or cultural shifts.

  - Example: In the macro trend of sustainability, key drivers include government regulations on emissions, consumer preference for eco-friendly products, and advances in sustainable technologies.

- Define Sub-Categories: Macro trends usually contain several sub-categories or focus areas. Breaking down these areas helps narrow the focus and identify where specific niches might emerge.

- Example: Within the sustainability trend, sub-categories include renewable energy, waste reduction, eco-friendly packaging, and sustainable fashion. Each of these areas may contain smaller, actionable sub micro-trends.

- Map Out the Ecosystem: Visualize the various stakeholders, technologies, and needs within a macro trend. This "ecosystem map" can reveal connections between sub-categories, helping to identify where emerging micro-trends may overlap or intersect.

  - Example: In digital health, mapping the ecosystem reveals connections among telemedicine, wearable devices, mental health apps, and data privacy solutions. This ecosystem approach can uncover niche opportunities where these areas intersect.

2. Recognizing Potential in Micro-Trends

Once you have mapped out the core areas of a macro trend, it is time to look for specific micro-trends with growth potential. Here are some strategies:

- Look for Emerging Consumer Preferences: Within each sub-category, identify shifts in consumer behaviour or preferences that indicate a need for new products, services, or solutions.

  - Example: Within plant-based diets, consumers increasingly seek plant-based snacks that are high in protein. This micro-trend highlights a desire for nutritious, convenient options within the larger movement of plant-based eating.

- Monitor Technology Advancements: Advances in technology often spur new micro-trends by enabling better solutions or more efficient processes.

  - Example: In renewable energy, improvements in battery storage technology have led to a micro-trend in home energy storage solutions. Consumers can now store solar energy at home, making this a high-potential niche within the larger renewable energy movement.

- Assess Regulatory Impacts: Legislative or regulatory changes can stimulate micro-trends within larger movements, especially in industries like finance, health, and environment.

  - Example: In the broader data privacy trend, regulatory requirements like GDPR have led to the micro-trend of "privacy-first" digital products and services, which focus on consumer data protection and transparency.

By analysing the broader sustainability movement, these specific niches reveal how consumer values, regulatory pressures, and technological innovation create micro-opportunities within the larger trend.

Why Micro-Trends Matter

Micro-trends, though smaller in scope, provide several strategic advantages:

1. Early Entry with High Growth Potential: Since micro-trends often go unnoticed in their initial stages, they offer an opportunity for early entry at lower competition levels. Early movers in a micro-trend can capture market share before others recognize its potential.

2. Less Competition and Higher Differentiation: Major companies tend to focus on large, established macro trends, leaving micro-trends with fewer competitors in their initial stages. This allows smaller or emerging players to establish a foothold and differentiate themselves without directly competing with industry giants.

3. Targeted Consumer Demand: Micro-trends address specific, often unmet needs within broader consumer demands, attracting passionate early adopters. These early adopters drive growth through word-of-mouth and help validate the micro-trend for broader markets.

4. Greater Agility and Adaptability: Smaller companies or nimble investors can respond to micro-trends faster, adjusting their offerings or portfolios as the trend evolves. This agility offers a competitive advantage, especially as micro-trends can shift rapidly.

5. Potential for High Returns with Moderate Risk: Because micro-trends are specific, they often involve less capital than large-scale macro trends, lowering the barrier to entry. Additionally, the potential for high returns remains, especially if the micro-trend matures and moves toward mainstream adoption.

Acting on Trends

Knowing about trends is valuable, but applying that knowledge effectively is what sets successful investors and business leaders apart. Here are some practical tips on how to act on trends:

1. Develop a Portfolio Approach to Trend Investing

- When investing in emerging trends, consider spreading investments across multiple sectors or companies related to the trend. This approach, often called "trend diversification," reduces the risk associated with any one company or product within the trend.

- Example: For a trend like clean energy, an investor could diversify by investing in solar panel companies, battery storage manufacturers, and electric vehicle producers rather than focusing solely on one.

2. Start with Small, Experimental Investments

- If you are unsure about a trend's long-term potential, begin by allocating a small portion of your capital to test its viability. This approach allows you to explore the trend without committing a large amount upfront, providing room to scale up if the trend proves sustainable.

- Example: Investing in an AI tech startups with small amount and track the performance would be better risk management while testing the trend's growth.

3. Stay Agile and Open to Adjustments

- Trends can evolve quickly, so agility is essential. Be prepared to pivot or adjust your investments if latest information suggests the trend's trajectory has shifted. Staying flexible enables you to capitalize on opportunities or cut losses if the trend shows signs of slowing down.

- Example: The rapid evolution of social media has shown how platforms rise and fall in popularity. Investors who adapted to new entrants like TikTok rather than holding onto legacy platforms were better positioned to capture growth.

4. Look for Early Indicators of Trend Sustainability

- Apply the "trend indicators" from earlier sections to track the trend's progress over time. Look for consistent consumer retention, ongoing innovation, and market expansion to determine if the trend is growing into a long-term movement.

- Example: Early indicators like rising customer lifetime value or an expanding user base can confirm that an e-commerce trend is sustainable and worth deeper investment.

5. Avoid "Shiny Object Syndrome"

- Not all trends are worth pursuing. Be mindful of "shiny object syndrome," where exciting, novel ideas can distract from more valuable, established trends. Focus on trends that align with long-term value creation and address real consumer needs.

- Example: While virtual reality (VR) had a strong early appeal, many investors found greater returns in adjacent trends like augmented reality (AR) in professional applications, which solved specific business needs rather than consumer novelty.

6. Monitor Trends through Key Metrics Regularly

- Tracking trend metrics consistently will help you stay up to date with market shifts. This approach ensures that you are acting based on current information and that your investments align with the trend's latest developments.

- Example: Regularly monitoring industry reports, search volume on Google Trends, and social media engagement can keep you informed about a trend's direction.

7. Consider Complementary Trends

- Some trends reinforce or accelerate each other. Look for complementary trends that can combine to create greater impact, as these "trend synergies" often point to sustainable growth and cross-industry applications.

- Example: The synergy between the remote work trend and cybersecurity solutions illustrates how two trends can reinforce each other, creating more investment opportunities across sectors.

8. **Engage in Ongoing Learning and Networking**

   - Stay curious and connected. Engaging with industry professionals, attending events, and participating in discussions keeps you informed and ahead of shifts within trends. Networking allows you to access firsthand information about new opportunities.

   - Example: Joining forums, attending webinars, or reading industry newsletters can provide you with the latest insights on trend development.

Flow for Validating/Analysing Any Trend

1. **Problem Identification**

   - What is the primary problem or need the trend/theme is addressing?

   - Who is affected by the problem, and how severe is it?

   - Is this problem widespread or niche?

2. **Available Solutions**

   - What are the current solutions available in the market?

   - Who are the key players providing these solutions?

   - How effective are these solutions in addressing the problem?

3. **Loopholes in Current Solutions**

   - Technology: Are the current solutions technologically limited or outdated?

- Affordability: Are the solutions cost-effective for most users?

- Availability: Are these solutions easily accessible in terms of geography or infrastructure?

- Accessibility: Are there barriers to adoption (e.g., education, awareness, technical skills)?

4. Proposed Solution

- What is the new trend/theme proposing as a solution to the identified problem?

- How does this solution improve upon the current ones?

- Is this solution disruptive, incremental, or a combination of both?

5. Proposed Solution Analysis

- Value for Money: Does the solution offer a good cost-benefit ratio?

- Availability: How readily can the solution be deployed or scaled?

- Ease of Use: Is it user-friendly, especially for the target audience?

- Sustainability: Does the solution align with long-term environmental, economic, and societal goals?

- Scalability: Can this solution grow and adapt to a larger audience or market?

6. Current Adoption

Is the solution already in use? If yes:

- Adoption Metrics: How many people are using it?

- Usage Patterns: How are users interacting with the solution?

- User Feedback: What challenges or complaints are users facing?

- Sustainability of Usage: Are users consistently adopting the solution or is it declining?

7. Market Feedback

- Are people having positive responses to the solution?

- Are the problems being solved gradually by the existing players?

- Are competitors entering the market or showing interest in the trend?

8. Government Policies and Regulations

- Are there any existing government policies or regulations supporting or hindering the trend?

- Are the companies in this space complying with legal and social norms?

9. Hurdle Identification

- What are the possible hurdles (technical, regulatory, social, or financial) in scaling the trend?

- How might these hurdles be addressed?

10. SWOT Analysis

- Strengths: What are the inherent advantages of the trend or theme?

- Weaknesses: What internal challenges or gaps exist?

- Opportunities: What external factors can be leveraged for growth?

- Threats: What external risks might impact the trend?

11. Industry Forces Analysis

- Competitive Rivalry: How intense is the competition in this space?

- Supplier Power: How dependent is the trend on specific suppliers or resources?

- Buyer Power: Do consumers have many alternatives, or is this trend unique?

- Threat of New Entrants: How easily can new competitors enter this space?

- Threat of Substitutes: Are there existing or emerging alternatives to the trend?

Once you cross the first phase/step of analysis, you need to start tracking various developments from diverse sources.

12. Cost-Benefit Analysis

- Merits (Benefits of adopting the trend/theme):

  - Reduction in costs (operational or consumer-level) or time saved.

  - Efficiency gains (technological or process improvements).

  - Positive environmental impact or alignment with sustainability goals.

  - Market expansion potential or new customer acquisition.

  - Alignment with government incentives or policy priorities.

  - Opportunity for differentiation or early mover advantage.

  - Scalability and adaptability for broader adoption.

- Demerits (Challenges or risks associated with the trend):
    - High initial capital expenditure (Capex) or development costs.
    - Complexity in implementation or integration with existing systems.
    - Regulatory hurdles or lack of established policies.
    - Market resistance or lack of consumer trust/awareness.
    - Potential technology obsolescence or reliance on emerging tech.
    - Environmental or ethical concerns if not managed properly.
    - Risk of saturation in an already competitive space.

13. **Continuous Monitoring of Trend Movements**

- **Media**:
    - Follow reputable media outlets covering technology, business, and industry updates.
    - Keep track of trending news or breakthrough developments in the trend/theme.
    - Analyse expert opinions or editorials discussing the future trajectory.

- **Management Calls**:
    - Listen to earnings calls or investor presentations from key players.
    - Pay attention to management's commentary on demand, challenges, and outlook.
    - Note any specific focus on the trend during Q&A sessions with analysts.

- **Industry Events and Conferences**:
    - Attend webinars, summits, or trade shows featuring discussions about the trend.
    - Gain insights from keynote speakers, panel discussions, or networking opportunities.

- **Specialized Magazines and Publications**:
    - Subscribe to magazines or journals focused on the relevant industry or technology.
    - Read case studies, white papers, and industry-specific articles for deeper insights.

- **Government Approach and Commentary**:
    - Track announcements about policies, subsidies, or incentives related to the trend.
    - Analyse any restrictions, sanctions, or regulatory developments.

- **Existing Players in the Related Space**:
    - Examine the strategies of existing players: Are they expanding into the trend space?
    - Look at their investment levels and R&D expenditure related to the trend.
    - Note any shifts in market positioning or product offerings.

- **User Feedback and Sentiment**:
    - Review customer feedback through social media, forums, and product reviews.
    - Track public sentiment to identify pain points or emerging demand areas.
    - Engage with early adopters for firsthand insights.

- **Capex Announcements**:
  - Note any capital expenditure announcements by companies investing in the trend.
  - Understand the scale of investment and the timeline for execution.

- **General Observations**:
  - Keep an eye on lifestyle shifts, emerging behaviours, and changes in societal norms.
  - Observe local adoption patterns, product availability, or service penetration in the market.

14. Decision-Making Framework for Investing or Tracking Further

- Compile all insights, data points, and trends identified through the above steps.
- Identify early signals of adoption or disruption within the trend.
- Look for leading indicators such as increased Capex, fresh players entering, or policy changes.
- Continuously evaluate whether the trend is progressing or fading.
- Decide whether to go for business identification and analysis or wait for the further clarity.

Trend Impact Matrix: Assessing the Influence of Trends

The Trend Impact Matrix is a tool for evaluating trends based on two key factors:

Impact: The potential influence of a trend on industries, consumer behaviour, or society at large.

Likelihood: The probability that the trend will succeed or become widely adopted.

By mapping trends within this matrix, readers can make more informed decisions about where to invest their time, energy, and capital. Here is a breakdown of the matrix categories:

1. **High Impact, High Likelihood – Priority Trends**

   These are trends with both a strong potential impact and a high probability of success. Trends in this quadrant are worth prioritizing as they offer substantial growth opportunities and are relatively reliable.

   - Examples: Renewable energy, digital payments, and e-commerce. Each of these trends has already proven its ability to transform industries and influence consumer behaviour, and their continued adoption is highly likely.

   - How to Act: For trends in this category, consider making more significant investments or dedicating resources to companies or sectors aligned with these trends. The combination of high impact and high likelihood often results in strong returns on investment over the long term.

2. **High Impact, Low Likelihood – Strategic Opportunities with Caution**

   Trends in this quadrant have transformative potential but face barriers to widespread adoption or success. This category may include trends that require new technology, regulatory support, or shifts in public behaviour.

   - Examples: Quantum computing for mainstream use, carbon capture technologies, and autonomous vehicles. These trends could reshape industries if successful but currently face technological, regulatory, or adoption challenges.

- How to Act: Approach these trends with caution but monitor their progress closely. Small, experimental investments or "watchlist" strategies allow you to stay informed about their developments without overcommitting. If a trend's likelihood of success increases over time (e.g., through policy support or technological breakthroughs), consider increasing your investment.

3. **Low Impact, High Likelihood – Safe but Modest Returns**

Trends in this category are likely to succeed but have limited potential to disrupt industries or create significant growth. These trends can provide safe, steady returns but may not offer substantial opportunities for transformative gains.

- Examples: Incremental improvements in fitness tech, certain lifestyle changes like minimalism, or trends like meal-prep services. These trends cater to specific needs and are easily adopted by consumers, but they do not drastically alter consumer behaviour or market structures.

- How to Act: Trends in this quadrant are suitable for low-risk investments or diversification within a portfolio. They may be ideal for steady returns without high volatility, providing stability while balancing more high-impact trends.

4. **Low Impact, Low Likelihood – Avoid or Limit Exposure**

Trends in this category have both a low likelihood of success and limited impact if they do succeed. Trends here are often speculative, emerging from niche interests or novelty-driven fads that do not address significant needs or offer long-term value.

- Examples: Certain viral social media challenges, highly specific niche products, or "gimmick" trends like brief fashion crazes. These trends might attract attention temporarily but do not fulfil a lasting demand or present a clear path to mass adoption.

- How to Act: In general, it is best to avoid or limit exposure to trends in this quadrant unless you are comfortable with high-risk, speculative investments. If you choose to explore these trends, consider small, experimental investments with the understanding that returns are uncertain.

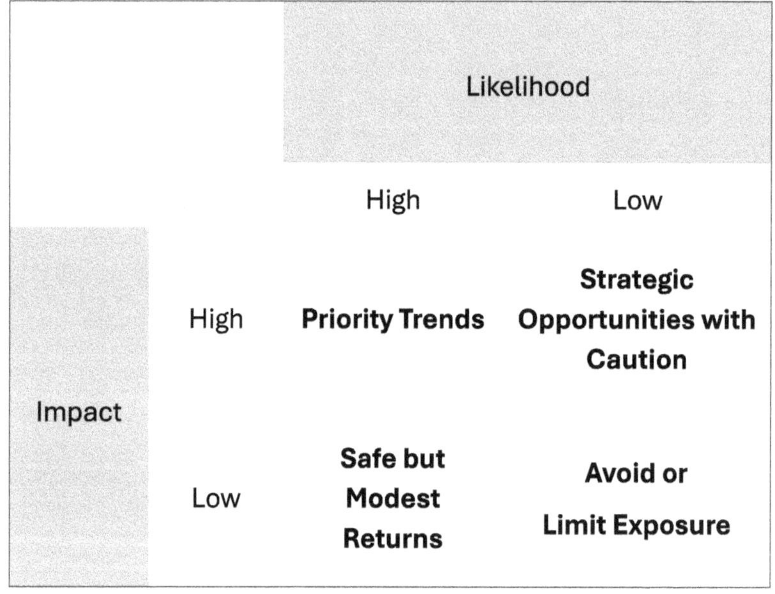

Illustration F.1 Trend impact matrix.

Mental Models of Trend-Investing

Investors often make basic mistakes when engaging in trend-based investing. To approach trend-based investing effectively, one must consider certain fundamental characteristics, inherent natures, and common occurrences associated with trends. Here are a few key points to keep in mind to ensure you not just a beginner while approaching trend-based investing.

Beyond the Buzz: Trend is Not Enough

Insight

Identifying a trend is an essential first step in trend investing, but it only accounts for a small portion of the overall process. The more challenging and crucial part is assessing the businesses within the trend to determine their viability as investments. This involves analysing key business fundamentals:

- **Management Quality**: Strong leadership is often the backbone of a successful company. Management with a clear vision and the ability to adapt quickly is crucial in rapidly evolving trends.

- **Strategic Planning**: Companies that can align their strategies with the trend's growth drivers are more likely to capitalize on opportunities.

- **Execution Capability**: The ability to implement plans effectively and achieve results is often what sets successful companies apart from competitors.

- **Balance Sheet Strength**: Financial health ensures a business can weather challenges and invest in growth.

- **Moat and Differentiation**: The advantage in terms of technology, skills, product differentiation or moat in terms of networking, distribution, stickiness.

Without this deeper analysis, even the most promising trends may lead to investments in companies that fail to execute effectively. Find more details in the upcoming chapter.

Examples and Case Studies

1. Electric Vehicles (EVs): Tesla vs. Other Players

- **Tesla**: Tesla's success in the EV market is not solely because it was part of the EV trend. Its strong leadership under Elon Musk, focus on technological innovation, and efficient execution enabled it to dominate the market.

- **Others**: Numerous other EV startups emerged around the same time, riding the trend, but many failed to scale due to poor management or financial struggles, such as Fisker Automotive's bankruptcy in 2013.

2. Streaming Platforms: Netflix's Focus on Execution

- Netflix capitalized on the OTT trend by effectively managing its transition from DVD rentals to online streaming. Its management identified the importance of original content early and strategically invested in it. Conversely, smaller players failed to compete, despite operating in the same trend, due to limited resources and weak strategies.

3.   Renewable Energy: SunEdison's Bankruptcy

- SunEdison was once a leader in the solar energy trend but filed for bankruptcy in 2016. While the renewable energy trend remains robust, the company's overly aggressive expansion and financial mismanagement led to its downfall, highlighting the importance of evaluating business fundamentals alongside the trend.

Recognizing a trend provides a starting point, but sustainable investment success comes from analysing the underlying businesses. Investors should prioritize companies with strong leadership, clear strategies, execution capabilities, Competitive advantage, and financial stability. Simply riding a trend without this analysis can lead to poor outcomes. In a later chapter, business related factors that need to be analysed have been mentioned and explained in detail.

The Mirage of Hype: Risks in Unsustainable Trends

Insight

One of the key risks in trend investing is that not all trends are sustainable or scalable enough to support substantial, long-term businesses. Many trends may appear promising in their initial stages but turn out to be temporary fads.

Investors must critically evaluate whether the trend is genuinely sustainable with a shift in behaviour and having alignment of supporting factors and has a long-term growth trajectory.

Examples and Case Studies

1. 3D Printing: A Fad with Limited Scalability

- **The Hype**: In the early 2010s, 3D printing was hailed as a revolutionary technology that would disrupt traditional manufacturing. Stocks of companies like 3D Systems and Stratasys soared as investors rushed into the trend.

- **Reality**: Over time, the market realized that 3D printing was better suited to niche applications rather than mass production. The hype faded, and many companies struggled to grow or achieve profitability. Today, 3D printing remains relevant but is far from the disruptive force it was expected to be.

2. Organic Foods and Beyond Meat

- **The Hype**: The plant-based food trend gained immense traction with the launch of companies like Beyond Meat, which promised to revolutionize the food industry with sustainable alternatives. At its peak, Beyond Meat's valuation exceeded $10 billion.

- **Reality**: While the trend remains relevant, intense competition, high production costs, and slower-than-expected adoption have led to significant valuation corrections. Beyond Meat's stock lost much of its value as the initial hype waned.

Trends driven by hype often attract overvaluation, which can harm investors even if the trend itself remains viable. Assessing scalability, sustainability, and realistic valuations is crucial for avoiding the pitfalls of overhyped trends. Trends like 3D printing and cryptocurrencies show how easily market enthusiasm can lead to excessive optimism, leaving investors vulnerable to losses.

The Bubble Effect: Avoiding Overvalued Trend Investing

Insight

When a new trend emerges, especially one with a futuristic appeal, it often generates significant excitement. This initial enthusiasm attracts businesses and investors alike, leading to a flood of market entrants and rising valuations. While this enthusiasm can drive rapid innovation and adoption, it can also inflate valuations to unsustainable levels, creating risks for investors.

Even if the trend itself is viable, entering at an overvalued stage can limit the potential for abnormal returns. Investors need to carefully evaluate the economics of participating businesses and ensure that valuations align with realistic growth projections.

Examples and Case Studies

1. Dot-Com Bubble (1999-2000)

- **The Hype**: The late 1990s saw a massive surge of interest in internet-based companies, as investors believed the internet would revolutionize commerce and communication. Companies without proven business models, like Pets.com, achieved billion-dollar valuations based on potential rather than actual performance.

- **The Collapse**: By two thousand, many companies failed to deliver sustainable profits, leading to a market crash that wiped out trillions of dollars in value. While the internet trend itself was sound, inflated valuations during the early hype phase led to significant investor losses.

- **Key Lesson**: The internet trend proved transformative, but only companies like Amazon, which had solid execution and realistic valuations, survived and thrived.

2. Blockchain and Cryptocurrency Boom of 2017

- **The Hype**: Blockchain technology and cryptocurrencies like Bitcoin and Ethereum attracted immense interest, with thousands of Initial Coin Offerings (ICOs) launched. Investors rushed to capitalize on what was seen as the future of finance.

- **The Collapse**: Many ICOs lacked viable business models, leading to a market crash in 2018. Although blockchain remains a promising technology, the hype around unproven projects hurt investors who entered at inflated valuations.

- **Key Lesson**: Early blockchain adopters who focused on companies with proven use cases, were better positioned for long-term gains compared to those chasing speculative projects.

3. Electric Scooters (2018-2019)

- **The Hype**: Companies like Lime and Bird introduced electric scooters as an urban mobility solution. Investors saw these as revolutionary for last-mile transportation, leading to billion-dollar valuations.

- **The Reality**: Many scooter companies struggled with unit economics, high maintenance costs, and regulatory pushback. While the micro-mobility trend continues, the initial hype overestimated the scalability and profitability of these models.

- **Key Lesson**: The early hype led to inflated valuations, and only companies that addressed operational inefficiencies have remained viable.

Early enthusiasm for a trend can lead to excessive valuations, even if the trend is fundamentally sound. Investors must be cautious about entering during the hype phase and focus on businesses with realistic growth prospects and sustainable economics. Trends like the dot-com boom, cryptocurrency mania, and electric scooters illustrate the risks of chasing speculative valuations without sufficient scrutiny.

Short-Term vs. Permanent: The Fine Line in Trend Investing

Insight

Trends often encounter challenges that create the perception of decline, but not all slowdowns signal a permanent shift. Some issues are temporary hurdles caused by external factors such as economic cycles, supply chain disruptions, or changing market conditions. Others may result from internal challenges within key businesses driving the trend, such as management missteps or execution inefficiencies. Investors must investigate the root causes of these challenges to determine whether they are transitory or indicative of a deeper issue.

Examples and Case Studies

1. **Netflix's Subscriber Loss in 2022**

    - **The Challenge**: Netflix faced a significant drop in subscriber numbers, with nearly 1.2 million cancellations in the first two quarters of 2022. This decline sparked concerns about the OTT trend's sustainability, particularly with increasing competition from platforms like Disney+ and HBO Max. Investors questioned whether streaming was losing its appeal.

    - **The Recovery**: Netflix identified key issues such as account-sharing practices and a lack of pricing flexibility. By introducing an ad-supported subscription tier and cracking down on password sharing, the company stabilized its subscriber base. The broader streaming trend remained robust, with global OTT consumption continuing to grow.

- **Lesson**: Temporary declines often require companies to adapt to external pressures. In this case, Netflix's actions ensured the trend resumed its growth trajectory.

2. **Electric Vehicles (EVs): Supply Chain and Economic Cycles**

- **The Challenge**: The EV market has periodically faced slowdowns due to raw material shortages, rising battery costs, or economic downturns. For instance, during the COVID-19 pandemic, supply chain disruptions limited production capacity, leading to reduced sales and a temporary decline in consumer confidence.

- **The Recovery**: As governments offered incentives and battery costs began to fall, adoption resumed. Companies like Tesla and BYD adapted to these challenges, while infrastructure improvements supported long-term growth in the EV trend.

- **Lesson**: Temporary hurdles like economic cycles or supply constraints are not always indicative of a fading trend. Strategic adaptation by key players can ensure growth continuity.

3. **E-commerce in the Post-Pandemic Era**

- **The Challenge**: E-commerce platforms experienced exponential growth during the pandemic, but as physical stores reopened, online sales growth slowed. Investors speculated that the trend might have peaked.

- **The Recovery**: While growth normalized, platforms like Amazon and Flipkart focused on hybrid models like click-and-collect and enhancing logistics for better consumer experiences. The overall penetration of online retail continues to rise globally.

- **Lesson**: A temporary slowdown often reflects market adjustments rather than the decline of a trend.

Temporary hurdles are common in any trend's lifecycle. Recognizing whether these challenges are short-term issues or permanent shifts requires a detailed understanding of growth drivers and external factors. By distinguishing between the two, investors can make better decisions and capitalize on opportunities during periods of doubt.

Not All that Glitters Scales: The Struggles Within Visible Trends

Insight

Not all businesses thrive, even within strong and visible trends. While a trend may appear sustainable and scalable, businesses operating within it may face challenges in scaling effectively or achieving profitability. This can occur due to factors such as intense competition, operational inefficiencies, excessive costs, or an inability to adapt to market dynamics. Sometimes, the trend itself may fade over time, leaving businesses struggling to find a viable market.

Investors need to evaluate whether companies within a trend can execute effectively and sustain growth. Key factors to assess include scalability, cost management, differentiation, and the ability to adapt to changing market conditions.

Examples and Case Studies

1. **Wearable Technology: High Growth but Narrow Profitability**

   - **The Trend**: Wearable devices like fitness trackers and smartwatches gained traction as consumers sought health and lifestyle monitoring tools. Companies like Fitbit initially captured significant market share.

   - **The Struggle**: Intense competition from larger players like Apple and Samsung, coupled with high production costs and limited differentiation, led to challenges for smaller players. Fitbit, for example, struggled with declining market share and was eventually acquired by Google in 2021.

   - **The Lesson**: A strong trend alone does not guarantee business success. Companies must differentiate themselves and manage costs to thrive within competitive markets.

2. **OTT Platforms: Subscription Fatigue and Fierce Competition**

   - **The Trend**: Streaming platforms like Netflix, Disney+, and Amazon Prime Video capitalized on the growing demand for on-demand entertainment, especially during the COVID-19 pandemic. The shift from traditional cable to OTT (over-the-top) platforms marked a visible and strong trend.

   - **The Struggle**: Smaller platforms, such as Quibi, failed to survive despite significant funding and high-profile launches. Challenges included subscription fatigue, poor content differentiation, and an inability to compete with larger, well-established players. Quibi shut down just six months after its launch, illustrating the perils of entering a saturated market without a clear edge.

- **The Lesson**: In trends like OTT, where the competition is intense, content quality, customer retention strategies, and strong execution are critical for long-term survival.

3. **EdTech (Byju's): Challenges Within a Booming Trend**

- **The Trend**: EdTech gained momentum as digital learning platforms emerged to meet the growing demand for flexible, accessible education. Companies like Byju's capitalized on this trend by offering online courses, personalized learning, and test preparation tools. The COVID-19 pandemic further accelerated the adoption of digital learning globally, with significant investor enthusiasm around the sector.

- **The Struggle**: Despite its early success and rapid growth, Byju's faced mounting challenges as it scaled. Key issues included Aggressive acquisitions, such as Whitehat Jr. and Aakash Institute, led to high debt and integration challenges. The company heavily invested in marketing, customer acquisition, and discounts to sustain its growth, leading to mounting operational losses. Allegations of aggressive sales tactics and complaints from parents about misleading practices tarnished the company's reputation.

- **The Lesson**: Byju's journey underscores the risks of prioritizing growth at all costs. In visible trends like EdTech, success requires balancing aggressive expansion with operational efficiency, transparency, and long-term profitability. It also highlights the importance of adapting to post-trend normalization as external factors (like the pandemic) evolve.

Visible and scalable trends do not guarantee successful businesses. Investors should focus on companies that demonstrate strong execution, cost efficiency, and the ability to differentiate in competitive environments. Understanding these dynamics can help identify winners within a trend rather than relying on the trend itself for investment success.

The Global Mosaic: How Trends Differ Across Geographies

Insight

Trends do not evolve uniformly across geographies. Differences in demographics, cultural norms, economic fundamentals, consumption habits, and technological readiness create distinct growth trajectories for trends in different regions. While a trend may thrive in one country, it may develop more slowly—or not at all—in another. Even when trends are similar across geographies, the timing of their adoption can vary significantly based on local conditions.

For investors, understanding these geographic nuances is critical to identifying opportunities and avoiding misjudgements. Trends need to be analysed through a localized lens to evaluate their scalability and sustainability in different markets.

Examples and Case Studies

1. **E-Commerce in India vs. the USA**

    - **India:** The e-commerce trend in India has been shaped by its mobile-first internet penetration, price-sensitive consumers, and reliance on cash-on-delivery payment methods. Platforms like Flipkart and Amazon India have tailored their offerings to cater to regional preferences, including deep discounts and regional language interfaces.

Growth has been fuelled by rising digital literacy and improved logistics networks.

- **USA**: In contrast, e-commerce in the USA matured earlier, with platforms like Amazon leading due to widespread credit card adoption, strong logistics, and consumer trust in online payments. The trend focused more on convenience and seamless digital experiences rather than affordability.

- **Lesson**: While e-commerce is a global trend, its development in India and the USA highlights how local factors—such as payment methods and consumer behaviour—can drive differences in growth trajectories.

2. Electric Vehicles (EVs) in China vs. Europe

- **China**: The Chinese government's aggressive push for EV adoption through subsidies, incentives, and support for domestic manufacturers like BYD has made China the largest EV market globally. The trend is driven by urban pollution concerns and a focus on reducing oil dependency.

- **Europe**: EV adoption in Europe is driven by stricter emission standards and the urgency of achieving carbon-neutral goals. Countries like Norway, where 80% of new car sales are EVs, have implemented high taxes on fossil fuel vehicles alongside extensive subsidies for EV buyers.

- **Lesson**: Both regions share the EV trend, but China's focus on domestic manufacturing and Europe's emphasis on sustainability reflect differing local priorities.

3. Cashless Payments in Japan vs. India

- **Japan**: Despite being a technologically advanced country, Japan has been slow to adopt cashless payments due to cultural preferences for cash and an efficient cash-handling system. Mobile payment adoption, while growing, remains secondary to physical cash use.

- **India**: The shift to digital payments in India accelerated after the 2016 demonetization initiative, which limited cash availability. Platforms like UPI, Paytm, and Google Pay have become dominant due to affordability, government support, and a young, tech-savvy population.

- **Lesson**: While cashless payments are a global trend, cultural and economic factors have created vastly different adoption curves in these regions.

4. Renewable Energy in Europe vs. the Middle East

- **Europe**: Renewable energy adoption in Europe is driven by strict environmental regulations and carbon-neutral goals. Countries like Germany and Denmark are pioneers in wind and solar energy adoption.

- **Middle East**: While the Middle East is beginning to invest in renewable energy, the region's abundant fossil fuel reserves and lower immediate need for energy diversification mean its focus is on long-term sustainability rather than immediate adoption.

- **Lesson**: The timing and emphasis on renewable energy differ significantly based on local resource availability and policy priorities.

Geographic differences in trends underscore the importance of localized analysis. Investors must consider factors like culture, economic conditions, and regulatory environments to understand how a trend will evolve in a specific region. Trends like e-commerce, EVs, and renewable energy demonstrate how the same trend can manifest differently across geographies.

The Waiting Game: When Trends Need Time, Resources, and Support

Insight

Certain trends, even when visible and scalable, often require the right conditions to play out fully. These conditions may include affordability, supportive infrastructure, regulatory support, technological readiness, or cultural acceptance. Recognizing a trend is only one part of the investment process; understanding whether the environment is conducive to its growth and sustainability is equally critical.

Investors must evaluate the timing of a trend by analysing factors like cost evolution, infrastructure readiness, and external catalysts that can accelerate or hinder adoption. Investing too early, before these conditions align, can result in missed opportunities or prolonged wait times for returns.

Examples and Case Studies

1. **Electric Vehicles (EVs): Waiting for Cost Parity and Infrastructure**

   - **The Trend**: EVs have been a visible trend for decades, with clear environmental and economic benefits. However, widespread adoption was delayed due to high battery costs and insufficient charging infrastructure.

   - **The Right Conditions**: The EV market gained momentum once battery technology improved, making EVs more affordable. Additionally, government incentives and investments in charging infrastructure created an ecosystem conducive to growth. Companies like Tesla benefited by scaling at the right moment when these conditions aligned.

- **The Lesson**: Early recognition of the EV trend was insightful, but waiting for affordability and infrastructure readiness was critical for large-scale adoption.

2. **Solar Power in Developing Markets: Innovation in Financing**

   - **The Trend**: Solar energy has been a viable alternative for decades, but adoption in developing countries was slow due to high upfront costs and limited access to financing.

   - **The Right Conditions**: The introduction of innovative financing models like pay-as-you-go solar systems, coupled with falling solar panel prices, enabled mass adoption in regions like Africa and India. Companies such as M-KOPA revolutionized access to solar power for low-income households.

   - **The Lesson**: Recognizing the potential of solar power was only part of the equation. Understanding affordability and financing challenges was key to unlocking its growth in underserved markets.

3. **5G Technology: Aligning Network and Device Compatibility**

   - **The Trend**: 5G networks promise transformative applications in IoT, autonomous vehicles, and smart cities. However, the rollout has been dependent on significant investments in network infrastructure and compatible devices.

   - **The Right Conditions**: The adoption of 5G accelerated as telecom companies invested in infrastructure and smartphone manufacturers began offering 5G-enabled devices at affordable prices. Regions like South Korea and China, which prioritized infrastructure development, became early leaders in 5G deployment.

- **The Lesson**: While the potential of 5G was evident early on, its scalability required infrastructure and device compatibility to reach mass adoption.

4. **Green Hydrogen: Technology and Policy Support**

- **The Trend**: Green hydrogen has the potential to decarbonize industries like steel, cement, and shipping. However, production costs and the lack of infrastructure have historically limited its adoption.

- **The Right Conditions**: Governments are now offering subsidies and investing in hydrogen production technology, creating a more favourable environment. For example, the European Union's Green Deal includes significant funding for hydrogen projects.

- **The Lesson**: Early-stage investments in green hydrogen depended heavily on the right combination of technology advances and supportive policies.

Visible trends often require specific conditions to scale sustainably. Investors must assess factors like cost, infrastructure, and external catalysts to determine the right timing for an investment. Trends like EVs, solar power, and 5G illustrate the importance of waiting for the environment to align before committing capital.

Small Giants: Betting on Companies with Proven Traction

Insight

When investing in trends, identifying small companies that are already profitable or gaining strong traction can be a winning strategy. These businesses often have the ability to adapt quickly to market demands and the scalability to grow as the trend expands. A proven, replicable concept significantly reduces the risks associated with execution and demonstrates that the company has found a product-market fit.

Focusing on profitability and traction ensures that the company has overcome early-stage hurdles, such as high customer acquisition costs or inefficient operations. By targeting such businesses, investors can capitalize on both the growth potential of the trend and the operational maturity of the company.

Examples and Case Studies

1. Tesla in the Early EV Trend

- **Why Tesla Stood Out**: In its initial stages, Tesla demonstrated traction through its innovative EV models like the Roadster and Model S. Although the EV trend was still developing, Tesla showed a scalable and replicable business model, supported by growing demand and proprietary battery technology.

- **The Result**: Tesla's early profitability and technological leadership allowed it to dominate the EV market, even as competitors struggled with scaling and cost management.

2. Nykaa in India's E-Commerce Trend

- **Why Nykaa Stood Out**: As a beauty-focused e-commerce platform, Nykaa differentiated itself by focusing on a niche market and demonstrating profitability before scaling further. Its omnichannel approach (online and offline stores) proved replicable in multiple cities and regions across India.

- **The Result**: Nykaa became a leader in India's beauty and personal care segment, showing that early profitability and strong traction can set the foundation for long-term success.

3. **Zoom During the Remote Work Boom**

    - **Why Zoom Stood Out**: While remote work tools like Microsoft Teams and Google Meet were competing in the same space, Zoom demonstrated early traction by focusing on simplicity, reliability, and ease of use. It scaled rapidly as the remote work trend accelerated during the pandemic.

    - **The Result**: Zoom's replicable and user-friendly model helped it capture significant market share and establish a strong brand identity, even in a crowded market.

Investing in small, profitable companies with proven, replicable business models allows investors to reduce risks while capitalizing on a trend's growth potential. Businesses like Tesla, Nykaa, and Zoom demonstrate how traction and scalability can set the stage for long-term success.

The Pivot Advantage: When Old Players Join New Trends

Insight

Not all trends require identifying fresh players for investment opportunities. Often, established businesses transition to adopt new technologies, offerings, or products as part of the trend. These transitions allow well-established companies to leverage their existing infrastructure, customer base, and brand recognition, enabling them to pivot or expand more efficiently than startups.

Small to mid-sized companies, in particular, tend to be more agile in adapting to new trends due to less bureaucratic inertia. Identifying which established players are transitioning faster can be a valuable approach, as these companies often combine the stability of proven business models with the growth potential of latest trends.

Examples and Case Studies

1. Microsoft's Pivot to Cloud Computing

- **The Transition**: In the early 2010s, Microsoft recognized the growing importance of cloud computing and transitioned its core business to focus on cloud-based services, including Azure. This shift allowed Microsoft to remain competitive as businesses moved away from traditional software licensing models to cloud-based subscriptions.

- **The Result**: By adopting cloud computing early, Microsoft became a leader in the trend, generating significant revenue growth and diversifying its business model.

2. Maruti Suzuki's Shift Toward Electric Vehicles

- **The Transition**: As the EV trend gained traction in India, Maruti Suzuki, a leader in the internal combustion engine market, began investing in hybrid and electric technologies. While startups were entering the market, Maruti leveraged its extensive dealer network and customer base to position itself for the transition.

- **The Result**: Maruti Suzuki demonstrated how established players can use their existing strengths to pivot into emerging trends while maintaining market dominance.

3. Nike's Digital Transformation

- **The Transition**: Recognizing the rise of e-commerce and digital-first consumer behaviour, Nike invested heavily in its direct-to-consumer (DTC) channels and digital ecosystem, including the Nike app and online customization tools.

- **The Result**: Nike successfully adapted to the e-commerce trend, growing its digital sales significantly and strengthening its brand loyalty, even as smaller competitors struggled to achieve similar scale.

4. **Tata Power in Renewable Energy**

- **The Transition**: As renewable energy gained momentum, Tata Power transitioned its focus from traditional power generation to solar, wind, and green energy solutions. It capitalized on its reputation and resources to lead India's renewable energy market.

- **The Result**: Tata Power became a key player in India's renewable energy sector, leveraging its existing capabilities to adapt to the trend.

Established players transitioning into latest trends can be excellent investment opportunities, especially if they adapt quickly and leverage their existing strengths. Companies like Microsoft, Maruti Suzuki, and Nike illustrate how agility within established businesses can lead to significant growth within emerging trends.

Mapping the Value Chain: Investing in Trend Ecosystems

Insight

When a trend begins, companies entering the market often rely on imported raw materials and underdeveloped supply chains. This dependence can increase costs and slow adoption. However, as the trend gains traction, ancillary players, intermediates, and raw material providers begin to establish themselves, creating a localized and more efficient value chain. Understanding the entire value chain economics is critical for investors to identify which players are best positioned to benefit as the trend matures.

Strategically betting on companies across the value chain—such as raw material suppliers, component manufacturers, or final product producers—can help investors diversify their exposure while maximizing returns.

Examples and Case Studies

1. **Electric Vehicles: The Evolution of Battery Supply Chains**

    - **Early Stage**: In the initial stages, EV manufacturers like Tesla relied on imported lithium-ion batteries, which added significant costs. The supply chain was dominated by a few global players, primarily from China, South Korea, and Japan.

    - **Later Stage**: As the trend grew, battery manufacturers like CATL and LG Chem expanded operations globally, and new players entered the lithium, cobalt, and nickel mining sectors. Companies focused on battery recycling also emerged, creating a more robust supply chain.

    - **Investor Opportunity**: Investors who identified opportunities in battery materials, recycling, or localized battery production benefited significantly as the EV trend matured.

2. **Solar Energy: From Imported Panels to Local Manufacturing**

    - **Early Stage**: Solar energy adoption in many countries began with importing photovoltaic (PV) panels from China, which dominated global production.

    - **Later Stage**: As adoption increased, local manufacturers like Adani Solar in India and First Solar in the USA began producing panels domestically, supported by government incentives. Ancillary industries such as inverters, mounting systems, and installation services also flourished.

- **Investor Opportunity**: Understanding the value chain dynamics allowed investors to capitalize on upstream opportunities like polysilicon production and downstream opportunities like installation services.

3. **Pharmaceuticals: Contract Manufacturing Organizations (CMOs)**

   - **Early Stage**: During the initial outsourcing wave, pharmaceutical companies relied on importing active pharmaceutical ingredients (APIs) from countries with strong manufacturing bases like China and India.

   - **Later Stage**: Over time, local CMOs and API manufacturers emerged, building efficient supply chains. Companies like Divi's Laboratories and Laurus Labs in India became global leaders in the pharmaceutical value chain.

   - **Investor Opportunity**: Betting on CMOs and API manufacturers provided consistent returns as these companies grew alongside the trend of pharmaceutical outsourcing.

Understanding the evolution of the value chain is essential when investing in emerging trends. As trends mature, players across the supply chain, from raw materials to final products, create new opportunities. Investors should assess the economics of each segment to strategically position themselves for long-term gains.

It is Cyclical Afterall: The Nature of Sector Matters

Insight

Evolving trends often have an inherent cyclical nature that investors must account for when evaluating their growth potential.

While a trend may represent a long-term structural shift, the industries it affects may experience periodic ups and downs due to external factors such as economic cycles, consumer sentiment, or resource availability. Recognizing these cycles allows investors to make more informed decisions, avoiding overestimation of short-term growth or mistaking temporary slowdowns for fading trends.

Understanding the interplay between long-term structural trends and short-term cyclical fluctuations is essential. For example, electric vehicles (EVs) represent a transformational trend shaping the future of mobility, but car buying remains cyclical, tied to economic conditions, interest rates, and consumer confidence.

Examples and Case Studies

1. **Electric Vehicles (EVs): Long-Term Growth Amid Cyclical Car Buying Patterns**

   - **The Trend**: EV adoption is driven by sustainability, technological advancements, and government incentives.

   - **The Cyclical Nature**: Despite the long-term upward trajectory, car sales are inherently cyclical, influenced by factors like economic slowdowns, high-interest rates, and fuel price fluctuations. For instance, during the COVID-19 pandemic, car sales declined globally, impacting EV sales as well, despite growing interest in sustainable transportation.

   - **The Lesson**: Investors in the EV trend must be mindful of broader automotive cycles while maintaining confidence in the trend's long-term potential.

2. **Renewable Energy: Solar Power's Sensitivity to Policy and Prices**

   - **The Trend**: Solar energy adoption continues to grow due to falling costs and climate change mitigation efforts.

   - **The Cyclical Nature**: Renewable energy investments are often tied to government policies and subsidy cycles.

When incentives are reduced or withdrawn, adoption may slow temporarily. For example, cuts in subsidies in Europe during the 2010s led to a short-term decline in solar installations.

- **The Lesson**: While solar energy remains a long-term trend, investors must consider the policy-driven cyclical dynamics that influence short-term adoption rates.

3. **Real Estate: Trends in Green Buildings and Sustainable Architecture**

- **The Trend**: Sustainable and energy-efficient buildings are becoming the norm in real estate development.

- **The Cyclical Nature**: Real estate cycles, driven by interest rates, inflation, and economic conditions, can impact the pace of adoption for green building practices. During economic downturns, developers may prioritize cost-cutting over sustainability investments.

- **The Lesson**: Understanding how macroeconomic factors influence adoption timelines helps investors time their entry into the green building trend.

Understanding the cyclical nature of segment/sub segment and alignment/dependence of related sector and their cyclicality would ensure the right investment timing and limited downside. Buying at the top of the cycle and waiting for the investment to realise returns becomes very painful and lead to limited returns.

It is not Static: Innovate to Stay Alive

Insight

Trends are dynamic and rarely remain static. As innovation continues to advance, even trends that appear well-established today can evolve, opening new opportunities for businesses and investors. What seems like a mature trend might still have untapped potential, whether through adjacent applications, emerging consumer behaviours, or technological breakthroughs. Conversely, trends that fail to adapt to changing contexts or innovations can fade into obsolescence.

Recognizing the evolving nature of trends helps investors identify opportunities that may not have been visible initially. It also emphasizes the importance of staying informed about advancements that could reshape or extend a trend's lifecycle.

Examples and Case Studies

1. Social Media: Orkut to Facebook to TikTok

- **The Orkut Era**: In the early 2000s, Orkut was a pioneer in social networking, especially in markets like India and Brazil. However, it failed to innovate, stagnating in user experience and engagement features.

- **The Facebook Revolution**: Facebook capitalized on Orkut's stagnation, offering continuous innovation through features like targeted advertising, integrated messaging, and better user privacy controls.

- **The TikTok Shift**: TikTok revolutionized social media by focusing on short-form video content and algorithm-driven engagement, which appealed to a younger demographic and created entirely new content consumption habits.

- **The Lesson**: Social media as a trend has continually evolved, with each platform addressing gaps in the previous generation's offerings. Investors who recognize such transitions early can capture emerging opportunities.

2. Renewable Energy: The Rise of Green Hydrogen

- **The Initial Trend**: Renewable energy initially focused on solar and wind power, driven by falling costs and rising climate awareness.

- **The Evolution**: With industrial decarbonization becoming a priority, green hydrogen emerged as a solution for hard-to-abate sectors like steel, shipping, and aviation. Governments and corporations worldwide are now investing in green hydrogen production and infrastructure.

- **The Lesson**: Renewable energy's evolution from electricity generation to industrial applications demonstrates how trends can expand into new dimensions, offering fresh opportunities for growth.

Trends evolve with innovation, creating new dimensions and opportunities over time. Staying attuned to these shifts allows investors to identify fresh opportunities and maintain relevance in rapidly changing markets. Let me know if you would like further refinements!

Why Top-Down Approach Makes More Sense

In investment analysis, **top-down** and **bottom-up** are two primary approaches used to identify profitable opportunities. Each method has its strengths, but the top-down approach tends to work better when identifying opportunities within emerging trends. Here is an in-depth look at why this is the case.

1. The Bottom-Up Approach

The **bottom-up approach** begins with an analysis of individual companies, focusing primarily on finding businesses that appear undervalued based on their intrinsic value. Investors using this approach concentrate on a company's fundamentals—its earnings, cash flow, management quality, and competitive position. Once they identify a company that seems undervalued, they may consider the sector or macroeconomic factors, but the primary focus is on the business itself.

- **Advantages of Bottom-Up**: The bottom-up approach is effective for finding undervalued companies, often at valuations below their intrinsic value. Investors who are skilled in company-level analysis can uncover overlooked gems that the market has undervalued, leading to potential gains as the market corrects.

- **Limitations of Bottom-Up**: Finding undervalued companies is challenging and rare. Additionally, bottom-up analysis is backward-looking, focusing heavily on past performance, which may not predict future growth. If the industry or broader market is in decline or facing headwinds, a company's fundamentals alone may not lead to sustained success.

- **Reliance on Sectoral Analysis for Growth**: Even after identifying undervalued companies, investors often need to analyse the sector to evaluate future potential. If a company is in a stagnant or declining industry, the investment's long-term prospects may be limited. In trend-based investing, this can be a disadvantage, as emerging trends usually drive sectoral or macro growth rather than isolated company growth.

2. The Top-Down Approach

In the **top-down approach**, investors begin with a broader view, analysing global, macroeconomic, or sectoral trends to identify areas with growth potential. Once they identify a promising trend or sector, they move down to company-level analysis, selecting individual businesses positioned to benefit from the trend. The top-down approach emphasizes future potential rather than past performance, making it a forward-looking strategy. Once investor identify the trend/sector, investor can look for other parameters to judge the quality and sustainability of the company. (Promoter, their focus, technology/capability, capex plans, balance sheet strength etc).

- **Forward looking**: The top-down approach allows investors to align with emerging trends and high-growth sectors, reducing dependence on past performance. By focusing on industries with strong growth drivers, investors position themselves for gains from broader market dynamics, especially in sectors experiencing transformation or high demand.

- **Flexibility with Market Conditions**: The top-down approach does not rely on finding undervalued companies within all sectors; instead, it emphasizes finding opportunities where macroeconomic conditions support growth. By identifying sectors with favourable market conditions, investors can improve their chances of success without relying solely on intrinsic valuation discrepancies.

- **Ideal for Trend-Based Investing**: Because the top-down approach emphasizes sector and macro analysis, it aligns well with trend-based investing. Investors can track broad movements, such as digital transformation, sustainability, or health tech, and invest in companies likely to benefit from these trends. This method also supports the identification of niche sectors that have growth potential within larger trends, even if they lack a history of high performance.

Why the Top-Down Approach Works Better for Trend Investing

- **Focus on Future Potential**: Trend investing relies on understanding where markets are heading, not where they have been. The top-down approach allows investors to capitalize on emerging trends by identifying sectors with high growth potential before evaluating individual companies.

- **Adaptability to Changing Market Conditions**: Trends evolve, and the top-down approach offers flexibility to pivot as new information emerges. Investors can monitor changing macroeconomic or regulatory factors, then adjust their portfolios to align with sectors that benefit from those shifts. This adaptability allows investors to stay relevant and make timely decisions in line with evolving trends, rather than relying on past performance.

- **Reduces Dependence on Historical Performance**: A top-down approach is inherently forward-looking, reducing the focus on historical metrics. When investing in emerging trends, historical performance may not reflect a company's future potential, especially in new sectors with limited performance history.

- **Minimizes the Risk of Value Traps**: Bottom-up analysis can sometimes lead to "value traps," where a company appears undervalued but lacks growth potential due to weak sector fundamentals or macro headwinds. By focusing on sectors and trends with strong tailwinds, top-down investors minimize exposure to companies that may look good on paper but lack sustainable demand.

- **Greater Alignment with Trend Cycles**: Top-down investing aligns with the life cycles of trends, allowing investors to enter sectors in their early growth phases, benefit through maturity, and exit as the trend declines. By tracking the broader trend cycle, investors can capture gains by aligning with growth sectors at the right time and diversifying as sectors reach peak maturity.

For investors interested in capitalizing on latest trends, the top-down approach offers a flexible, forward-looking strategy that emphasizes adaptability and minimizes risk. As trends evolve and new sectors emerge, this approach provides a reliable framework for navigating complex markets and capturing the full potential of future growth.

Evaluating Early Stage and Growth Businesses (After Trend Identification)

Investing in early-stage and growth businesses is a unique challenge, especially for investors accustomed to assessing mature companies with robust financial histories. Unlike established firms, these businesses often lack the traditional metrics that provide a sense of stability and predictability, such as consistent revenue streams, past execution records, or long-term profitability trends. This makes evaluating them a more nuanced process, blending qualitative judgment with calculative foresight.

One of the most significant challenges is the absence of historical financial data. Established companies typically offer a track record of revenue growth, Return on Equity (ROE), and profit margins that help investors gauge their performance and efficiency over time. In contrast, early-stage companies often operate with little to no profit, cash flows as they prioritize growth and market capture over immediate returns.

Another hurdle is the unproven execution capability. While founders might have ambitious plans and market-disrupting ideas, their ability to execute those plans effectively remains largely speculative. Investors must rely on indirect indicators, such as the management team's background, experience, and demonstrated passion, to assess the likelihood of successful execution.

The lack of operating leverage data also complicates matters. Early-stage businesses may not yet have reached the scale where fixed costs decline as a percentage of revenue, leaving their cost structures relatively inefficient. This absence of clarity can make it difficult to forecast future profitability or operational efficiency.

Customer validation and market acceptance are other areas where clarity is often missing. Unlike mature businesses that have built brand loyalty and a solid recurring customer base, early-stage firms are still in the process of proving product-market fit or they are yet to establish a concrete brand. Even with initial traction, the sustainability of their growth often remains uncertain.

Further, external economic and industry forces are unpredictable at this stage. Disruptive technologies, competitive threats, or regulatory changes could drastically alter the trajectory of these businesses. Without past performance as a buffer, these companies are especially vulnerable to external shocks.

Lastly, the valuation conundrum looms large. Valuing early-stage companies is often more of an art than a science. With limited financial metrics to rely on, investors must estimate market potential, growth trajectories, and competitive positioning—all of which involve significant subjectivity and risk.

In summary, early-stage and growth businesses may operate with high upfront costs, limited historical data, and uncertain scalability, making conventional valuation methods like DCF inadequate.

Evaluating early-stage and growth businesses requires investors to step outside their comfort zones, adopting a mindset that blends analytical rigor with a strong capacity for envisioning the future.

While the lack of traditional metrics adds complexity, it also presents opportunities for those willing to embrace the challenge and recognize potential before it becomes widely apparent.

Young businesses in trend-driven markets often trade more on future potential than current performance. This requires investors to focus on forward-looking indicators such as market size, trend momentum, and scalability rather than profitability. Additionally, valuations in such cases may be influenced heavily by market sentiment and competitive pressures, leading to overvaluations or underestimations.

Examples

- **Challenge of Valuing Tesla in Its Early Days**: In its early years, Tesla faced scepticism due to high capital requirements and long timelines to profitability. Traditional models would have undervalued the company, failing to account for its disruptive potential in the EV trend.

- **Overvaluation of WeWork:** WeWork was valued at nearly $47 billion at its peak, driven by hype around the co-working space trend. Traditional profitability metrics were overlooked, leading to a valuation bubble that eventually burst.

Investors evaluating early-stage and growth businesses face a dual challenge: assessing **qualitative aspects** that provide a holistic understanding of the business's foundation and **quantitative aspects** that anchor decisions in data. Since early-stage businesses often lack detailed financial records, it is crucial to prioritize qualitative evaluation and attempt to translate these insights into actionable numbers.

1. Qualitative Evaluation: Laying the Foundation

Qualitative factors form the backbone of early-stage business evaluation, providing essential insights into the company's potential, team dynamics, and strategic alignment with its market.

1.1 Vision and Growth Potential

Understanding the company's vision and its potential for growth is critical to evaluating whether it can sustain and thrive in the long run.

- **Problem-Solution Fit**: Assess if the business addresses a real, pervasive problem with a clear, unique value proposition. Validate the relevance and scalability of the problem and whether the proposed solution will remain viable in the foreseeable future. Ask:

  - Is this a current and future pain point for a sizable market?

  - Is the solution simple, effective, and adaptable to changing market needs?

- **Market Opportunity:**

  - Estimate the Total Addressable Market (TAM), Serviceable Addressable Market (SAM), and Serviceable Obtainable Market (SOM).

  - Evaluate the business's ability to penetrate the market effectively. Is there room for the company to carve out a significant niche?

- **Market Growth**:

  - Study trends in the target market, factoring in the scale of the problem and anticipated adoption of the proposed solution.

  - Identify macro and micro tailwinds (e.g., regulatory shifts, societal behaviour changes) and headwinds (e.g., economic slowdowns, competition) that could affect growth.

- **Trend Alignment**: Ensure the company aligns with sustainable trends rather than fads. Look for trends with:

- Clear long-term viability.

- Evidence of growing or consistent consumer demand.

- Tailwinds that indicate compounding growth opportunities.

1.2 Management Team

A strong management team is often the cornerstone of successful execution. Analyse their capabilities, experience, and strategic approach.

- **Experience and Expertise**:

  - Review the team's track record, domain knowledge, and success in similar roles.

  - Assess whether the leadership team is diverse, including operational, technical, and strategic expertise.

- **Ambition and Vision**:

  - Observe the leadership's ability to think long-term and articulate a clear vision for scaling the business.

  - Ensure the ambition is balanced with realistic expectations and a structured approach to execution.

  - Check whether the entrepreneurs (especially third generation) are hungry and motivated.

- **Integrity and Transparency**:

  - Look for consistent communication with stakeholders (investors, employees, customers).

  - Evaluate whether the leadership displays accountability during challenging situations.

- **Execution Capability**:

  - Look for successful execution of early strategies, such as launching MVPs, acquiring early customers, or securing initial funding.

- Assess whether the team quickly learns from failures and iterates effectively.

- **Resilience:** Evaluate how the management navigates major events, including macroeconomic or industry-specific challenges. Leaders who make sound decisions during turbulent times are more likely to succeed long-term.

- **Skin in the Game**:

  - Check the promoters' investments and equity proportions to gauge their commitment.

  - Assess whether compensation structures are performance-linked, signalling alignment with company success.

1.3 Competitive Advantage

The presence of sustainable competitive advantages ensures the company can maintain a strong position in its market.

- **Unique Differentiators**:

  - Identify features like proprietary technology, intellectual property (patents), or operational efficiencies that set the company apart.

  - Evaluate whether these advantages create tangible value for customers.

- **Barriers to Entry**:

  - Assess the difficulty for competitors to replicate the business model or product quality.

  - Look for high switching costs or first-mover advantages in niche markets.

- **Customer Loyalty**:
  - Look for signs of customer retention and repeat business.
  - Assess whether early customers are becoming advocates or evangelists for the product/service.

1.4 Customer Validation and Market Feedback

Feedback from actual users and the market offers valuable validation of the company's early efforts.

- **Customer and Personal Reviews**:
  - Analyse customer testimonials, ratings, and reviews.
  - If possible, use the company's product/service to gain firsthand insight into its quality and value.

- **Retention Metrics**:
  - Early customer retention can signal satisfaction and potential for recurring revenue.
  - Look at Net Promoter Scores (NPS) or Customer Lifetime Value (CLV) as indicators.

- **Client/Customer Diversification**:
  - Assess whether the business relies on a small number of large clients or has diversified its customer base.
  - Diversification reduces dependency risk and signals scalability potential.

- **Client, Supplier, Employee, and Competitors' Feedback**
  - Feedback and reviews from the stakeholders associated with the organization can tell you lot more about their quality and ethics of work

- Competitors can tell you about how different/unique their offerings and associated risks.

1.5 Scalability and Operational Model

A scalable business model with operational robustness is critical for long-term success.

- **Business Model Robustness**:

  - Examine how the company generates revenue and whether its pricing strategies are sustainable.

  - Ensure the operational model supports scalability without significant dilution of quality or efficiency.

- **Technology Adoption**:

  - Evaluate how the company leverages technology for growth, whether in automation, customer acquisition, or operational efficiency.

  - Check for forward-looking strategies like AI integration or platform scalability.

- **Staying Ahead of the Curve**:

  - Determine whether the company is proactive in understanding customer pain points and offers solutions that address evolving needs.

  - Assess their ability to anticipate market shifts and pivot or innovate accordingly.

2. Quantitative Evaluation: Validating the Foundation

While qualitative factors provide a narrative, quantitative metrics validate whether the business can execute its vision. These data points highlight financial health, scalability, and operational efficiency, enabling more precise investment decisions.

2.1 Revenue Growth and Patterns

Revenue trends are a direct indicator of market traction and the company's ability to capture demand.

- **Top-Line Growth**:

  - Monitor monthly, quarterly, or annual revenue growth rates. Consistent and accelerating growth suggests strong demand and effective market execution.

  - Pay attention to seasonality or cyclical trends to assess whether growth is sustainable.

- **Recurring Revenue**:

  - Businesses with subscription-based or contractual revenue models often provide predictable and stable income streams, reducing revenue volatility.

  - Evaluate customer retention rates and churn rates, as they directly affect recurring revenue stability.

2.2 Margins

Margins reflect the company's operational efficiency and ability to generate profits.

- **Gross Margins**:

  - High gross margins indicate strong pricing power and efficient cost management of goods sold.

  - Compare margins with industry benchmarks to determine competitive positioning.

- **Contribution Margins**:

  - Evaluate the profit generated per unit of product sold or service rendered, after deducting variable costs.

  - Positive contribution margins suggest that scaling will improve overall profitability.

- **Future Margin Potential**:
  - Identify opportunities for margin improvement, such as achieving economies of scale, reducing input costs, or optimizing processes.
  - Consider whether the business can command higher margins as it gains market dominance.

2.3 Operating Leverage

Operating leverage assesses the business's ability to improve profitability as it scales.

- **Fixed vs. Variable Costs**:
  - Analyse the proportion of fixed costs (e.g., rent, salaries) versus variable costs (e.g., materials, commissions). Higher fixed costs can lead to greater profit gains as revenue grows.

- **Break-Even Analysis**:
  - Calculate the break-even point, where revenue covers all fixed and variable costs. This helps in understanding the minimum scale required for profitability.
  - Assess whether the business has passed or is close to its break-even stage.

2.4 Market Share and Traction

These metrics reflect the company's competitive position and growth potential.

- **Market Penetration**:
  - Compare the company's revenue or customer base to the total addressable market (TAM). A low penetration rate indicates significant room for growth.

- **Early Traction**:
  - Evaluate key indicators like user adoption rates, sales velocity, or expansion into new geographies.
  - Monitor customer acquisition trends and how effectively the company is expanding its customer base.

2.5 Financial Resilience

Financial stability is critical, especially for early-stage companies operating in competitive or volatile markets.

- **Burn Rate**:
  - Measure monthly cash consumption. A high burn rate relative to revenue growth could indicate inefficiencies or unsustainable operations.

- **Cash Runway**:
  - Calculate how long the business can sustain operations without raising additional capital.
  - Assess whether the company's cash runway aligns with its growth and funding milestones.

2.6 Efficiency Metrics

Efficiency metrics assess how effectively the company allocates resources to drive growth.

- **CAC to LTV Ratio**: Compare the Customer Acquisition Cost (CAC) to the Customer Lifetime Value (LTV). A healthy ratio (e.g., 1:3 or higher) indicates efficient customer acquisition and long-term profitability.

- **Sales Efficiency**: Evaluate the amount of revenue generated per dollar spent on sales and marketing. High sales efficiency suggests strong demand generation and effective marketing strategies.

2.7 Valuation Metrics

Valuation metrics ensure the business is priced appropriately compared to peers and market expectations.

- **Comparable Valuations**: Use multiples like Enterprise Value (EV) to Revenue, EV to EBITDA, or Price-to-Sales ratios of similar companies within the same industry. Adjust for growth rates, margins, and market positioning when comparing. Comparing market value or entire business valuation against the possible size of opportunities is another rough way to check the valuation.

- **Revenue Multiples**: Early-stage companies are often valued based on revenue rather than earnings. High-growth sectors might command higher revenue multiples, but these should still align with fundamentals.

- **Discounted Cash Flow (DCF)**: For more established growth businesses, project future cash flows and discount them to present value. This method is more comprehensive for assessing intrinsic value. Do not prefer this method for early-stage businesses and early growth businesses.

- **Replacement/Cost to Duplicate:** Time, opportunity cost and money required to duplicate the similar kind of business define the value of the business.

2.8 Scalability and Growth Indicators

Quantitative measures that indicate whether the business can scale profitably over time.

- **Productivity Metrics**:
  - Revenue per employee or revenue per user can highlight operational productivity.

- Evaluate whether growth leads to proportionate increases in productivity or whether operational inefficiencies emerge at scale.

- **Geographic Expansion**:

  - Revenue or user growth across regions indicates scalability and adaptability to new markets.

  - Assess whether the company has established strategies for entering and sustaining operations in new geographies.

- **Customer Concentration**:

  - Analyse whether revenue is overly dependent on a few key clients. A diversified customer base reduces risk and improves resilience.

By combining these quantitative metrics with earlier qualitative insights, investors can create a comprehensive picture of a company's financial health, growth trajectory, and ability to scale. This structured approach ensures a balanced evaluation of potential opportunities and risks. Let me know if you would like further refinements!

3. Blending Qualitative and Quantitative Insights

3.1 Prioritizing What Matters

Investors need to identify which qualitative factors can most directly influence quantitative metrics. For example:

- A strong management team (qualitative) can accelerate top-line growth (quantitative).

- High customer satisfaction (qualitative) correlates with retention and lifetime value (quantitative).

3.2 Building a Narrative

Integrating qualitative and quantitative aspects allows investors to construct a cohesive narrative:

- **The "What"**: What problem is the company solving? (Qualitative)

- **The "How"**: How prudently is the company solving it? (Qualitative)

- **The "Proof"**: What data validates its success? (Quantitative)

Evaluating early-stage businesses requires a delicate balance between understanding the vision and measuring its execution potential. By focusing on qualitative aspects while striving to translate them into quantifiable metrics, investors can make informed decisions that capture the essence of the business and its potential for growth.

Evaluating early-stage and early growth business requires a level approach which enables you to filter the businesses efficiently and save time, and efforts.

Due Diligence Process and Levels

Establishing diligence levels is crucial to expedite, streamline, and optimize the investment filtration process. By implementing a structured due diligence process and segmenting it into distinct tiers, clarity is conferred at the management level regarding sourcing, filtering, and investment decisions.

This approach not only enhances the efficiency of the investment process but also ensures that each stage is comprehensively addressed. The breakdown into various levels facilitates a systematic evaluation, enabling informed decision-making while minimizing risks and maximizing productivity.

The delineation of levels is based on specific parameters guiding the filtration process, the depth of diligence applied, and the sequential steps taken to ascertain the business's potential.

Level – 1: Fundamental Diligence

Following is the data points/ information that the Analyst will have to extract at Level – 1

1. Problem Statement

2. Possible Solution/ Current Available Solution (Market Size, Market Growth)

3. Solution provided by the company (focus area)

4. Business Model and Revenue Model

5. Market size

6. Basic Process Flow/ Value Chain

7. Competition (Basic)

8. Current Traction (Revenue, Margin, User-base, Geography) (Basic)

9. Fund Requirement & Deployment Roadmap (Basic) (When they are looking to raise)

10. Fund Raising History

11. Promoter and Team information (Basic)

12. Expected Valuation

Level – 2: Comprehensive Diligence

Following is the data points/ information that the Analyst will have to extract at Level – 2.

1. Detailed Process Flow/ Value Chain/ Stakeholders, their involvement, and where the product/ service fits in exactly in the value chain.

2.   Detailed analysis of market/segment/sub-segment size (TAM/ SAM/SOM) and growth

3.   Detailed Competitive Scenario (Business Model & Revenue Model of the competitors)

4.   History check – Fundraising, investors, Valuation history, Promoters

5.   Fund Deployment Roadmap

6.   Unit economics analysis and financial analysis

7.   Detailing of Time, Effort, and Money invested in developing MVC, carrying out PoC and areas of Fund Deployment so far (For very early-stage venture).

8.   Analysis of vision, outlook, and business plans

9.   Shareholding pattern

10.   Valuation Check/ Validation

11.   Likely Exit Strategies

Level – 3: Health Check and on Ground Diligence

Following is the data points/ information that the Analyst will have to extract at Level – 3

1.   Financial Modelling and projections

2.   Valuation justification & validation

3.   Cross-verification of data/information

4.   Meeting relevant vendors/suppliers/customers etc

5.   Company visit – Understanding operation and culture.

6.   Cross-Validation of Documents, patents, registrations, licenses

Level – 4: Verification, Negotiations & Decisions (For unlisted)

Following are the actions that the Analyst/lawyer will have to perform at the Level – 4

1. FDD (Financial Due diligence)

2. LDD (Legal Due diligence)

3. Defining the terms, negotiating, and agreeing

4. Comparative analysis with available opportunities/portfolio companies (Portfolio Analysis)

5. SHA (Shareholder agreement)

Method to Calculate Revenue Multiple (RMEV Method)

Evaluating early-stage businesses can be challenging, especially when financials like profitability or historical data are limited. A structured approach that incorporates qualitative parameters and financial metrics can help investors estimate a company's revenue multiple. Additionally, integrating other factors like time and money invested into the business can provide deeper insights into valuation, particularly for companies with insufficient revenue relative to their front-end investments. RMEV method (Revenue Multiple for Early-Stage Ventures) has been developed by the author.

Step 1: Qualitative Parameters as the Foundation

Start by ranking the business on five key qualitative parameters to understand its potential. Each parameter can be scored as High, Medium, or Low, offering clarity on the company's strengths and weaknesses.

1. **Market Size – Problem Size**

   Evaluate the size of the problem the business is solving and the corresponding market opportunity.

   - **High**: The problem affects a large population or industry, offering substantial scalability.

   - **Medium**: Moderate market size or a niche with growth potential.

   - **Low**: Small or localized market with limited expansion opportunities.

2. **Scalability & Competitiveness**

   Examine how easily the business can scale its operations and compete effectively.

   - **High**: Low customer acquisition cost (CAC), minimal investments, and strong competitive positioning.

   - **Medium**: Moderate CAC and investments, with growth potential amidst competition.

   - **Low**: High CAC and substantial investment requirements, with intense competition.

3. **Innovation & Moat**

   Assess the company's ability to stand out with its unique value proposition (UVP) or defensible competitive advantage.

   - **High**: Strong differentiation, barriers to entry, and potentially proprietary technology or IP.

   - **Medium**: Some differentiation, but partially vulnerable to replication.

   - **Low**: Minimal uniqueness, with no substantial competitive edge.

4. Execution

Analyse the management team's capabilities and track record in executing strategies effectively.

- **High**: Strong execution history, good capital allocation, and a well-rounded, capable team.

- **Medium**: Competent team with some gaps in expertise or execution experience.

- **Low**: Limited track record and weak operational management.

5. Revenue Generation Probability

Evaluate the likelihood of generating sustainable revenue through clear pathways like order books, user base, or sales channels.

- **High**: Clear, proven revenue generation with strong client commitments or traction.

- **Medium**: Some visibility into revenue streams but limited traction or market validation.

- **Low**: Uncertain or unclear revenue potential, with no significant user or client base.

Step 2: Evaluate Margins and Growth Potential

After scoring the qualitative parameters, move to financial metrics to validate the company's operational and growth potential:

1. **Operating Margins**: Analyse current or likely gross margins, contribution margins, and their improvement potential through operational leverage or cost optimization.

2. **Growth Trajectory**: Assess current or likely monthly or quarterly revenue growth rates, user acquisition patterns, and market share expansion.

Step 3: Integrating Additional Parameters

For businesses that are not yet generating significant revenue, traditional revenue multiples may not fully reflect their value. In such cases, investors can add additional parameters to enhance their analysis:

- **Money Invested**: Consider the capital already deployed in building the product, brand, or market presence.

- **Time Invested**: Account for the time spent in R&D, building customer relationships, or establishing operational networks.

- **Idea value**: Put in the number as per the uniqueness, differentiation, and innovation in the business idea.

By factoring in these elements, investors can address the limitations of revenue multiples and better understand the company's front-end investments relative to its growth potential.

Final Step: Create a Comprehensive Evaluation

Combine the qualitative parameters, financial metrics, and additional factors to gain a holistic view of the business. Businesses with high qualitative scores, robust margins, and substantial growth are likely to command higher revenue multiples. Conversely, businesses with low scores or insufficient traction may warrant caution or further analysis. This method provides a flexible yet structured framework, helping investors gauge early-stage businesses effectively, even in the absence of extensive financial data. It also allows room for customization based on the unique nature of each investment opportunity.

Valuation Mantra

The Price of Certainty

Investing involves navigating a delicate balance between certainty and uncertainty. The core principle of the valuation mantra lies in understanding that markets assign higher valuations to businesses with predictable, stable futures, while businesses with uncertain trajectories are often undervalued but hold the potential for outsized returns.

When a business's future appears certain—marked by stable cash flows, clear competitive advantages, and proven scalability—it often trades at a premium. Certainty reduces risk for investors, but this reduction comes at a price.

The reason certainty commands premium is predictable businesses minimize downside risk, making them attractive to a wide range of investors. Also, Certainty attracts institutional investors who are willing to pay a premium for safety and stability. In an ever-changing market, truly stable businesses are rare, driving their valuations higher.

Companies like Nestlé or Hindustan Unilever command high valuations because of their consistent demand and established market position. Firms like Apple or Microsoft valued at premiums due to their predictable revenue streams and strong moats.

Premium valuations leave little room for exponential gains unless there's unexpected growth or innovation. When certainty is overestimated, it can lead to inflated prices, making it harder to achieve above-average returns.

The Opportunity in Uncertainty

Uncertainty creates opportunities for discerning investors who can identify businesses with strong fundamentals and alignment with emerging trends. These businesses, while undervalued due to perceived risks, often offer the potential for significant returns.

The reason uncertainty creates value opportunities is market tends to overestimate the risks associated with uncertainty, leading to undervaluation. Businesses in uncertain environments often operate in nascent industries or are on the cusp of scaling. The potential upside in uncertain businesses can far outweigh the risks, especially when aligned with robust trends.

Early investments in electric vehicles (e.g., Tesla in 2010) or renewable energy companies (e.g., First Solar) carried significant uncertainty but offered exponential returns as the trends materialized. Companies like Zoom or Shopify were initially perceived as risky but proved their value as their business models scaled rapidly.

The downside of uncertainty is many businesses fail to overcome the challenges associated with uncertainty, leading to losses for investors. Realizing returns from uncertain businesses often takes time, as they need to prove their viability and scalability.

Balance Certainty and Uncertainty in Valuation

Investors must carefully weigh the price of certainty against the opportunity in uncertainty to construct a well-balanced portfolio. Certainty offers predictability but often comes with limited upside due to high valuations, while uncertainty carries greater risk but can yield exponential rewards when aligned with strong growth drivers. Here are some strategies to approach both effectively:

When investing in businesses with predictable futures, it is essential to focus on fairly valued opportunities with strong competitive moats and consistent cash flows. These companies provide stability and reduce downside risk, making them an attractive component of a portfolio. However, investors should be cautious about paying excessively high premiums for certainty, as it can limit potential returns. Striking a balance between fair valuation and stability ensures a strong foundation for long-term growth.

Uncertainty presents an opportunity to capitalize on undervalued businesses operating in industries with clear growth drivers but facing temporary challenges or scepticism. Investors must assess qualitative factors such as the quality of the management team, the company's alignment with emerging trends, and its scalability potential. These businesses often require patience and a deep understanding of their long-term trajectory to unlock their true value.

Diversification is the Key. A diversified portfolio is essential to balance risk and reward. Combining investments in stable, predictable businesses with a smaller allocation to high-growth opportunities in uncertain markets can create a robust strategy. This approach ensures exposure to exponential growth potential while safeguarding against volatility. Diversification allows investors to capture gains from both ends of the spectrum—certainty and uncertainty.

Valuation strategies must incorporate practical considerations to ensure sound investment decisions. Regardless of the certainty level, maintaining a margin of safety is crucial. This buffer protects against unforeseen risks and ensures that investments are made at reasonable prices. Additionally, investors should focus on the fundamentals of businesses operating in uncertain markets, looking beyond short-term volatility to assess their long-term viability. It is also essential to monitor shifts in businesses, as they can transition from uncertainty to certainty—or vice versa—as they mature or face new disruptions.

Case Studies: Certainty vs. Uncertainty

Infosys, a mature IT services company, exemplifies the stability associated with certainty. Its strong cash flows, proven track record, and competitive moat make it a reliable investment option. However, the premium valuation attached to such predictability often caps the upside potential. Investors in Infosys benefit from steady, consistent returns, but they are unlikely to experience exponential growth.

Zomato represents the potential rewards of uncertainty. Initially, the company faced scepticism due to profitability concerns, but its alignment with the growing food delivery trend and ability to scale effectively captured significant value over time. Early investors who recognized the long-term opportunity amidst uncertainty were rewarded with substantial gains as the business transitioned into a more stable phase of growth.

Chapter **1**

2040 and Famous Trend Predictions

How 2040 May Look Like: A Vision of the Future

2040 is likely to be defined by profound transformations in demographics, technology, climate, geopolitics, and the global economy. Based on current trends, here is a speculative view of what the world might look like:

1. Global Demographics: An Uneven World

    - Countries like Japan, South Korea, Italy, and much of Europe will have some of the oldest populations, with average ages exceeding 50 years.

    - The challenges of supporting aging populations through pensions, healthcare, and shrinking workforces will dominate policy agendas.

    - Automation and AI are expected to play significant roles in addressing labour shortages.

    - Africa will emerge as a demographic powerhouse, with its population doubling to nearly 2.5 billion. The median age will still be under twenty-five, making it the youngest continent.

- South Asia, especially India, will continue to benefit from its demographic dividend, maintaining a relatively young population and becoming a global supplier of talent.

- This youth-driven growth will propel consumer markets, innovation, and entrepreneurship in these regions.

- Countries such as China and Russia will experience significant population declines due to low fertility rates and aging demographics. China's population could drop below one billion by 2040, shifting global economic dynamics.

2. Technological Revolution: The Rise of the Smart Age

- Artificial Intelligence (AI) will permeate nearly every aspect of life, from personalized healthcare to autonomous transportation.

- Routine tasks will be fully automated, and human effort will focus on creativity, problem-solving, and strategic thinking.

- Quantum technology will revolutionize sectors like pharmaceuticals, cryptography, and material science, unlocking previously unattainable solutions.

- Green hydrogen, fusion energy, and advanced battery storage technologies will become mainstream, drastically reducing dependence on fossil fuels.

- Energy will be cheaper, more accessible, and almost entirely renewable in many parts of the world.

- Space exploration and commercialization will expand, with asteroid mining, space tourism, and lunar colonies becoming feasible industries.

- Wearable and implantable technology will enhance physical and cognitive capabilities, blurring the line between human and machine.

3. Climate and Environmental Impact: A World in Transition

- Most countries will aim for net-zero emissions, and climate adaptation technologies will become a trillion-dollar industry.

- Renewable energy will dominate, with solar, wind, and hydrogen taking the lead.

- Water scarcity will remain a critical issue in regions like Sub-Saharan Africa and South Asia, driving innovation in water conservation and desalination.

- Coastal cities like Mumbai, New York, and Jakarta will face significant challenges due to rising sea levels, leading to increased investment in resilient infrastructure and potential climate migration.

- Carbon capture and storage technologies will become standard practice, and global carbon trading markets will mature into a key economic sector.

4. Economic and Geopolitical Shifts

- India is projected to become the second-largest economy by 2040, driven by its youthful population, innovation, and infrastructure development.

- Key industries like pharmaceuticals, technology, and renewable energy will thrive.

- Africa's economic potential will begin to materialize, fuelled by urbanization, technological adoption, and investments in education and infrastructure.

- With an aging population and slowing growth, China's focus will shift from being the "world's factory" to high-tech innovation and services.

- The world will become more multipolar, with power centres in North America, Europe, China, India, and Africa.

- International relations will emphasize resource sharing, climate action, and economic partnerships.

5. Society and Lifestyles

- Over 70% of the world's population will live in urban areas, creating megacities with populations exceeding fifty million.

- Smart cities with integrated AI systems for transportation, healthcare, and governance will dominate.

- Advances in medicine and biotechnology will extend life expectancy, creating a new economic sector catering to health, leisure, and productivity for older adults.

- Traditional employment structures will shift toward gig and project-based work, with remote and hybrid setups being the norm.

- Lifelong learning will be critical as individuals adapt to ever-changing job requirements.

- Global connectivity will create a blend of cultures, but local traditions will remain strong in regions with deep historical roots.

The world in 2040 will be vastly different, shaped by the interplay of demographic shifts, technological advancements, environmental challenges, and geopolitical realignments. For investors, policymakers, and individuals, navigating this future will require adaptability, vision, and a commitment to sustainable and inclusive growth.

Trend Predictions of Some Notable Personalities

Here are some long-term trend and theme predictions made by notable business leaders, personalities, and industrialists from around the world, based on their insights and public statements:

1. **Reid Hoffman (LinkedIn)**

   - **End of Traditional 9-to-5 Jobs**: Hoffman has predicted that by 2034, the traditional 9-to-5 job might become extinct. He envisions a future where work is more flexible, with individuals engaging in multiple gigs across different industries rather than having a single full-time job.

   - **AI's Impact on Work:** He has highlighted how AI will disrupt and reshape the workforce. AI technologies are expected to automate many routine tasks, leading to a workforce that focuses on higher-level, creative, and strategic roles. AI might also facilitate new forms of work, like AI-assisted jobs or roles that manage AI systems.

   - **Lifelong Learning and Networking:** With the rapid pace of technological change, he believes workers will need to constantly update their skills to stay relevant. Hoffman has always emphasized the importance of professional networking. He predicts that networking will become even more crucial as traditional job structures fade.

   Source: Yahoo Article - LinkedIn Co-Founder Predicts the Death Of 9-to-5 Jobs By 2034 – How AI & The Gig Economy Will Reshape the Workforce

2. **Elon Musk (Tesla, SpaceX, X Corp)**

   - **Sustainability and Renewable Energy**: Musk has consistently predicted that the future will be dominated by sustainable energy, with a significant shift towards electric vehicles, solar power, and batteries. He envisions a future where energy is stored and used efficiently, reducing dependency on fossil fuels.

- **Space Travel**: He foresees humans becoming a multi-planetary species, with Mars colonization as a long-term goal, emphasizing the importance of space exploration for the survival and expansion of human consciousness.

Sources: X posts of Elon Musk's, Tesla's Annual Reports

3. **Bill Gates (Microsoft, Bill & Melinda Gates Foundation)**

- **Healthcare and Biotechnology**: Gates has emphasized the importance of healthcare technology, predicting advancements in personalized medicine, vaccines, and global health initiatives. He is particularly focused on eradicating diseases through technology and innovation.

- **Climate Change**: He has been vocal about tackling climate change through technological innovation and policy changes, predicting that clean energy solutions will become economically competitive with fossil fuels.

Source: GatesNote Article - We are not ready for the next epidemic

4. **Jeff Bezos (Amazon)**

- **E-commerce Expansion**: Bezos predicted that e-commerce would continue to grow, fundamentally changing how commerce is conducted worldwide, with personalized, AI-driven shopping experiences.

- **Space Tourism**: Through Blue Origin, Bezos has invested in making space travel accessible to civilians, predicting a future where space tourism becomes a common experience.

Sources: Amazon's shareholder letters and Blue Origin discussions

5. **Jack Ma (Alibaba)**

    - **Digital Transformation**: Ma has been a proponent of the digital economy, predicting that everything from retail to manufacturing would undergo digital transformation, emphasizing the role of technology in every aspect of life.

    - **AI and Data**: He has spoken about the rise of AI, suggesting that data would become a key resource, with AI playing a vital role in shaping future businesses.

    Source: Fast Company Article - AI will cause people "more pain than happiness," says Alibaba founder

6. **Indra Nooyi (Former PepsiCo CEO)**

    - **Health and Wellness**: Nooyi highlighted the trend towards healthier living, predicting that companies would need to pivot towards offering healthier products to meet consumer demand, integrating sustainability into business models.

    Source: BCG Article - Indra K. Nooyi on Performance with Purpose

7. **Richard Branson (Virgin Group)**

    - **Customer Experience**: Branson has always emphasized the importance of exceptional customer service, predicting that as technology advances, the focus on personalized and memorable customer experiences would become even more critical for brand differentiation.

    - **Space Travel**: Similar to Bezos, he is invested in space tourism with Virgin Galactic, predicting a future where space travel becomes part of human adventure and tourism.

    Source: CNBC article - Billionaire Richard Branson defends space travel, argues it can benefit planet

8. **Muhammad Yunus (Grameen Bank)**

   - **Social Business**: Yunus has predicted the rise of social businesses, where the aim is not profit maximization but solving social problems, particularly poverty alleviation through microcredit and entrepreneurship.

   Source: BCG Article - Professor Muhammad Yunus on the Power of Social Business

9. **Anand Mahindra (Mahindra Group)**

   - **Electric Mobility**: In India, he has predicted a significant shift towards electric vehicles, with Mahindra Group investing heavily in electric SUVs and last-mile mobility solutions.

   - **Digital India**: He sees India's digital transformation as a massive opportunity, with technology enabling growth in rural areas and enhancing urban services.

   Source: Forbes India Article: Anand Mahindra gets future ready by N Madhavan (2017)

10. **Satya Nadella (Microsoft)**

    - **AI and Cloud Computing**: Nadella has steered Microsoft towards becoming an AI-first company, predicting that AI will be the defining technology of our time, integrated across all industries, with cloud computing as its backbone.

    Source: Microsoft CEO Satya Nadella's Keynote Address on The Potential of Next-generation AI | N18L

11. **Tim Cook (Apple)**

    - **Privacy and AR**: Cook has emphasized privacy as a fundamental human right in the digital age, predicting that the demand for privacy will drive technological innovation. He also sees augmented reality (AR) as the next big computing platform.

Source: Article by Techradar - Apple's Tim Cook: 'AR has the ability to amplify human performance

These predictions reflect themes like sustainability, digital transformation, health and wellness, space exploration, working ecosystem and AI integration, showing a broad consensus on how technology, environment, and human-centric approaches will shape future trends. However, remember that these are based on their visions and the dynamic nature of technology and global markets means these trends can evolve or shift due to unforeseen changes or innovations.

Here are some predictions made by notable non-business figures, including scientists, academics, and entertainers, whose insights can provide a distinct perspective on future trends:

Yuval Noah Harari (Historian and Author)

- **Prediction**: Harari predicts that humans might merge with machines in the future, with biotechnology, AI, and data potentially leading to a new class divide between those who can enhance themselves and those who cannot.

- **Implications**: This could lead to profound societal changes, where enhancements might offer significant advantages, potentially exacerbating inequality. Ethical, privacy, and identity issues would become central, as would the question of what it means to be human.

  Source: Harari, Y.N. (2018). 21 Lessons for the 21st Century

Ray Kurzweil (Futurist and Google's Director of Engineering)

- **Prediction**: Kurzweil famously predicted the singularity, a point where artificial intelligence will surpass human intelligence, potentially leading to exponential technological growth. He also predicted that by 2030, nanobots will roam freely inside our bodies, repairing damage and keeping us healthy.

- **Implications**: The singularity could revolutionize every aspect of life, from medicine to economics, but it also brings existential questions about control, ethics, and the future role of humans in society. Health improvements via nanobots could lead to extended lifespans but would require addressing safety, accessibility, and the societal impact of such longevity.

    Source: Kurzweil, R. (2005). The Singularity is Near: When Humans Transcend Biology.

Jane Goodall (Primatologist and Conservationist)

- **Prediction**: Goodall has predicted that without significant changes in how we treat the environment, especially deforestation and loss of biodiversity, many species could face extinction, impacting ecosystems globally.

- **Implications**: This dire prediction underscores the urgency of conservation efforts, potentially leading to a global movement towards sustainability, reforestation, and biodiversity protection. However, it also highlights the need for economic models that value ecological services and the challenge of balancing human development with environmental preservation.

    Source: Goodall, J. (2020). Various interviews and speeches on conservation issues.

Neil deGrasse Tyson (Astrophysicist)

- **Prediction**: Tyson has discussed the future of space exploration, predicting that humans will eventually colonize other planets, not just for survival but for the expansion of human knowledge and experience.

- **Implications**: Space colonization could open new scientific and resource frontiers but would also pose ethical, legal, and financial challenges. The motivation for such endeavours might shift from exploration to resource exploitation, raising questions about ownership and stewardship of extraterrestrial environments.

  Source: Tyson, N.d.G. (2019). Accessory to War: The Unspoken Alliance Between Astrophysics and the Military

Stephen Hawking (Theoretical Physicist)

- **Prediction**: Before his passing, Hawking made several predictions, including the potential danger of AI unless properly controlled, and the need for humanity to become a multi-planetary species to ensure survival against events like natural disasters or pandemics.

- **Implications**: The warnings about AI highlight the need for ethical AI development and governance to prevent misuse or unintended consequences. His vision for space exploration suggests a future where human survival depends on our ability to adapt and expand beyond Earth, necessitating international cooperation and technological advancement.

  Source: Hawking, S. (Multiple interviews and publications, especially towards the end of his life).

Esther Dyson (Technology Analyst and Investor)

- **Prediction**: Dyson has predicted that technology will increasingly focus on health, with personalized medicine and health data becoming central to individual and societal well-being.

- **Implications**: A health-focused tech boom could lead to longer, healthier lives through preventative care and tailored treatments. However, this also raises privacy concerns, the potential for data misuse, and the need for equitable access to these technologies.

  Source: Dyson, E. (2012). Release 2.1: A Design for Living in the Digital Age

These predictions by non-business individuals often focus on broader societal, ethical, and existential themes, reflecting concerns about the intersection of technology with human values, the environment, and the very nature of humanity itself.

How These Personalities Predict Things with Conviction

Deep Domain Expertise

These individuals have extensive experience in their respective fields, which gives them an intuitive grasp of market dynamics, consumer behaviour, and technological advancements. For example, Elon Musk's work in electric vehicles (Tesla) and space exploration (SpaceX) equips him to predict advancements in renewable energy and space travel.

Access to Cutting-Edge Data and Insights

They have access to data from research, operations, and their extensive networks. This enables them to identify patterns, emerging technologies, and shifts in consumer demand early. Bill Gates, through the Bill & Melinda Gates Foundation, is deeply involved in global health initiatives, providing him insights into healthcare trends.

Innovative Mindset

Visionaries like Richard Branson and Jeff Bezos are known for challenging the status quo and thinking beyond conventional boundaries. This helps them envision transformative possibilities others might overlook.

Influence Over Industry Direction

Many of these leaders are not just observers but active participants shaping industry trends. Their companies often spearhead innovations that set the tone for broader industry changes. Satya Nadella's leadership at Microsoft, for instance, has driven the adoption of cloud computing and AI across industries.

Holistic Thinking

Their predictions often consider a combination of technological, social, environmental, and economic factors. This holistic perspective allows them to anticipate interconnected changes. For example, Indra Nooyi connects the shift towards healthier products with sustainability trends and evolving consumer preferences.

Constant Learning and Curiosity

These leaders are lifelong learners who actively engage with latest ideas, research, and trends. This curiosity helps them stay ahead of the curve. Reid Hoffman's emphasis on lifelong learning reflects his own practice of staying updated with technological and workforce trends.

Pattern Recognition

With years of experience, they can recognize subtle patterns and anticipate how they might evolve over time. This skill is crucial for predicting long-term changes. Ray Kurzweil's ability to foresee technological milestones stems from analysing historical patterns of innovation and extrapolating them into the future.

Global Perspective

Many of these figures operate on a global scale, giving them exposure to diverse markets, cultures, and innovations. This broad perspective helps them identify universal trends. Jack Ma, for instance, has a global view of digital transformation, drawing on insights from both developed and emerging economies.

Focus on Long-Term Vision

These leaders are not bogged down by short-term challenges. They focus on long-term possibilities, enabling them to make predictions that might seem ambitious today but are achievable over decades. Elon Musk's vision of Mars colonization is a prime example of long-term strategic thinking.

Involvement with Think Tanks and Collaborations

Many of these individuals collaborate with experts, academics, and think tanks, giving them access to multidisciplinary insights and perspectives. Tim Cook's predictions about privacy and AR are informed by collaborations with technology and policy experts.

Challenges and Imperfections in Predictions

While these factors lend credibility to their predictions, it is worth noting that not all predictions come true. Factors such as unforeseen technological challenges, regulatory changes, and shifts in consumer behaviour can derail even well-informed forecasts. Nevertheless, their predictions often serve as valuable frameworks for understanding potential future directions.

Closure

Recap of Key Takeaways

Throughout the book, we have explored the intricacies of identifying and capitalizing on emerging trends. Key insights include understanding the country demographics, lifecycle of trends, navigating risks like overvaluation or short-term setbacks, and evaluating businesses with a combination of quantitative metrics and qualitative factors. We emphasized the importance of timing, infrastructure, and recognizing geographic and industry-specific nuances. Together, these tools form a comprehensive framework for mastering trend investing and creating sustainable opportunities in the rapidly changing global economy.

Inspiring Readers to Start Their Journey

Trends are the harbingers of transformation, shaping industries, consumer behaviour, and entire economies. The ability to spot and act on trends early is not reserved for seasoned investors or insiders; it is a skill that can be cultivated by anyone with curiosity and persistence.

Let this book serve as a starting point for your journey. Begin by observing shifts in your surroundings—consumer habits, technological advancements, or policy changes—and connect them to the larger forces at play. Start small, think critically, and build your conviction as you learn to recognize the patterns that drive change. Remember, the most successful trend investors are those who remain lifelong learners, adapting their approach as the world evolves.

Final Thoughts on Navigating Future Trends in India and Beyond

As India emerges as a global economic powerhouse, its trends will increasingly shape the world's future. The interplay between technology, sustainability, and innovation will create opportunities that were unimaginable just a decade ago. At the same time, India's unique demographic, cultural, and economic characteristics mean that trends here will often evolve differently from global patterns.

The journey of identifying and investing in trends is not without challenges, but it is also deeply rewarding. By combining insight, patience, and action, you can position yourself at the forefront of change, creating value not just for yourself, but for the communities and industries you engage with.

The future belongs to those who recognize its shape today. Go out, explore, and embrace the endless possibilities that future offer.

Your journey starts now.

References

Philosophies
* Dalio, R. Principles: Life and Work. Simon & Schuster. 2017 (Extract of his philosophy)
* Marks, H. The Most Important Thing: Uncommon Sense for the Thoughtful Investor. Columbia University Press. 2011 (Extract of his philosophy)
* Buffett, W, Letters to Shareholders 1991, Berkshire Hathaway Inc.
* Vijay Kedia. X post, Nov 20, 2020

Introduction
* Article, Blockbuster Could Have Bought Netflix for $50 Million, but the CEO Thought It Was a Joke, Inc.com, website
* Profile of Netflix, Britannica, Website.

Chapter A

Understanding Trends and Their Evolution
* Kahneman, Daniel. *Thinking, Fast and Slow*. Farrar, Straus, and Giroux, 2011.
* Christensen, Clayton M. *The Innovator's Dilemma: When New Technologies Cause Great Firms to Fail*. Harvard Business Review Press, 1997.
* Rogers, Everett M. *Diffusion of Innovations*. Free Press, 5th Edition, 2003.
* Schumpeter, Joseph A. *Capitalism, Socialism and Democracy*. Harper & Brothers, 1942 – The concept of "creative destruction."
* Brown, Tim. *Change by Design: How Design Thinking Creates New Alternatives for Business and Society*. Harper Business, 2009 – Understanding user behaviour and market trends through design thinking.

Identification and Categorization of Trends
* Gladwell, Malcolm. *The Tipping Point: How Little Things Can Make a Big Difference*. Little, Brown, and Company, 2000 – For insights into the adoption stages and tipping points of trends.
* Osterwalder, Alexander, and Pigneur, Yves. *Business Model Generation: A Handbook for Visionaries, Game Changers, and Challengers*. Wiley, 2010 – Understanding the impact of trends on business models.
* Trend Watching. *Trend Reports*. Website – For examples of emerging consumer trends and patterns.
* Gartner. *Hype Cycle Reports*. Website – For insights into technology adoption and the lifecycle of trends.

References

Tools and Methods for Trend Identification
- Nielsen. *Consumer Insights Reports.* Website – For insights into the consumer behaviour trends globally.
- Statista. *Trend Data and Statistics.* Website – For data on the emerging trends across industries.
- Google Trends. Website – A widely used tool to track the popularity of search terms and identify trends.
- Social Media Platforms: Twitter, Instagram, LinkedIn – For identifying emerging conversations, hashtags, and influencer-driven trends.

Evolution of Trends
- Bass, Frank M. *A New Product Growth Model for Consumer Durables.* Management Science, 1969 – Bass Diffusion Model for understanding adoption stages.
- Mahajan, Vijay, et al. *Innovation Diffusion Models of New Product Acceptance.* Marketing Science, 1990 – Academic insights into the lifecycle of trends.
- McKinsey & Company. *Emerging Consumer Trends Reports.* Website

Observing Global and Local Trends
- Hofstede, Geert. *Culture's Consequences: Comparing Values, Behaviours, Institutions, and Organizations Across Nations.* Sage Publications, 2001 – For understanding cultural influences on trend adoption.
- UNCTAD. *Reports on Global Economic Trends and their Implications.* Website
- World Economic Forum. *Global Risks Report.* Website

Visualizing Trends
- Heath, Chip, and Heath, Dan. *Made to Stick: Why Some Ideas Survive and Others Die.* Random House, 2007 – For understanding how trends gain attention and stick in public consciousness.
- Gartner. *Emerging Trends Reports.* Website

Risks Associated with Trends
- Taleb, Nassim Nicholas. *The Black Swan: The Impact of the Highly Improbable.* Random House, 2007 – Understanding risk in trend investing and adoption.
- Levitt, Theodore. *Marketing Myopia.* Harvard Business Review, 1960 – For understanding how businesses misinterpret trends and fail to adapt.

Chapter B
- World Population Prospects 2022: A comprehensive resource on global population trends, fertility rates, and demographic projections. UN DESA Website.
- Comprehensive data on fertility rates, urbanization, and global demographic shifts. World Bank Website.
- The World in 2050: A detailed report on long-term GDP growth projections and the rise of emerging economic powers. PwC Website.
- Country-specific economic forecasts and insights into global economic stability and growth prospects. IMF Website.
- Analysis focusing on political stability, governance, and the shifting balance of global power dynamics. EIU Website.

- Global economic shifts, demographic transitions, and the emerging market opportunities. Harvard Business Review Website.
- Africa's demographic trends, labour market opportunities, and economic challenges. McKinsey Website.
- Insights into Africa's economic potential and demographic growth opportunities. African Development Bank Website.
- In-depth reports on aging populations, labour market challenges, and policy frameworks. OECD Website.
- Research on aging trends and their socioeconomic implications in developed economies. Pew Research Centre Website.
- Global migration patterns, workforce redistribution, and the economic effects of remittances. International Organization for Migration Website.
- Migration's influence on global labour markets and demographic transitions. Brookings Institution Website.

Chapter C

Historical Evolution of India

- Guha, Ramachandra. *India After Gandhi: The History of the World's Largest Democracy*. HarperCollins, 2007.
- Ministry of Statistics and Programme Implementation (MOSPI). *Historical Data on Socio-Economic Development in India.*
- Reserve Bank of India. *Handbook of Statistics on the Indian Economy*. Website
- *Economic and Political Weekly* (EPW): Articles on India's industrialization, policy shifts, and globalization efforts.

Economic Liberalization and Reforms

- Ninan, T.N. *The Turn of the Tortoise: The Challenge and Promise of India's Future*. Allen Lane, 2015.
- Ministry of Finance, Government of India. *Economic Survey of India*. Website
- Planning Commission of India (now NITI Aayog). *Five-Year Plans and Reports.*
- Rodrik, Dani, and Subramanian, Arvind. *From "Hindu Growth" to Productivity Surge: The Mystery of the Indian Growth Transition*. IMF Working Paper, 2004.

India's IT and Digital Revolution

- Prahalad, C.K., and Krishnan, M.S. *The New Age of Innovation: Driving Co-Created Value Through Global Networks*. McGraw-Hill, 2008.
- Pande, Aparna. *Making India Great: The Promise of a Reluctant Global Power*. HarperCollins, 2020.
- Nasscom. *Annual Reports on India's IT Sector*. Website
- World Bank. *India and the Knowledge Economy: Leveraging Strengths and Opportunities*. 2005.

Key Global Events Shaping India

- World Bank. *India Development Update*. Semi-Annual Reports. Website
- IMF. *World Economic Outlook*. International Monetary Fund. Website
- WTO. *Reports on India's Integration into Global Trade*. Website
- UNCTAD. *India's Role in Global FDI and Emerging Markets Reports*. Website

References

Socio-Political and Demographic Changes
- Acemoglu, Daron, and Robinson, James A. *Why Nations Fail: The Origins of Power, Prosperity, and Poverty.* Crown Business, 2012.
- Naipaul, V.S. *India: A Million Mutinies Now.* Penguin Books, 1990.
- United Nations Development Programme (UNDP). *Human Development Index Reports for India.* Website

Ongoing Trends and Potential
- McKinsey Global Institute. *India's Turning Point: An Economic Agenda to Spur Growth and Jobs.* 2020. Website
- World Economic Forum (WEF). *India's Role in Global Sustainability and Technology Trends.* Website

Chapter D:
Digital Transformation in Consumer Services
- Deloitte. (2020). The future of retail: The future of the consumer experience. [REPORT]
- Statista. (2024). E-commerce worldwide - Statistics & Facts. Retrieved from [URL]
- McKinsey & Company. (2023). The future of payments: A shift to digital and innovative solutions. [REPORT]
- World Bank Group. (2021). The Global Findex Database 2021: Financial Inclusion, Digital Payments, and Resilience in the Age of COVID-19. [REPORT]
- Euromonitor International. (2023). Top Trends in E-commerce for 2023. [REPORT]
- McKinsey & Company. (2022). The next normal in grocery: From survival to revival. [REPORT]
- PwC. (2023). Global Entertainment & Media Outlook 2023–2027. [REPORT]
- Forbes. (2023). The Rise of OTT Platforms and the Future of Entertainment. [Article]
- Uber Technologies Inc. (2022). Uber's Annual Report 2022. [REPORT]
- CB Insights. (2023). The Mobility Revolution: Ride-Hailing. [Research Brief]
- World Bank Group. (2023). Digital Public Infrastructure as a Catalyst for Economic Growth. [Report]
- Reserve Bank of India. (2022). Payment Systems in India: Vision 2025. [REPORT]
- McKinsey Global Institute. (2019). Notes from the AI frontier: Tackling Europe's gap in digital and AI. [Report]
- Deloitte Insights. (2022). The rise of the data economy. [Article]
- McKinsey & Company. (2021). How live commerce is transforming the shopping experience. [REPORT]
- eMarketer. (2023). Live Commerce: The New Frontier for Retail. [Report]
- Forrester. (2022). The State of Omnichannel Retail. [Report]
- Salesforce. (2023). State of the Connected Customer. [REPORT]
- Gartner. (2023). Hype Cycle for Emerging Technologies, 2023. [Report]
- Accenture. (2022). The Rise of 'As-a-Service' Solutions. [REPORT]

Renewable Energy and Sustainability
* International Renewable Energy Agency (IRENA). *Global Renewables Outlook.* Website
* Ministry of New and Renewable Energy (MNRE), India. *Annual Reports.* Website
* The Energy and Resources Institute (TERI). *Reports on Solar and Wind Energy in India.* Website
* International Energy Agency (IEA). (2023). Renewables 2023. [Report]
* IEA. (2023). Global EV Outlook 2023. [Report]
* McKinsey & Company. (2022). Charging ahead: Electric-vehicle infrastructure demand. [Report]
* Ellen MacArthur Foundation. (2023). The Circular Economy: A Transformative Solution. [Report]
* UN Environment Programme. (2023). Global Waste Management Outlook 2023.
* Grand View Research. (2023). Biodegradable Plastics Market Size & Share Report, 2023-2030. [Report]
* The Sustainable Brands. (2023). Consumer Insights on Sustainability. [Survey]
* World Bank. (2023). State and Trends of Carbon Pricing 2023. [Report]
* Gold Standard. (2023). Carbon Credit Market Insight Report. [Report]
* IRENA. (2023). Green Hydrogen: A guide to policy making. [Report]
* Hydrogen Council. (2022). Hydrogen Insights 2022. [Report]

Contract Research, Development, Manufacturing, and Outsourcing
* Frost & Sullivan. (2024). Global Pharmaceutical CRAMS Market Outlook.
* MarketsandMarkets. (2023). Pharmaceutical Contract Manufacturing Market - Global Forecast to 2028.
* IPC - Association Connecting Electronics Industries. (2024). Global EMS Market Report.
* Grand View Research. (2023). Electronics Manufacturing Services Market Size, Share & Trends Analysis Report.
* Everest Group. (2024). Service Provider Landscape with PEAK Matrix™ Assessment.
* Deloitte. (2023). Global Outsourcing Survey.
* NASSCOM. (2024). GCC Landscape Report.
* Gartner. (2024). Consumer Electronics Market Analysis.
* Statista. (2024). Global Consumer Electronics Industry Report.
* SEMI. (2024). World Fab Forecast.
* McKinsey & Company. (2023). The Semiconductor Decade: A Trillion-Dollar Industry.
* TrendForce. (2024). Global Semiconductor Market Analysis.
* Deloitte. (2024). Precision Engineering: A Global Perspective.
* MarketsandMarkets. (2023). Precision Engineering Market - Global Forecast to 2028.
* Make in India: Progress and Challenges - www.clearias.com. ClearIAS. Retrieved from [clearias.com]

References

- China Plus One Strategy - An Imperative to Achieve Supply Chain Resilience - www.beroeinc.com. Beroe Inc. Retrieved from [beroeinc.com]

Bio Innovation and Wellness

- Nature. (2023). AI in Drug Discovery. Citation: (Nature, 2023)
- McKinsey & Company. (2024). The Role of AI in Healthcare. Citation: (McKinsey & Company, 2024)
- PwC. (2023). AI in Healthcare: The Future is Now. Citation: (PwC, 2023)
- American Hospital Association. (2024). Telehealth Trends. Citation: (American Hospital Association, 2024)
- Deloitte. (2023). Telehealth: A Path to Transformation. Citation: (Deloitte, 2023)
- Nature Medicine. (2023). Advances in Gene Editing. Citation: (Nature Medicine, 2023)
- McKinsey & Company. (2023). The Rise of Personalized Medicine.
- MarketsandMarkets. (2024). 3D Printing Medical Devices Market. Citation: (MarketsandMarkets, 2024)
- Deloitte. (2023). 3D Printing: Healthcare's New Frontier. Citation: (Deloitte, 2023)
- Nature Reviews Genetics. (2024). Genomics and Personalized Healthcare. Citation: (Nature Reviews Genetics, 2024)
- Deloitte. (2023). Genomics in Healthcare: Opportunities and Challenges. Citation: (Deloitte, 2023)
- Forbes. (2023). The Impact of Wearables on Health. Citation: (Forbes, 2023)
- Deloitte. (2023). Wearable Technology in Healthcare. Citation: (Deloitte, 2023)
- Headspace. (2024). Mental Health Apps Impact Report. Citation: (Headspace, 2024)
- PwC. (2023). Digital Health and Mental Wellness. Citation: (PwC, 2023)
- Indian Council of Medical Research (ICMR). Reports on Lifestyle Diseases. Website
- Mintel. (2023). Consumer Trends in Natural Products. Citation: (Mintel, 2023)
- Nutrition Business Journal. (2024). State of the Supplement Industry. Citation: (Nutrition Business Journal, 2024)
- Statista. Health and Wellness Industry Trends. Website

Smart Home Gadgets and Home solutions

- Lardinois, F. (2024). Integrating Services into Smart Homes: The Next Frontier. TechCrunch. Retrieved from [techcrunch.com]
- Lunden, I. (2024). Smart Home Security: The Future Is Now. Forbes. Retrieved from [forbes.com]
- Tuohy, J. P. (2024). The Rise of Home Robots: A New Era for Household Automation. The Verge. Retrieved from [theverge.com]
- Energy Efficiency in Homes. (2024). U.S. Department of Energy. Retrieved from [energy.gov]
- Tuohy, J. P. (2024). Smart Home Devices Get Smarter with New AI Features. The Verge. Retrieved from [theverge.com]

- Brewster, T. (2024). The Invisible AI Watching Your Home: Privacy Concerns in Smart Devices. WIRED. Retrieved from (wired.com)
- The Verge. (2024). The Future of Gaming Consoles: More Than Just Games. Retrieved from [theverge.com]
- Modular Home Office Furniture - The Upcoming Trend | by Pinkapple Designs | Medium. (2018). Retrieved from [medium.com]
- Will Virtual Reality Change the Design World? Architectural Digest. (2018). Retrieved from [architecturaldigest.com]
- Modern Marvels: The Evolution of Advanced Cookware. Gourmet Sleuth. (2024). Retrieved from [gourmetsleuth.com]

Digital Education and Skill Development
- World Economic Forum. (2024). The Future of Education: Lifelong Learning Platforms. Retrieved from [weforum.org]
- Coursera. (2024). Lifelong Learning: The New Normal in Education. Retrieved from [blog.coursera.org]
- Training Industry. (2024). Top Trends in Corporate Training and Development for 2024. Retrieved from [trainingindustry.com]
- Forbes. (2024). The Future of Corporate Learning: Trends in Training Platforms. Retrieved from [forbes.com]
- World Economic Forum. (2024). The Future of Jobs Report 2024. Retrieved from [weforum.org]
- McKinsey & Company. (2024). Skills Shift: Automation and the Future of the Workforce. Retrieved from [mckinsey.com]
- EdSurge. (2024). Trends in K-12 Education Technology. Retrieved from [edsurge.com]
- Inside Higher Ed. (2024). The Future of Higher Education Platforms. Retrieved from [insidehighered.com]

Urbanization and Real Estate Transformation
- Managing and Reducing Wastes: A Guide for Commercial Buildings. US EPA. (2016). Retrieved from [epa.gov]
- ASHRAE. (2024). Combining Efficiency with Indoor Air Quality: The Role of Centralized HVAC Systems. Retrieved from [ashrae.org]
- Elevator World. (2024). Latest Trends in Elevator Technology for Multistorey Buildings. Retrieved from [elevatorworld.com]
- Architectural Digest. (2024). The Most Innovative Glass Buildings. Retrieved from [architecturaldigest.com]
- McKinsey & Company. (2024). The Value of Digital Twins in Industrial Applications. Retrieved from [mckinsey.com]
- Construction Dive. (2024). Trends in Alternative Building Materials: The Push for Sustainability. Retrieved from [constructiondive.com]
- Coworking Insights. (2024). The Evolution of Coworking Spaces: Trends and Forecasts for 2024. Retrieved from [coworkinginsights.com]
- Allwork.Space. (2024). The State of Coworking: 2024 Market Analysis. Retrieved from [allwork.space]

References

- McKinsey & Company. (2024). Smart Cities: Digital Solutions for a More Livable Future. Retrieved from [mckinsey.com]
- AARP. (2024). The Future of Senior Living: Trends, Challenges, and Opportunities. Retrieved from [aarp.org]
- Property Review SG. (2024). Co-Living Spaces: The New Trend In Singapore's Housing Market. Retrieved from [propertyreview.sg]

Technology and Artificial Intelligence (AI) Adoption

- Gartner. (2024). Magic Quadrant for Cloud Infrastructure and Platform Services. Retrieved from [gartner.com]
- Statista. (2024). Cloud Computing - Statistics & Facts. Retrieved from [statista.com]
- Google AI Blog. (2024). Advances in Voice Recognition: Understanding and Intent. Retrieved from [ai.googleblog.com]
- TechCrunch. (2024). The Future of Voice Interfaces: Beyond Recognition to Intent. Retrieved from [techcrunch.com]
- Harvard Business Review. (2024). The Art of Platform Strategy: Navigating the New Business Landscape. Retrieved from [hbr.org]
- MIT Sloan Management Review. (2024). The Future of Platforms: Challenges and Opportunities. Retrieved from [sloanreview.mit.edu]
- GSMA. (2024). The State of Mobile Internet Connectivity Report. Retrieved from [gsma.com]
- Ericsson. (2024). Ericsson Mobility Report. Retrieved from [ericsson.com]
- Gartner. (2024). Magic Quadrant for Enterprise SaaS Applications. Retrieved from [gartner.com]
- McKinsey & Company. (2024). The Future of SaaS: Trends, Challenges, and Opportunities. Retrieved from [mckinsey.com]
- IFR. (2024). Top 5 Robot Trends 2024. Retrieved from [ifr.org]
- Robotics Tomorrow. (2024). Trends in Industrial Robotics to Watch in 2024. Retrieved from [roboticstomorrow.com]
- Forbes. (2024). AR, VR, and MR: The Future of Immersive Technology. Retrieved from [forbes.com]
- Statista. (2024). Global Augmented and Virtual Reality Market Size. Retrieved from [statista.com]
- How Generative AI Is Changing Creative Work - hbr.org. Harvard Business Review. Retrieved from [hbr.org]
- Generative AI in Content Creation: Benefits & Tips - www.docebo.com. Docebo. Retrieved from [docebo.com]
- IBM. (2024). Blockchain for Business: Use Cases and Applications. Retrieved from [ibm.com]
- Deloitte. (2024). Blockchain and Distributed Ledger Technologies: A Deloitte Perspective. Retrieved from [deloitte.com]
- McKinsey & Company. (2024). The Future of Manufacturing: Automation and Robotics. Retrieved from [mckinsey.com]
- IFR. (2024). World Robotics Report: Industrial Robots. Retrieved from [ifr.org]

- SAS. (2024). Predictive Analytics: What it is and why it matters. Retrieved from [sas.com]
- IBM. (2024). What is Big Data Analytics? Retrieved from [ibm.com]
- Forbes. (2024). The Impact of AI Chatbots on Customer Service. Retrieved from [forbes.com]
- HubSpot Blog. (2024). Future of AI in Customer Service: Trends, Statistics, and Insights. Retrieved from [blog.hubspot.com]
- McKinsey & Company. (2024). Quantum Technology: The Next Frontier for Industry. Retrieved from [mckinsey.com]
- Nature. (2024). Quantum Computing: The Path to Practicality. Retrieved from [nature.com]

Agri-Tech and Sustainable Agriculture

- UN/DESA Policy Brief #105: Circular Agriculture for Sustainable Rural Development. (2024). Retrieved from [un.org]
- Ellen MacArthur Foundation. (2024). Circular Economy in Agriculture. Retrieved from [ellenmacarthurfoundation.org]
- CEAC. (2024). Advances in Controlled Environment Agriculture. Retrieved from [ceac.arizona.edu]
- Greenhouse Grower. (2024). The Future of Controlled Environment Agriculture. Retrieved from [greenhousegrower.com]
- USDA. (2024). Organic Agriculture. Retrieved from [ers.usda.gov]
- The Organic Research Centre. (2024). The Global Rise of Organic Farming: Trends and Insights. Retrieved from [efrc.com]
- FAO. (2024). Digital Technologies in Agriculture and Rural Areas. Retrieved from [fao.org]
- McKinsey & Company. (2024). The Digital Transformation of the Agriculture Supply Chain. Retrieved from [mckinsey.com]
- USDA. (2024). Precision Agriculture: Opportunities and Challenges. Retrieved from [usda.gov]
- McKinsey & Company. (2024). How IoT is Revolutionizing Agriculture. Retrieved from [mckinsey.com]
- BPIA. (2024). Biological Products in Agriculture: Market Trends and Opportunities. Retrieved from [biocontrols.org]
- Nature Biotechnology. (2024). Biotechnology in Agriculture: Hybrid Seeds and Biological Control. Retrieved from [nature.com]

Financial and Wealth Management

- Microinsurance Network. (2024). The Landscape of Microinsurance 2024. Retrieved from [microinsurancenetwork.org]
- World Bank. (2024). Microinsurance: A Tool for Financial Inclusion and Risk Management. Retrieved from [worldbank.org]
- U.S. Financial Literacy and Education Commission. (2024). National Strategy for Financial Literacy. Retrieved from [mymoney.gov]
- OECD. (2024). Financial Literacy and Education: Promoting Financial Well-being. Retrieved from [oecd.org]

References

- Preqin. (2024). Alternative Investments: Market Overview and Trends. Retrieved from [preqin.com]
- Forbes. (2024). The Rise of Alternative Investments for Retail Investors. Retrieved from [forbes.com]
- Financial Planning Association. (2024). The Evolution of Holistic Financial Planning. Retrieved from [financialplanningassociation.org]
- Forbes. (2024). The Rise of Holistic Financial Advisors: What Clients Really Want. Retrieved from [forbes.com]
- Statista Market Forecast (2024) for Wealth Management in India. Retrieved from Website.

Cybersecurity and Data Protection
- Fraud and Identity Trends to Watch in 2024. LexisNexis Risk Solutions. Retrieved from [risk.lexisnexis.com]
- Socure. (2024). What is Identity Fraud Detection in Banking? Retrieved from [socure.com]
- Cybernews. (2022). Best Threat Intelligence Solutions. Retrieved from [cybernews.com]
- Palo Alto Networks. (2024). What Is the Role of AI in Threat Detection? Retrieved from [paloaltonetworks.com]
- Article. Gartner Identifies Top Five Trends in Privacy Through 2024. Gartner. Retrieved from [gartner.com]
- Article. 5 Emerging Data Privacy Trends in 2024 | Osano. Osano. (2023). Retrieved from [osano.com]
- Article. Only 2% of businesses have implemented firm-wide cyber resilience, even as cyber security concerns are top-of-mind and the average data breach costs US$3.3M. PwC. Retrieved from [pwc.com]
- Article. Staying current on cybersecurity trends and best practices is critical for cybersecurity leaders to manage threats. Gartner. Retrieved from [gartner.com]

Tourism and Experience Consumption
- Elevated Experiences: 2024 Global Trends In Luxury Travel And Hospitality - www.forbes.com. Forbes. Retrieved from [forbes.com]
- These Are 2025's Most Exciting Luxury Travel Trends - www.luxurygold.com. Luxury Gold. Retrieved from [luxurygold.com]
- Best Luxury Cars for 2024 and 2025. MotorTrend. Retrieved from [motortrend.com]
- Luxury Car Market Size, Share, Trends | Growth Report [2032]. Fortune Business Insights. Retrieved from [fortunebusinessinsights.com]
- Eventbrite Blog. (2024). The Future of Events: Trends Shaping the Industry. Retrieved from [eventbrite.com]
- Wedding Wire. (2024). 2024 Wedding Trends: What's Hot in Weddings. Retrieved from [weddingwire.com]
- 4DX: The Ultimate Cinema Experience. CJ 4DPLEX. Retrieved from [cj4dx.com]
- The Verge. (2024). The Future of Cinema: Beyond 3D. Retrieved from [theverge.com]

* India Tourism Statistics. Ministry of Tourism, Government of India. Retrieved from [tourism.gov.in]
* Number of domestic tourist visits in India from 2000 to 2022. Statista. Retrieved from [statista.com]
* IATA. (2024). Air Connectivity: A Key Driver for Economic Growth. Retrieved from [iata.org]
* Air Connectivity Ranking 2023: Steady Improvement in Middle East; Asia-Pacific Records Gradual Recovery. ACI Asia-Pacific & Middle East. Retrieved from [aci-asiapac.aero]

New-Age Logistics
* Elastic logistics strengthen 21st century supply chains | Supply Chain Magazine. Supply Chain Digital. Retrieved from [supplychaindigital.com]
* Elastic logistics is the new normal way to get customer retention, meet fluctuating market demands, and more. Visit here and learn the benefits ... GEP. Retrieved from [gep.com]
* Predictive Analytics in Global Trade: Forecasting Market Trends with AI. Global Trade Magazine. Retrieved from [globaltrademag.com]
* Top 5 Predictive Analytics Models and Algorithms. Insightsoftware. Retrieved from [insightsoftware.com]
* The Future of Warehouse Management: Trends and Innovations. Englishlush.com. Retrieved from [englishlush.com]
* 6 Trends to Transform the Industry Using Warehouse Automation. Global Trade Magazine. Retrieved from [globaltrademag.com]
* Last-mile delivery: How to win the race. McKinsey & Company. Retrieved from [mckinsey.com]
* The future of last-mile delivery: Drones, robots, and micro-fulfilment centres. TechCrunch. Retrieved from [techcrunch.com]
* Posts found on X discuss the Indian government's initiative to set up 400 new cold chain facilities, highlighting investment in states like Maharashtra, Gujarat, and Uttar Pradesh.
* Trending on X, discussions around logistics parks emphasize their role in enhancing connectivity, streamlining operations, and revolutionizing supply chain strategies, with events like the Warehouse Logistics Cold Chain Expo being highlighted for showcasing these advancements.

Youth and Lifestyle
* 12 Dating App Trends 2024: Based on Big Data. SplitMetrics.
* 11 Top Dating Trends for 2024: What You Should Know. Marriage.com.
* Fast Fashion Industry: Market Trends and Future Outlook 2024, Wright Research. Retrieved from [wrightresearch.in]
* Fast Fashion Statistics 2024 - www.uniformmarket.com. UniformMarket. Retrieved from [uniformmarket.com]
* Top Trends Shaping Beauty and Personal Care Industry in 2024 - Euromonitor.com. Euromonitor International. Retrieved from [euromonitor.com]
* The Biggest Beauty Trends to Watch in 2024 | BoF - www.businessoffashion.com. Business of Fashion. Retrieved from [businessoffashion.com]

References

- 5 Influencer Marketing Trends Set to Take Off in 2025 - www.forbes.com. Forbes. Retrieved from [forbes.com]
- Top Influencer Marketing Trends You Can't Afford to Miss in 2025 - influencity.com. Influencity. Retrieved from [influencity.com]
- Fitness Trends for 2024: What's New in the Workout World - www.menshealth.com. Men's Health. Retrieved from [menshealth.com]
- Health and Wellness Trends 2024: Diet, Fitness and Well-being - www.forbes.com. Forbes. Retrieved from [forbes.com]

Chapter E

1. Health and Biotechnology
- National Institutes of Health (NIH). *CRISPR Technology Advancements.* Website
- World Economic Forum (WEF). *Future of Health and Precision Medicine.* Website
- Nature. *Articles on Neuroprosthetics and Brain-Computer Interfaces.* Website
- MIT Technology Review. *Emerging Technologies in Epigenetics and Personalized Medicine.* Website
- IEEE Spectrum. (2024). Human Augmentation Trends. Website

2. Technology and Computing
- Gartner. *Reports on Quantum Internet and Neuromorphic Computing.* Website
- IEEE Spectrum. *Holographic Data Storage and Advanced Computing Trends.* Website
- CB Insights. *Tech Startups in Emerging Computing Technologies.* Website

3. Energy and Environment
- International Energy Agency (IEA). *Future Technologies for Green Energy.* Website
- American Chemical Society (ACS). *Research on Artificial Photosynthesis and Bio-Photovoltaics.* Website
- World Resources Institute (WRI). *Reports on Sustainable Materials and Thermoacoustic Refrigeration.* Website

4. Materials Science
- Advanced Materials Journal. *Self-Healing Materials and 4D Printing Innovations.* Website
- Materials Today. *Sustainable Materials and Smart Polymers.* Website

5. Transportation
- Hyperloop One. *Technological Advancements in Hyperloop Systems.* Website
- Aviation Week. *Personal Air Vehicles and eVTOL Market Trends.* Website

6. Economical and Social Trends
- Brookings Institution. *Reports on Universal Basic Income Trials.* Website
- PwC. *Decoupling of Economies and Global Trade Reports.* Website
- McKinsey & Company. *The Metaverse: Opportunities and Risks.* Website

7. Space Industry
- NASA. *Lunar Resource Utilization and Asteroid Mining Reports.* Website

- Indian Space Research Organisation (ISRO). *In-Orbit Manufacturing and Commercial Space Trends.* Website
- SpaceX. *Advancements in Commercial Space Technologies.* Website

8. Agriculture and Food

- Food and Agriculture Organization (FAO). *Genetically Engineered Pollinators and Regenerative Agriculture.* Website
- The Good Food Institute (GFI). *Plant-Based and Cultivated Meat Market Reports.* Website

9. Experiential and Entertainment

- Harvard Business Review. *The Rise of Immersive Reality in Education and Training.* Website
- World Economic Forum (WEF). *Digital Detox Solutions and Mindfulness Trends.* Website

Rest of the Chapters

1. Understanding and Identifying Trends

- Harvard Business Review. *How to Spot a Trend Before It's a Trend.* Website
- Forbes. *Trend Analysis in Business and Investing.* Website
- Gartner. *Hype Cycle Reports for Emerging Trends.* Website

2. Evaluating Trends for Investment Potential

- McKinsey & Company. *Megatrends and the Art of Navigating Market Cycles.* Website
- World Economic Forum (WEF). *Emerging Trends in Global Markets.* Website
- Bain & Company. *Investment Strategies for New and Emerging Trends.* Website

3. Building a Strategic Framework

- Deloitte. *Strategic Investing in Disruptive Times.* Website
- Nasscom. *Frameworks for Leveraging Digital Disruption in India.* Website
- Accenture. *Playbook for Future-Ready Investments.* Website

4. Evaluating Qualitative Aspects of Early-Stage Businesses

- Y Combinator. *Startups and Early-Stage Business Metrics.* Website
- CB Insights. *Analysing Startups for Scalability and Growth Potential.* Website
- Investopedia. *Qualitative Factors in Investment Analysis.* Website

5. Quantitative Analysis and Metrics

- Morningstar. *Financial Metrics and Investment Evaluation.* Website
- Seeking Alpha. *Analysing Revenue Growth and Operating Margins.* Website
- Bloomberg. *Data-Driven Investing in Growth and Emerging Trends.* Website

6. Risk Management in Trend Investing

- CFA Institute. *Managing Risk in Trend-Based Investment Strategies.* Website
- BlackRock. *The Role of Diversification in Trend Investing.* Website
- Morgan Stanley. *Assessing Long-Term Viability and Trend Risks.* Website

7. Practical Tips for Trend Investing

- The Intelligent Investor by Benjamin Graham. *Principles of Value Investing in a Changing World.* [Book Reference]

References

- Zero to One by Peter Thiel. *Insights on Identifying Transformational Ideas and Trends.* [Book Reference]
- The Little Book That Builds Wealth by Pat Dorsey. *Understanding Economic Moats in Emerging Trends.* [Book Reference]

8. Real-World Case Studies and Lessons Learned
- McKinsey Global Institute. *Case Studies on Emerging Market Trends.* Website
- Harvard Business School. *Investment Strategies in Emerging Sectors: Case Studies.* Website
- Financial Times. *Lessons from Investors Who Navigated Disruptive Trends.* Website

9. 2040 and Predictions
- United Nations Department of Economic and Social Affairs, "World Population Prospects 2022," UN DESA Website.
- PwC, "The World in 2050" report, PwC Website.
- McKinsey Global Institute, Reports on disruptive technologies and future industries, McKinsey Website.

Illustrations
- Illustration A1, A2, A3, B1 – Authors work
- Japan population chart, 1899 - 2023 | Yearly | Person mn | CEIC Data, Website
- United Nations Department of Economic and Social Affairs (UN DESA), Average age of population.

Acknowledgements

This book is the result of long hours of thought, effort, and unwavering support from those who have been part of my journey.

To My Parents

For trusting my abilities, standing by me through every venture, and being my unwavering pillar of support. Your belief in me has been my greatest source of strength.

To My Friends and Cousins

For believing in my vision, inspiring me to dream bigger, and nurturing in me the attitude that "Anything is Possible." Your encouragement has fuelled my ambition at every step.

To Professor Jaimin Patel

I would like to extend my heartfelt thanks for your invaluable assistance with the illustrations in this book.

Lastly, I am deeply grateful to every reader who picks up this book. Your curiosity and passion for learning drive me to create content that inspires and informs. Thank you for being part of this journey.

Modern Publishing Practice Disclaimer:

This book has benefited from the assistance of AI tools for proofreading and language enhancement. These tools were employed to refine the clarity, grammar, and readability of the content while ensuring the ideas and concepts remain authentic and author driven.

Have a successful Investing Journey!